W.H. CRAWFORD (1932–2014) was arch
education at the Public Record Office of N
Keeper of Material Culture at the Ulster
retired as Development Oficer for the Feder
an honorary research fellow at the Institu   ~ueen's
University Belfast, he lectured on the regiona   _ .ocal history of Ulster for
which he had been awarded a Ph.D. in 1983. He pioneered research in the
creation and evolution of estates, towns, and markets and fairs in Ulster;
relations between landlords and tenants on these estates from c. 1600 to
1820; and the development of the linen industry in Ulster. His archival and
museum experience is reflected in several case studies of social life in Ireland.

'Bleaching field, near linen mills (s.e.), Lisburn, near Belfast, Ireland', Underwood and Underwood, Library of Congress, Prints and Photographs Division

The Domestic
Linen Industry
in Ulster

W.H. Crawford

ULSTER HISTORICAL
FOUNDATION

ACKNOWLEDGEMENT TO THE 2005 EDITION
This publication has been supported by the Ulster Local History Trust.
Ulster Historical Foundation is also pleased to acknowledge support for this
publication provided by the Miss Elizabeth Ellison Charitable Trust.

FRONT COVER
Wellbrook Beetling Mill, Kildress, County Tyrone (2018).
Courtesy of Oliver Molloy, www.facebook.com/slatequarryphotography

BACK COVER
'Spinning flax in Ireland', Keystone View Company, Library of Congress, Prints
and Photographs Division; trade mark of The Blackstaff Flax Spinning and
Weaving Co. Ltd, *Linen Trade Circular*, vol. XLI, no. 10, 12 Mar. 1955

The Hincks prints are reproduced courtesy of
the Ulster Folk and Transport Museum

First published in 2005 as *The Impact of the Domestic Linen Industry in Ulster*,
republished in 2021 as *The Domestic Linen Industry in Ulster*
by Ulster Historical Foundation
www.ancestryireland.com

ISBN 2005: 978-1-903688-37-3
ISBN 2021: 978-1-913993-31-3

Design by Dunbar Design
Printed by SPRINT-print Ltd.

Contents

1

Introduction

PLATE 1

*Taken near Scarva in the County of Downe, representing Ploughing,
Sowing the Flax Seed and Harrowing*

WILLIAM HINCKS 1783

ALTHOUGH EVERY ULSTERMAN identifies the linen industry with the economic development of the province, he can have little real conception of the indelible imprint it has left on its society and its culture. In the eighteenth century the domestic linen industry expanded so rapidly across the province that annual exports increased from less than a million to forty million yards of cloth. Flax was grown on every small farm, prepared and spun into linen yarn and woven into webs of cloth by families in their own homes, and sold in linen markets in towns to the linendrapers and bleachers who finished the linens and marketed them in Dublin or in Britain. As linen transactions were conducted in coin, money percolated through Ulster society so that in time many families managed to get their feet on to the property ladder and Ulster became noted for the density of its family farms. The trade was well organised under the aegis of the Linen Board and then dominated by the bleachers who managed the industrialisation of the spinning and weaving sectors during the nineteenth century. Nevertheless, the domestic linen industry survived into the twentieth century, producing linens of the finest quality such as damasks and cambrics.

Such a phenomenon was bound to attract historians. In 1925 Conrad Gill, then a lecturer in economic history in the Queen's University of Belfast, published *The Rise of the Irish Linen Industry*. In this pioneering work Gill was interested in the linen industry chiefly as Ireland's contribution 'towards that great transformation of industry and society' popularly known as the Industrial Revolution, and so he was concerned mainly 'to trace the change from domestic to factory production'. As he wanted also to investigate the role of successive governments in this process, he paid considerable attention to the history of the Board of Trustees of the Linen and Hempen Manufactures (known as the Linen Board) set up by the Irish Parliament to regulate the industry. Although his comments on this source in his bibliography indicate that he had not studied it systematically before the destruction of the whole archive in the burning of the Four Courts in Dublin in 1922, Gill deplored in the preface to his book the loss of this 'best of his sources … in the catastrophe of the Dublin Record Office'. It has to be admitted that the loss of the manuscript volumes of the 'Proceedings of the Board of Trustees of the Linen Manufacture in Ireland 1711–1828' has made it impossible to produce a detailed history of the Irish Linen Board in spite of the survival of a printed volume of *Precedents and Abstracts* selected from the early minute books from 1711 to 1737 and later the publication of the *Proceedings* from 1784.

The loss of such a vital source in Dublin was, however, discounted to some extent by the success of the new Public Record Office of Northern Ireland (PRONI, established in 1924) in locating and processing government and private archives throughout the province. One of the first academic historians to exploit these archives was a local polymath, Rodney Green, who published *The Lagan Valley 1800–1850: a local history of the industrial revolution* (Manchester, 1949) and *The Industrial Archaeology of County Down* (Belfast, 1968); after he became Director of the Institute of Irish Studies in Queen's University Belfast in 1970 he encouraged several students to carry on research. Harry Gribbon, who came from a Coleraine family long engaged in textiles, published several papers on the history of the Linen Board as well as *A History of Water Power in Ulster* (Newton Abbot, 1969). Both Green and Gribbon were well acquainted with the industrial history of the province. Their work was complemented by Alan McCutcheon's *Industrial Archaeology of Northern Ireland* (Belfast, 1980), based on the regional survey of industrial archaeology that he conducted for the Ministry of Finance.

I was introduced to historical research in the records of the Brownlow estate (then held in a solicitor's office in Lurgan, County Armagh, but now available for study in PRONI). After working on these records for several years I approached Professor J.C. Beckett to supervise me in preparing a doctoral thesis. He introduced me to Professor K.H. Connell, who passed on to me an invitation to contribute to a symposium in England on the role of landowners in the development of industry. My first paper on the linen theme, 'Ulster landlords and the linen industry', was later published in *Land and Industry: the Landed Estate and the Industrial Revolution* (Newton Abbot, 1971). While it owed much of its basic argument to the reprint in 1964 of Conrad Gill's classic, *The Rise of the Irish Linen Industry* (Oxford, 1925), it did include some corroborative evidence from the Dublin Registry of Deeds and the Brownlow estate papers.

Both these sources, as well as records of the Society of Friends, were used more extensively about this time in the preparation of a paper on 'The development of the linen industry in the Lurgan area of County Armagh 1660–1760', which was finally published in *Ulster Folklife* 17 (1971) as 'The origins of the linen industry in north Armagh and the Lagan valley'.

In December 1966, I joined the staff of PRONI, then based in the Law Courts in Belfast. The year 1967 saw the publication in *Ulster Folklife* 13 of an analysis of the contents of 'The market book of Thomas Greer, a Dungannon Linendraper, 1758–59' and the preparation of a script of a Thomas Davis lecture for Radio Eireann, subsequently published as 'The rise of the linen industry' in *The Formation of the Irish Economy*, edited by L.M. Cullen (Cork, 1969). This phase of research culminated in the publication in Dublin in 1972 by Gill and Macmillan of *Domestic Industry in Ireland: The Experience of the Linen Industry* in a series, 'Insights into Irish History', edited by L.M. Cullen for schools. In 1994, it was reprinted with a new introduction and a bibliographical essay, by the Ulster Historical Foundation as *The Handloom Weavers and the Ulster Linen Industry*.

A great impetus had been given to research in Irish history by the creation of the Economic and Social History Society of Ireland in 1970, with Ken Connell as President and Louis Cullen as Secretary. Many of us benefited also from attending seminars hosted by Cullen for British and foreign scholars in Trinity College Dublin. They in turn inspired conferences with first the Scots in Dublin in 1976 and then the French in Dublin in 1977. For a conference in Bordeaux in 1978 I was encouraged to pursue my research into the growth of the linen industry in the linen triangle and received much advice and assistance from two academics in Scotland, Brenda Collins and Alastair Durie. This paper was published as 'Drapers and bleachers in the early Ulster linen industry' in the collection of conference papers edited by Louis Cullen and Pierre Butel, *Négoce et Industrie en France et en Irlande aux XVIIIe et XIXe Siècles* (Bordeaux, 1980).

The third phase of my research into the history of the linen industry coincided with the preparation of an exhibition, 'Our Linen Industry', in the Ulster Folk and Transport Museum in 1987, taking advantage of the fine collection of textiles and the knowledge of the staff. Among the spin-offs was 'The introduction of the flying shuttle into the weaving of linen in Ulster'. For the exhibition I prepared an illustrated brochure, *The Irish Linen Industry*, which was published with the support of the Irish Linen Guild. It contained a commentary on the dozen prints made by William Hincks and published in 1783, illustrating the several stages then employed in the production and marketing of the finished cloth. In retrospect I realise that these illustrations conditioned my conclusions in the preparation of a paper on the role of women in the domestic linen industry contributed to a volume of essays, *Women in Early Modern Ireland*, edited by Margaret MacCurtain and Mary O'Dowd and published in 1991.

It was about this time too that I realised the significance of two parliamentary reports on the Irish linen industry in the early 1820s that confirmed some of my impressions about the evolution of the domestic linen industry in those important years before James Kay introduced mechanisation into the wet spinning of linen in 1825. In 1988 the results of this research were published in *Irish Economic and Social History* XV with the title 'The evolution of the linen trade of Ulster before industrialisation'. The year 1989 saw the publication of *Ulster: an Illustrated History*, a collection of essays by several specialists edited by Ciaran Brady, Mary O'Dowd and Brian Walker on behalf of its sponsors, the Dublin Historical Association and the Ulster Society for Irish Historical Studies, to satisfy 'a demand from both teachers of history and the general public for an accessible and up-to-date history of the province'. It included 'The political economy of linen: Ulster in the eighteenth century', an essay that tried to explain how the great expansion of the domestic linen industry helped to politicise several social groups in the province. A further opportunity to develop this theme was presented in 1995 in seminars commemorating the 1798 Rebellion. 'The "Linen Triangle" in the 1790s', published in *Ulster Local Studies* in 1997, introduced several fresh factors requiring consideration in any discussion about the eruption of sectarian violence between Orangemen and Defenders in the north-west corner of Armagh in the closing years of the eighteenth century.

Other important evidence had come to light about changing dimensions in the linen trade. In 1784 a statistical survey of the state of the linen markets in Ulster was submitted by John Greer soon after his appointment by the Linen Board as Inspector General for Ulster and published by the Board. A copy of this printed report, with detailed annotations in manuscript about the condition of the markets in Ulster in 1803, was found among the papers of John Foster, the last Speaker of the Irish House of Commons, who was sometimes referred to as the 'Chief Trustee of the Linen Manufacture' because he dominated the Board, although no such office existed. This valuable document I have edited in full for publication here.

I have added transcripts of three other pamphlets for the light they throw on important aspects of the industry. Thomas Turner's *New methods of improving flax and flax-seed and bleaching cloth* (Dublin, 1715) secured the approval of the Linen Board in its early years and marked an initial stage in the improvement of the finishing process. About twenty years later water power was harnessed to drive machinery in the bleach mills. *The case of the linen manufacture of Ireland, relative to the bleaching and the whitening the same* (c. 1750) provides a contemporary account of this very significant development that changed the whole character of the Irish linen industry and set it on the road to international success. *Serious considerations on the present alarming state of agriculture and the linen trade, by a farmer* (Dublin, 1773) is especially interesting because it both reinforces and elucidates the critical comments made about farming in Ulster by the noted traveller Arthur Young in that same decade. Although the author could not foresee the period of prosperity that lay before the farmer/weavers of Ulster, he did identify the fundamental economic dangers that would continue to haunt rural life.

The character of Ulster rural life still reflects the impact of the domestic linen industry to a greater or lesser extent. In the early 1960s when I was living in the townland of Corcreeny on the Armagh/Down border near Lurgan town, I became aware that some of those relics were still surviving: several damask weavers produced superb linen cloths while Swiss embroidery still flourished. Thirty years later I investigated these phenomena and their context in 'A handloom weaving community in County Down', using the census returns of 1901 and 1911 and valuation records. It proved to be a very satisfying exercise.

2

The origins of the linen industry in north Armagh and the Lagan valley [1]

PLATE 2

Taken near Hillsborough in the County of Down, representing pulling the Flax when grown, Stooking or putting it up to dry, Ripling or saving the Seed, and boging or burying it in water.

WILLIAM HINCKS 1783

N O SERIOUS STUDY has yet been made of the origins of the
linen-weaving industry in Ulster in the late seventeenth century. In the standard work, *The Rise of the Irish Linen Industry*, Conrad
Gill dealt in a very summary and allusive fashion with its early history, using a small number of quotations from later printed sources to
suggest that the industry was established by Scots settlers and vastly
improved by Huguenots.[2] This picture has been generally accepted
even by recent writers and the only modification to it has been by Dr
E.R.R. Green in the essay on 'The Linen Industry in County Down'
in his book *The Industrial Archaeology of County Down*. He thought
there was no doubt that 'The industrial development of this region
originated with the English and Scottish settlers and their desire to
exploit properties which they had acquired.' In support of this theo-
ry Green quoted a 1738 reference: 'In Ireland they had little or no
manufactures of linen, even for home consumption, till towards the
end of King Charles II's reign, when the persecution then raised
against the dissenters in Scotland forced many of them over to the
north of Ireland.' Green also noted the contribution of two local
landowners, Arthur Brownlow of Lurgan and Samuel Waring of near-
by Waringstown. He did, however, lay rather more emphasis than
Conrad Gill on the value of the Huguenot contribution although he
thought it reasonable to assume that Crommelin settled in Lisburn
'because the linen manufacture was in a more flourishing state there
than anywhere else in the country'.[3]

Green's analysis represents quite accurately the extent of the knowledge of the origins of the industry that can be gained from printed
sources, for these have been pretty effectively combed by succeeding
generations of students intrigued by the problem. But there are other
sources which have been largely neglected and which do light up hid-
den facets of these well-worn quotations and enable us to test the
validity of many conjectures in order to produce a more substantial
overall picture of the origins of the industry. The records of the
Quaker meetings of Lisburn and Lurgan survive from the mid-
1670s and contain incidental references to the linen trade and to

[1] First published in *Ulster Folklife* 17 (1971), pp. 42–51.
[2] Gill, Conrad, *The Rise of the Irish Linen Industry* (Oxford, 1925, reprinted 1964),
    pp. 15–20.
[3] Green, E.R.R., *The Industrial Archaeology of County Down* (Belfast, 1963), pp. 1–2.

personalities in the industry.[4] Among the few surviving seventeenth-century parish registers for Ulster are those for Blaris (Lisburn) and Shankill (Lurgan):[5] they reveal the size and structure of the population in these areas. Almost unknown, too, except to genealogists, are the treasures of the Registry of Deeds established in Dublin about 1708: huge volumes contain memorials of deeds, leases, mortgages, wills and marriage settlements, providing a useful measure of the extent of economic activity in many periods in many parts of Ireland. Finally, there are estate records and although they are not numerous for the seventeenth century they do exist as a valuable supplement to the sources for re-creating the economic and social pattern of that period.

The earliest reference to a considerable domestic weaving industry in Ulster dates from 1682.

> The Scotch and Irish in that province [Ulster] addicting themselves to spinning of linen yarn, attained to vast quantities of that commodity, which they transported to their great profit, the conveniency of which drew thither multitudes of linen weavers, that my opinion is, there is not a greater quantity of linen produced in like circuit in Europe: and although the generality of their cloth fourteen years since was sleisie and thin yet of late it is much improved to be a good fineness and strength, and will in all probability increase daily both in quantity and quality …[6]

This estimate was made by Colonel Richard Lawrence, who had himself unsuccessfully managed a linen manufactory for the Duke of Ormonde at Chapelizod near Dublin. Its accuracy is supported by the evidence we have. There had been for many years in Ulster a substantial production of yarn and after the 1660s it was worked up by immigrants from the north of England into a product well-known and respected in the London market before the arrival of the Huguenots. The industry was by then technically far enough advanced to hold its own with that of the Huguenot immigrants and

[4] See Goodbody, O.C. and Hutton, B.G., *Guide to Irish Quaker Records* 1654–1860 (Dublin, 1967).

[5] The surviving Church of Ireland parish records are in the custody of the rectors of each parish. Microfilms of them are held by the Public Record Office of Northern Ireland.

[6] Lawrence, Richard, *The Interest of Ireland in its trade and wealth stated* (Dublin, 1682), pp. 189–90.

to absorb their ideas very rapidly. At the same time the expansion of the agricultural economy, the wealth of the butter trade, and the consequent creation of a network of good markets made it easy for the more specialised activities of linendrapers to develop. The industry was indeed so firmly based that when England gave the Irish linen industry a favoured position in her markets after 1696, Irish exports of linen yarn and cloth rose by leaps and bounds.

Colonel Lawrence had attributed the establishment of the linen-weaving industry in Ulster to the production by spinners of large surpluses of linen yarn for export. This was not a new phenomenon. At the time of the plantation of Ulster it was claimed by a propagandist for the scheme that linen yarn was 'finer there and more plentiful than in all the rest of the kingdom'.[7] On the eve of the destruction of the British colony in 1641 Ireland exported 2,921 cwt. of linen yarn while there was as yet no considerable export of linen cloth.[8] A pamphlet published in the same year contained this comment: 'The town of Manchester buys the linen yarn of the Irish in great quantity, and weaving it returns the same again into Ireland to sell.'[9] In the 1660s another observer could still state with accuracy: 'We send abroad little linen cloth and less that is good, though store of linen yarn which is an imperfect sort of country manufacture, and sheweth we have more spinners than weavers.'[10] In 1673 Sir William Temple wrote: 'Linen yarn is a commodity very proper for this country but made in no great quantities in any part besides the north nor anywhere into linen in any great degree or sorts fit for the better uses at home or exportation abroad.'[11]

Since the existence of a spinning industry had not created a significant weaving industry in the period before 1660, it would not be convincing to argue that it did of itself attract 'thither multitudes of linen weavers' in the decades following 1660. The immigrants were attracted mainly by the prospect of obtaining land on good terms and at cheap rents from landlords whose estates had been depopulated during the 1640s, while many Cromwellian soldiers and 'adventurers'

---

[7] *Cal. State Papers Ire., 1608–10*, p. 208.
[8] *Cal. State Papers Ire., 1669–70*, p. 54.
[9] 'The Treasure of Traffike' (London, 1641), quoted by William Pinkerton in 'Contributions towards a history of Irish commerce', *Ulster J. Archaeol.*, 1st ser., 3 (1855), 193.
[10] *Cal. State Papers Ire., 1662–6*, p. 693.
[11] Temple, William, *Essay on Trade of Ireland* (Dublin, 1673).

who had been compensated for their services with grants of Irish land, especially on the Magennis estate in north Down, unloaded their land on the market.[12] A study of the surnames of these immigrants and of the Quaker records suggests that the majority of the settlers in the Lagan valley were from northern England. Indeed, the English character of Lisburn and the subsequent bitter rivalry between Lisburn and Belfast is the substance of a letter from Lisburn written in 1679 by a local merchant:

> Through the overpowering trade of the Scottish merchants of Belfast the English trade of Lisburn is upon its ruin. To demonstrate the same, those Scotch have got all the general commissions from the London merchants for trade into their hands and not one Englishman in these parts is so employed and those Scotch merchants of Belfast for the encouragement of their countrymen in this town allow and pay about 12d. per pound for commodities more than to any Englishman ...[13]

The trade of the region was based on agricultural products. In 1683 Belfast exported 7,017 barrels of corn, 12,445 hides, 4,610 barrels of beef, 3,769 cwt. of tallow, 766 cwt. of cheese and 33,880 cwt. of butter.[14] The accumulation of provisions to meet this demand created an extensive network of markets in the Belfast hinterland. The location of the markets is defined in a letter explaining the struggle between Belfast and Lisburn for control of the butter trade in 1679. Sir George Rawdon of Lisburn feared that 'the butter trade, the chief business here, will inevitably be forestalled and Belfast merchants will have agents at Lurgan and Moira for all Armagh butter and at Hillsborough and Dromore for Down, and as it began to look like a war between these two towns formerly on this account, so it will renew on this occasion ...'[15] However, Lisburn market not only survived but prospered so that many improvements were carried out in the market place in the 1680s with the intention of making it the best in Ireland.[16] The customs of Lurgan market, sixteen miles away, also

12 *Register of the Privy Council of Scotland, 1676–8*, 3rd ser., V, 397; Smout, T.C., *Scottish Trade on the Eve of Union, 1660–1707* (Edinburgh, 1963), pp. 90–93; see calendar of Waring papers, PRONI D/695.
13 *Cal. State Papers Domestic, 1679–80*, p. 298.
14 Benn, George, *A History of the town of Belfast* (Belfast, 1877), pp. 317–8.
15 *Cal. State Papers Domestic, 1679–80*, p. 282.
16 *Cal. State Papers Domestic, 1683*, p. 249.

rose from £5 in 1658 to £10 in 1675, £14 in 1682 and £30 by 1702.[17]

These markets, however, served not only as collection points for goods to supply Belfast but as service depots for the local people who brought to them their linen and woollen manufactures as well as their crops. Although in 1683 Belfast exported only 341 pieces of linen (about 17,000 yards) and 181 cwt. of yarn,[18] the linen industry was already well established in the province. In 1682 Colonel Lawrence had given as his opinion that in the north of Ireland more linen was produced than 'in like circuit in Europe' and in the same year a Portadown clergyman reckoned that in and about Lurgan was managed the greatest linen manufacture in Ireland.[19] This production therefore must have been absorbed by the home market and there is evidence that even it was insufficient to meet local demands, for 163,000 yards of Scottish linen were imported into Belfast in 1683.[20] Although in those years Lisburn merchants visited Chester and Dublin, which suggests that Dublin was the outlet for their linen cloth,[21] any export trade through Dublin was still not considerable since Sir William Petty noted that the total number of pieces of linen exported from Ireland in 1685 was only 1,851 (about 92,000 yards).[22] The demands of Dublin itself, however, may have been a factor in the development of the industry, especially of the finer branches. 'Black' George Macartney, the eminent Belfast merchant, did not himself deal in linen except to oblige special customers, but his orders included several requests for locally woven broad diaper for tablecloths and napkins. He wrote to one customer in 1680: 'There is but one weaver here [in Belfast] that weaves diaper here of ten feet wide and he makes all of one work and sells commonly at six shillings per yard. The above fourteen yards is but 1¼ yd. wide at twenty pence per yard.'[23]

[17] Arthur Brownlow's lease book (PRONI, T970), 54.
[18] Benn, op. cit., pp. 317–8.
[19] 'An account of the Barony of O'Neiland, Co. Armagh in 1682', ed. R.M. Young, *Ulster J. Archaeol.*, 2nd ser., 4 (1898), 241.
[20] Benn, op. cit., p. 319. This is suggested too by the quotation in note 10.
[21] *Cal. State Papers Domestic*, 1671, 313, 349.
[22] Hull, C.H. (ed.), *Economic Writings of Sir William Petty* (Cambridge, 1899), II, 595.
[23] Letter from George Macartney, Belfast, to 'My Lady Steward' [Dublin?], 11 August 1680. PRONI Mic./19/2.

12

Recognition of the quality of Ulster cloth spread. A London compendium of trade in 1696 referred specifically to linens 'made in the north of Ireland, some yard wide, some three-quarters, and some half-ell [22¹/2 inches], which are of great use for shirts and wear very white and strong'.[24] The growth of the trade encouraged more men to deal in linens. Arthur Brownlow, the squire of Lurgan from 1665 to 1710, claimed in 1708 that 'on his first establishing the trade here, [he] bought up everything that was brought to the market of cloth and lost at first considerably; but at length the thing fixing itself, he is now by the same methods a considerable gainer …'.[25] It is probable, too, that the butter merchants were shrewd enough to invest in cloth when the price was right and it is certain that markets stimulated by agricultural profits would have cradled the young linen industry. Dealers did not specialise strictly in their own commodities and even as late as 1745 it was reported from Lurgan 'that the breaking of so many factors in London has so discouraged this [linen] manufacture of late in this place where I best know it, that many substantial dealers are turning their money to other business; and the great plenty of the hides of the cattle of the poor which died this spring has induced them to turn tanners …'.[26] Occasionally we even find shopkeepers or merchants referring to themselves as linendrapers, a certain sign that this branch of their interests was then exercising their thoughts.[27]

Conrad Gill thought that linendrapers were becoming a distinct class around 1720. Yet in the Lurgan area alone twenty men were described in leases and other legal documents as linendrapers before 1720, the earliest reference being to the comparatively wealthy Quaker, Robert Hoope, in 1696.[28] Before 1732 no man in Lurgan

24 Quote from pamphlet 'The Merchant's Warehouse Laid Open' in *Ulster J. Archaeol.*, 1st ser., 3 (1855), 198.
25 Molyneux, Dr Thomas, 'Journey to the North in 1708' in Young, R.M. (ed.), *Historical Notices of Old Belfast* (Belfast, 1896), p. 154.
26 Letter from Rev. Richard Barton, Lurgan, to Walter Harris, 27 May 1745, in the Harris MSS, Muniment Room, Armagh Public Library.
27 Notes 27 to 29, and 31 are based on an analysis of records relating to the Brownlow estate in the neighbourhood of Lurgan in North Armagh. The estate papers are held by Messrs Watson & Neill, solicitors, High Street, Lurgan, while there are many memorials relating to the estate in the Registry of Deeds, Henrietta Street, Dublin.
28 Mordecai Barrow 1711; James Bradshaw 1711; James Bullock 1716; William Cave 1718; Charles Corner 1718; Robert Corner 1711; Thomas Fletcher 1719; Henry Greer 1711; James Greer 1718; John Greer 1718; Richard Holden 1711; Robert Hoope 1696; William Matthews 1715; John Robson 1709; Henry Sands 1714; Henry Spence 1713; Oliver Turkington 1718; Thomas Turner 1709; Thomas Usher 1711.

was referred to as a 'bleacher', although some of the men referred to as linendrapers owned bleachgreens. William Matthews, a shopkeeper, was the owner of a bleachgreen in Lurgan according to a memo added to a lease dated 1678: the bleaching house was certainly in existence in 1692.[29] In 1697 the Quakers set to Ninian Simson 'the plot of ground between the graveyard and the river called a bleaching yard with a bucking house'.[30] In 1711 a part of Dougher townland was renewed to Robert Corner, linendraper, 'whereon he has built his dwelling house and other office houses, planted an orchard and made a bleaching yard'.[31] On the other hand, although Michael Quinn and William Douglas are referred to as bleachers in 1732 and 1735 respectively, we have no evidence that they owned bleachgreens. It may be, therefore, that the term 'bleacher' was at that time applied to an expert who supervised a bleachgreen for one of the linendrapers. Indeed, the men who were known as 'linendrapers' in Ulster in the eighteenth century were almost always bleachers or their employees.

Other signs of specialisation had been creeping into the industry since the 1690s at the latest. A single case history taken from the minutes of the Quaker provincial men's meeting will illustrate this. In 1689 the Quakers consented 'that Samuel Hall be an apprentice with James Pottifar, if his mother be willing, for nine years, said James to instruct him in the trade of linen-weaving, soap-boiling and chandling, and to find the said apprentice meat, drink and clothes, bedding and washing, shoes and stockings, fitting for an apprentice of such trade'.[32] In 1697, however, because James Pottifar had not 'fully instructed the said Samuel his apprentice in the said arts of soap-boiling and chandling', it was agreed by both sides to terminate the indenture a year early.[33] At the same time, however, the extent of specialisation within the industry is revealed by references in property leases in Lurgan, granted by the Brownlow family who owned the estate: John Turner and Thomas Chapman were described as chandlers in 1702 and 1708 respectively, Thomas Bullock as a reedmaker

---

29 Arthur Brownlow's lease book, 102, 107.
30 Quaker records: LGM/1/1. Lurgan Men's Meeting, 16 January 1698.
31 Lease from William Brownlow to Robert Corner.
32 Quaker Records: LGM/1/1. Lurgan Men's Meeting, 28 November 1689.
33 Quaker Records: Q/1/1. Ulster Quarterly Meeting held in Lurgan 26 December 1697.

in 1712, David Robinson as a cardmaker in 1715, and Robert Hind as a threadmaker in 1717.

It is important to stress that there is no evidence for the existence of guilds of weavers in any of the Ulster towns. The corporations of Ulster boroughs were controlled tightly by local landlords and provided no scope for guilds. An apprentice was indentured to a master-weaver and, after serving his time, became a journeyman who in his turn might set up as a master-weaver if he had the mind and the capital. In 1697 when a Lisburn master-weaver fell ill the Quakers requested two of their number 'to use their best endeavours to get Robert Hull cured of his malady and to get a journeyman to keep the looms going and take home again the said Robert's apprentice and supply them with yarn to weave, provided that the meeting kept them indemnified in their undertakings therein'.[34]

In the countryside, however, the industry was taken up by farmers and their families to supplement their income from agriculture. On the Brownlow estate around Lurgan in the first twenty years of the eighteenth century, fifteen out of seventeen weavers leased land outside the town. We do not know if any of them served an apprenticeship. On the Castledillon estate in mid-Armagh a surveyor remarked about the inhabitants of the townland of Mullinasallagh in 1696: 'The inhabitants are all very poor. They are so far from selling corn that they can hardly get bread. They pay their rent with linen cloth, having no other way.'[35] It could be argued that such people were being depressed into the weaving trade. However, when the industry began to expand rapidly in the second half of the eighteenth century, many farming families were attracted to participate by the prospect of better and more reliable incomes.

What were the sources of the industry's capital? Where did linen-drapers obtain capital to trade and to establish bleachgreens? This problem is really not as serious as it seems, since in pre-industrial society a small amount of capital went a long way in setting up a business. Green has pointed out that in the Banbridge area along the river

---

[34] Quaker Records: LBM/1/1. Lisburn Men's Monthly Meeting, 3 April 1697.
[35] Lease book of the manor of Castledillon, County Armagh. PRONI Mic/80/3, f. 54.

Bann bleachgreens were established by farmers.[36] It was easy for linen-drapers to become bleachers and for bleachers to become linendrapers, and in the early years there was no advantage to be gained by specialisation since the main requirement of both was to secure enough webs for bleaching by what were at best primitive methods. It is probable that in the early years profits from the provision trade were invested in linen and whenever provisions were scarce dealers were more tempted to buy linens. Obviously Brownlow's action in purchasing all the linens brought to Lurgan market must have played a very important role in establishing and promoting the industry as he claimed. Not until the second half of the eighteenth century, when bleaching became more specialised and the bleachgreens more considerable in size and output, is there any evidence of an English factor investing in an Ulster linen enterprise in an attempt to control quality and price. Whenever an entrepreneur from Ulster required capital he approached either contacts in Dublin or local people who had money to invest.

Money was usually raised by mortgaging or selling a lease of property. Indeed, the fact that a lease was a piece of property which could be sold or mortgaged was of vital importance to the expanding Ulster linen industry because it enabled a linendraper to raise capital easily. The records of many of these sales and mortgages as well as leases lie in the Registry of Deeds in Dublin awaiting analysis. There are, for example, more than sixty references to Lurgan property for the decade 1711–20 (the Registry only opened in 1708 although it did register earlier deeds). They show that in 1715 Hugh Mathews, a linendraper, mortgaged a Lurgan tenement for £100, Miles Reilly sold a 1672 lease for £109 16s., and John Turner sold his interest in a three-life lease for £70. Sometimes larger sums were involved: in 1720 John Nicholson, a Lurgan merchant, bought property in the town from a brother merchant, Joseph Robson, for £450, while yet another merchant, Philip Barry, mortgaged some property for £260 and sold a house for £480. For even larger sums the Lurgan drapers tapped landowners, clergy, and Dublin merchants. John Nicholson mortgaged property near Lurgan for £1,500 to Archdeacon Jenny of Dromore who also held bonds from Henry Greer for £185. In 1726

---

[36] Green, op. cit., p. 2. One of the basic materials for bleaching was buttermilk for souring the linens.

Thomas Greer mortgaged Lurgan property for £500 to the Earl of Londonderry while James Bradshaw borrowed from the Earl of Duncannon.[37]

Certain legends have grown up around the origins of the linen industry and especially that legend which attributes the success of the industry to the Huguenot immigrants introduced to Lisburn in 1698. Genealogical evidence can establish that the weaving industry was established in Lisburn and Lurgan by men from the north of England who flocked into Ulster in the decades following the troubles of the 1640s. The most reliable genealogical records for the identification of their origins are the seventeenth-century Quaker family records which apparently survive only for Lurgan and Ballyhagan (Richhill) meetings but not for Lisburn. The Lurgan records note the origins of twenty families who emigrated to Ulster: one is from Scotland, nine from Yorkshire, four from Cumberland, two from Lancashire, two from Northumberland, and one each from Westmoreland and Durham. Very few of their trades are recorded but William Porter 'learned to weave in Ireland' after he arrived from Yorkshire and Thomas Walker was also a weaver. Robert Hoope, who was to become a linendraper and the richest of the Lurgan Quakers, had arrived from Yorkshire in 1660 as a twenty-one-year-old tailor, and the list includes three other surnames eminent in Ulster linen in the eighteenth century: Turner, Greer, Bradshaw.[38]

Fortunately for our purpose several relevant Church of Ireland parish registers have survived. They show an overwhelming preponderance of English names. Indeed, Presbyterian congregations were not established in Lisburn and Lurgan until the 1680s: that in Lurgan

---

[37] In the Registry of Deeds, Dublin, the memorials are in large MS volumes and the references here are to volume number/page number/memorial number.

15/14/6652	Hugh Mathews to Roth Jones.
15/130/6964	Miles Reilly to John Nicholson.
14/272/6215	John Turner to Samuel Johnston.
27/409/17586	Joseph Robson to William and John Nicholson.
28/99/16683	Philip Barry to Oliver Anketell.
29/10/15820	Philip Barry to Robert Hawkins.
47/272/30549	John Nicholson to Henry Jenny, 1725.
52/139/33927	John Nicholson to Henry Jenny, 1726.
50/297/33087	Henry Greer to Henry Jenny, 1726.
52/160/34023	Thomas Greer to Earl of Londonderry, 1726.
58/439/40097	James Bradshaw to Lord Duncannon, 1728.

[38] Quaker Records: LGM/5/1. Lurgan Record Book 'No. 1'.

especially was very small throughout the eighteenth century.[39] The parish registers of Blaris show that Lisburn was certainly not 'the ruined village of Lisnagarvey, later called Lisburn'.[40] In the seven years from 1696 to 1702, 710 children were baptised in the parish, an average of just over 100 per year. This suggests a population for the parish in the region of 3,000.[41] It was no wonder that in 1697 the parish vestry decided 'to raise £60 for the repair of the church and church-yard of Lisburn, also for enlarging the said church, and other pious uses'.[42] In the same decade in Lurgan the parish church was also enlarged[43] and the Quaker meetinghouse rebuilt because it was too small.[44] It is especially significant also that the figures for births in Blaris do not show any marked increase after the arrival of the Huguenots, although the register does contain a few recognisable Huguenot surnames such as Boomer and Brethet.

The significance of the Huguenot colony in promoting the linen industry in Ulster has been so overestimated as to distort the history of the origins of the linen trade. Yet the Huguenots left almost no permanent mark on the character of the industry: on its organisation, its marketing procedure, or in improved techniques. Louis Crommelin established a 'linen manufactory' and a bleachyard on a pattern which was to have little lasting success wherever it was tried in Ireland throughout the eighteenth century: the Joncourt scheme at Dundalk, and those of Sir Richard Cox at Dunmanway in County Cork, and the Smith family in Waterford are the most notable examples.[45] Crommelin tried to confine the weaving trade to skilled tradesmen. By 1727, however, the acts of 1705 and 1709 prescribing a five-year apprenticeship followed by two years' service as a journeyman for every master weaver were a dead letter. The industry was not to be

---

[39] Killen, W.D., *History of Congregations of the Presbyterian Church in Ireland* (Belfast, 1886), pp. 178, 186. Lisburn meeting may have been established in 1681 *(Cal. State Papers Domestic, 1680–1, p. 193).*

[40] Charles Wilson, *England's Apprenticeship, 1603–1763* (London, 1965), p. 197, based his account on Samuel Smile's fanciful picture.

[41] Blaris parish register: PRONI T679/112. See Wrigley, E.A., *An Introduction to English Historical Demography* (London, 1966), p. 54.

[42] Blaris vestry book 19 April 1697 quoted in Carmody, W.P., *Lisburn Cathedral and its past rectors* (Belfast, 1926), p. 32.

[43] Shankill vestry book, 14 April 1697.

[44] Quaker Records: LGM/1/1. Lurgan Men's Meeting, several references in 1695 and 1697 with detailed subscription list totalling £208.

[45] Gill, op. cit., pp. 83–5, 89.

confined in the towns, which would ultimately have strangled it, but burst out into the rural parts of several Ulster counties.[46] Any special Huguenot skills in marketing were restricted by the need to sell the linens through Dublin factors since they alone could afford to provide the credit which the English buyers demanded. As for technical innovations, Louis Crommelin's treatise, *An Essay towards the Improving of the Hempen and Flaxen Manufactures in the Kingdom of Ireland* (1705), which explained all his processes from flax-growing to bleaching, was analysed and criticised by Robert Stephenson, an eminent eighteenth-century expert in the linen trade: in his opinion, Crommelin's ideas were certainly not revolutionary.[47] It is worth noting in this context that Crommelin failed to persuade the Irish spinners to adopt the French hand-driven spinning wheel instead of the traditional treadle-driven wheel.[48] This would have been a retrograde step. Even the claim that the French introduced the weaving of fine linens into Ireland should be read in conjunction with Crommelin's own admission in his 1707 petition:

> That the said Crommelin and French colony have been necessitated much to the prejudice of their private fortunes to satisfy themselves with one single branch of establishment [mainly Holland diaper], and were ready even to abandon that, if a sense of honour and reputation had not engaged them to pursue it, but could not for want of proper encouragement to meddle with the other branches of the linen manufacture, as cambric, lawns (making but few for want of spinners and weavers), sewing thread, lace thread and tape, of which there is a very great consumption, which might have been brought to perfection, and would have been very advantageous to this kingdom.[49]

Indeed, the Huguenot colony was never really a success. Crommelin and his associates had promised by the patent of 1700 to invest £10,000 in capital in the scheme but they could not carry out their promise.[50] Therefore in 1701, when a new patent for a ten-year

---

[46] Ibid., p. 19. But note that the 1689 apprentice's indenture quoted in note 33 was for nine years.

[47] Stephenson, Robert, *An Inquiry into the State and Progress of the Linen Manufacture of Ireland* (Dublin, 1757), pp. 57–68, 112–3.

[48] Gill, op. cit., p. 19.

[49] *Journal of the House of Commons, Ireland* (1692–1713), II, 505–6.

[50] *Cal. State Papers Domestic, 1702–3*, pp. 331–2.

period was granted by Queen Anne, the conditions were revised slightly and the original offer of eight per cent interest on investments in the industry was extended to anyone who would introduce new sorts of looms, to the manifest annoyance of Crommelin. When this patent expired in 1711 both the Linen Board and Parliament recognised the services of Crommelin but felt that the trustees appointed by the government to administer the patent had 'in a just and equal manner performed the several conditions and agreements made with the said Louis Crommelin, in behalf of himself, his assistants, and colony'. They said nothing about continuing the pensions of £380 per annum and the allowance on the capital invested.[51] According to his 1711 petition Crommelin and his colony really needed the money, but it was not until 22 January 1715 that his old patron, the Earl of Galway, secured for him a pension of £500 per annum with £400 for his colony.[52] When Galway was appointed Lord Justice in Ireland in August 1715 he must have prodded the Linen Board into action, for on 24 February 1716 they examined a further petition submitted by Crommelin and recommended him for a pension of £400 'in consideration of all the expences he has been at, and the services he has already done, and hereafter proposes to do, to the flaxen and hempen manufacture of this kingdom', with £60 for the pastor of the French Protestant church in Lisburn.[53]

Louis Crommelin's reputation, in fact, depends on the coincidence that the linen industry began to boom soon after his arrival in Lisburn. In his several petitions of 1703, 1707, 1711 and 1716 he always stressed the value of his services and linked them to the great progress of the industry. He naturally did not mention the conclusion of the 1709 committee of Irish House of Commons that 'they observe the linen manufacture is now in a declining condition by reason the acts already passed for the encouragement thereof have not fully answered the ends for which they were made'.[54] Nor did he ever refer to the statement made by the Linen Board in 1713 that 'the linen trade here has languished since the year 1707; they [the Trustees]

---

[51] *Precedents and Abstracts from the Journals of the Trustees of the Linen and Hempen Manufactures of Ireland* (Dublin, 1784), p. 4.
[52] Transcripts of State Papers Ireland (PRONI T448/9).
[53] *Precedents and Abstracts*, p. 15.
[54] *Journal House of Commons Ireland* (1692–1713), II, appendix, cc.

easily imagine that this must proceed from some false steps which the people conversant in these trades have made with relation to the manufactures.'[55]

The Huguenot colony in Ulster had never been large. Crommelin reckoned in 1711 that the total number was one hundred and twenty persons (who may have composed fewer than thirty families).[56] The great fire which destroyed Lisburn on Sunday, 20 April 1707 had scattered the original colony. Some of the colonists, he reported to the Duke of Ormonde, had gone to his brother's establishment at Kilkenny while others lodged in Lurgan or stayed in the ruins and cabins.[57] The records of the Brownlow estate, however, contain very few traces of the Huguenots in this town, which recovered from Lisburn its role as 'the greatest linen manufactory in the North'. Gill was imprudent in accepting the estimate of Hugh McCall (a nineteenth century Lisburn historian of the Ulster linen industry) that the Huguenot colony in Ulster was estimated at five hundred families.[58] Even in Lisburn in 1728, according to a rental of the Hertford estate, no more than thirty out of five hundred surnames could be considered as French in origin.[59]

Crommelin's colony had been of most value to the linen industry when it was settled in Lisburn in 1698 because it was excellent publicity for the government's intentions to help the industry. Crommelin had great confidence in his own abilities and he told the Irish government what it wanted to hear: 'That if the people of this kingdom come heartily into this trade there is no danger but that their goods will find a market according to their value: for it is worth and real goodness that engages chapmen and not name.'[60] In practice, too, the local weavers must have benefited from the newcomers, for the weaving of fine linens received especial encouragement from the government.

The Huguenot colony has stolen the limelight from other figures in the industry. One of the most interesting must have been the Quaker

---

[55] *Precedents and Abstracts*, p. 8.
[56] Ibid., p. 8.
[57] *HMC Ormonde Papers*, new ser., VIII, 299.
[58] Gill, op. cit., p. 19.
[59] Hertford Estate papers, PRONI D427/2.
[60] Crommelin, Louis, *An Essay towards the Improving of the Hempen and Flaxen Manufactures in the Kingdom of Ireland* (Dublin, 1705), p. 3.

linendraper from Lurgan, Thomas Turner. Third son of an immigrant from Northumberland, Thomas Turner was born near Lurgan in 1662.[61] As early as 1704 he received a grant of £220 from the Trustees for the Management of the Linen Manufacture and in 1709 he was engaged by them 'in contriving an engine for dressing hemp and flax'. In 1715 he published for the Linen Board *New methods of improving flax and flax-seed, and bleaching cloth* [Appendix 1] and was employed to travel round the bleachyards to instruct bleachers in his new methods. In 1728 he secured a further subsidy to develop a new technique for bleaching and twisting yarn, for which he received a reward in 1735.[62] Tradition in the industry also recognised a Turner as the inventor of an improved spinning-wheel.[63]

These and other inventions, especially in the finishing processes,[64] were stimulated by the rapid growth of the Irish linen industry in the early eighteenth century. The immediate cause of the expansion of the industry, however, was the abolition by the British government in 1696 of the import duties on Irish plain linens entering England. Cheaper Irish linens gradually drove the Germans and Dutch out of the English home market. As John Cary of Bristol wrote in 1704:

> The people in the North of Ireland, make good cloth, sell it at reasonable rates, and would every year make much more, had they a vent for it … It is necessary for a new undertaking to be attended with some lucky accident; the linen manufacture can never be begun in Ireland at a more reasonable time than now, being imported custom free when all the other linens of Europe pay considerable duties.[65]

When the English market began to expand very quickly in the eighteenth century the linen industry in Ulster was able to respond so that Irish exports of linen climbed from less than 1½ million yards in 1712 to 5½ million in 1734, 11 million in 1750, and 46 million in 1796.[66]

---

[61] Quaker Records: LGM/5/1. Lurgan Record Book 'No. 1'.
[62] *Precedents and Abstracts*, p. 93, 114, 144.
[63] Smith, F.W. (ed.), *Irish linen trade handbook and directory* (Belfast, 1876), p. 45.
[64] Gribbon, H.D., *The History of Water Power in Ulster* (Newton Abbot, 1969), chapter 5.
[65] Cary, John, *Some Considerations relating to the Carrying on the Linen Manufacture by a Joint Stock* (London, 1704), pp. 12–13.
[66] Gill, op. cit., pp. 341–2.

3

Drapers and bleachers
in the early
Ulster linen industry[1]

CONRAD GILL'S *The Rise of the Irish Linen Industry* was published more than half a century ago but even now little is known about the early progress of the industry and especially about its capital and technology.[2] No substantial collection of linen business records has survived from the pre-1750 period and, as for the Journals of the Trustees of the Linen and Hempen Manufactures of Ireland, they survive only in an abridged form for the period of its inception in 1711 until 1737 in the *Precedents and Abstracts* (1784). Such poverty of basic sources compels us to search for another approach and for sources that might be pieced together to construct an accurate picture of the development of the linen trade in the early eighteenth century. The answer lies in more detailed investigation of case studies. Evidence about the development of the industry in the Lurgan area in the north-east corner of County Armagh suggests that several members of the Quaker community resident there did play significant roles in the early history of the linen trade. The family records of the Lurgan Quaker meeting enable us to identify and to keep track of not only individual members of this community but also their kin and family connexions.[3] In addition the minutes kept by both provincial and local meetings are wide-ranging and more comprehensive than the contemporary records of any other sect in Ireland. The details from them can be supplemented by wills and other legal documents lodged in the Registry of Deeds in Dublin since its inception in 1708, and by estate records. From these sources it has been possible to construct a chronology of some technical changes in the practice of bleaching and to shed light on the organisation of both the trade and the business community.

The venerable tradition that ascribes the successful promotion of the linen industry in Ireland to Louis Crommelin and his colony of Huguenot immigrants cannot be substantiated.[4] When they arrived in 1698 the industry was already well established in various parts of

---

[1] First published in Louis Cullen and Pierre Butel (eds), *Négoce et Industrie en France et en Irlande aux XVIIIe et XIXe Siècles* (Bordeaux, 1980).

[2] Gill, Conrad, *The Rise of the Irish Linen Industry* (Oxford, 1925, reprinted 1964).

[3] The records of the Quaker meetings in Ulster are held in the Meeting House, Railway Street, Lisburn. The references in this article are to copies held in the Public Record Office of Northern Ireland (hereafter PRONI), reference number T1062.

[4] See pages 18 to 21.

Ulster. A report written only a year previously to the Board of Trade and Plantations from Lisburn, where the Huguenots settled, claimed that there were at least five hundred looms working commercially in the counties of Down, Antrim, Armagh, Tyrone, and Londonderry and that County Down produced well made linens 'little inferior to French cloth'.[5] A London compendium of trade published in 1696 referred to linen 'made in the north of Ireland, some yard wide, some three-quarters, and some half-ell [22^1/$_2$ inches], which are of great use for shirts and wear very white and strong'.[6] It is true that Louis Crommelin did publish *An Essay towards the Improving of the Hempen and Flaxen Manufactures in the Kingdom of Ireland* (1705), and that his claim about his prominent role in the promotion of the industry was accepted by the Linen Board in 1716, but other contemporary evidence reveals that he owed much of his reputation to the favour and patronage of the Huguenot Earl of Galway, especially while he was Lord Lieutenant.[7] About forty years after its initial publication the contents of Crommelin's pamphlet were analysed by a recognised expert, Robert Stephenson. He concluded that Crommelin's knowledge of weaving was limited to the sort of fine linen cloth in which his home district in France had specialised, such as cambrics, kentings, and holland diapers:[8] Crommelin himself had admitted in his 1707 petition that he and his colony had concentrated on the weaving of Holland diaper alone.[9] It could be argued that Crommelin's colony by its example stimulated the weaving of Holland diapers, especially when it was admitted in 1722 that a bounty on the weaving of hollands had produced a glut on the market.[10] As for bleaching, however, Stephenson reckoned Crommelin's knowledge of bleaching was slight and argued that 'by the improvements of our

---

5 Public Record Office, London. CO 389/40, pp. 71, 87, George Stead, Lisburn, to Philip Bayley, London, 8 September 1697, and John Molyneux, Liverpool, to the Lords Commissioners of the Council of Trade, 19 November 1697; CO 391/10 Evidence of Philip Bayley, 23 August 1697, and Mr Bennett, 30 September 1697, to the Lords Commissioners. I am indebted to Dr David Dickson for these references.

6 Quoted from pamphlet 'The merchant's warehouse laid open' in *Ulster Journal of Archaeology*, 1st series, 3 (1855), 198.

7 See page 20.

8 Robert Stephenson, *An inquiry into the state and progress of the linen manufacture of Ireland* (Dublin, 1757), 60.

9 *Journal of the House of Commons*, Ireland (hereafter *JHCI*) (1692–1713), part i, 505–6.

10 Anon, *Remarks on the present state of the linen manufacture of this Kingdom* (Dublin, 1745), p. 15.

machinery for washing and rubbing, and saving expense of hands, sowers [sours] and ashes, we have gained more in a few years on foreigners in our finest branches of the manufacture than it would be possible to have effected for ages by pursuing his schemes'.[11]

Among the men who helped to bring about this transformation in the Irish linen industry were several members of the Quaker community in Lurgan: Thomas Turner, James Bradshaw, John Nicholson and John Christy. The names of the first two appear regularly in *Precedents and Abstracts* because they were employed by the Linen Board and so it might be argued that their projects were not representative of the weavers and bleachers in their native district. It can be demonstrated from the evidence, however, that both Turner and Bradshaw spent most of their life in the Lurgan area, while the experiences of both John Nicholson and John Christy confirm that Turner and Bradshaw were typical of the innovators of that part of Ulster. The fact that several members of the Quaker community in Lurgan appear often in *Precedents and Abstracts* is not a reason for arguing that the Lurgan area led the way in innovations in the Ulster industry. It is a moot point, for example, whether Turner innovated, or developed, or merely took the credit for other people's ideas that he had picked up on his tours through the province as a representative of the Linen Board. Did he only put into words the accumulating experience of the bleachers? Whatever Turner's role was, it cannot be doubted that these men were busy adapting practices from related industries, improving equipment, and experimenting with new varieties of bleaching agents in their drive for efficiency.

Thomas Turner was the most prominent. As early as 1704, a year before Crommelin published his treatise, the journals of the Irish House of Commons record that Turner had received £220 from the Trustees for the Management of the Linen Manufacture in Ireland although no reason is given for the payment.[12] In May 1709 he petitioned the Irish Parliament about the repayment of £200 lent to him by the Trustees and a few days later asked for some recompense for his expenses in contriving 'an engine for dressing hemp and flax'.[13] That he was regarded as an expert in all branches of the industry is clear

[11] Stephenson, op. cit., pp. 62–3.
[12] *JHCI* (1692–1713), part ii, appendix, ccii.
[13] *JHCI* (1692–1713), part i, 595, 599.

from the range of commissions given to him by the new Board of Trustees of the Linen and Hempen Manufactures of Ireland created in 1711: he prepared ground for sowing hemp, devised a scutch mill, reproduced foreign methods of weaving, and contrived improved bleaching techniques.[14]

James Bradshaw, who was married to a niece of Thomas Turner, was equally versatile. Appointed in 1712 as an 'itinerant hemp and flax man' to propagate new methods in the industry, he sowed hemp seed, copied linens for foreign markets, inspected premises for grants, and was sent to the Continent to study Dutch, Flemish, and French practices, first in 1721 and again in 1729.[15] By then Bradshaw appears to have concentrated on the weaving of fine linens while Turner became noted for his knowledge of bleaching methods and materials.

In 1715, when Turner's pamphlet *New methods of improving flax and flax-seed and bleaching cloth* was published, he was described as 'a person well-skilled in bleaching.'[16] Robert Stephenson, who had been so critical of Crommelin as a bleacher, reckoned that the publication of Turner's pamphlet marked a significant advance in techniques for that date: 'the utensils and apparatus recommended by him are easily provided, and best suited to the wealth of our manufacturers and dealers at that time', a pragmatic assessment.[17] Whereas Crommelin and others had been used to spreading their cloth on the bleach-green with the lyes still in it and relied on subsequent watering to flush out the chemicals, Turner urged bleachers to rinse the lyes out of the cloth after each immersion, or 'bucking', as it was termed. He devised a simple wooden batting plank on which the cloth was to be first lightly beaten to loosen the lye and then rinsed on a wooden planking floor with the aid of planking poles such as dyers used. The Linen Board sponsored a tour by the author to instruct bleachers from Antrim as far as Cootehill and Monaghan and it was widely adopted. This method of bleaching must have been that described as the 'bat

---

14 *Precedents and abstracts from the Journals of the Trustees of the Linen and Hempen Manufactures of Ireland* (Dublin, 1784), pp. 2, 9, 14, 15, 18, 22, 28, 29.

15 Quaker records, T/1062/37/60 recording that James Bradshaw of Lurgan married Ann Turner in 1707, that they had their first child in Lurgan in 1710 and their next four children at Naas between 1713 and 1716 and their last four children at Lurgan 1720 and 1725. *Precedents and abstracts*, pp. 2, 5, 12, 20–1, 22, 23, 29, 43, 49, 102–3, 106, 108, 109.

16 *JHCI* (1715–30), appendix, xxxv. Pamphlet published as Appendix 1.

17 Stephenson, op. cit., pp. 113–14.

staff' which was said to have been superseded by the 'tuck mill' about 1730.[18] Evidence that Turner continued to devise improvements in bleaching methods can be found in *Precedents and Abstracts*. In 1719 he was rewarded for a flax mill and claimed that he was working on a 'possing' or washing mill. This may have been comprised in 'the new method' of bleaching for which he was rewarded in 1728 but no details of it have been recorded.[19] In the same year another Lurgan Quaker, John Nicholson, was awarded £150 as well as equipment for his bleachgreen, which was situated on the River Bann, but again there is no mention of a wash mill.[20] However, yet another Quaker, John Christy, was later to claim that when he moved to Scotland in 1731 from his father's green at Moyallen, close to Nicholson's green, he had brought with him the design of a 'washing mill or put [*sic*] stock mill': he reckoned that it 'was the first in Scotland made use of in a bleachfield'.[21] This last phrase is significant because several writers have suggested that the wash mill for linens was simply an adaptation to the linen industry of machinery from the existing woollen tuck mills. It may be significant in this context that in 1730 John Nicholson was the owner of a tuck mill at Knocknagore townland on the river Bann.[22] John Christy is also credited with introducing to Scotland the drying house (a shed equipped with louvred sides to allow air to circulate round the cloth):[23] before he left Ireland in 1731 he must have seen the new 'dry house' 92 feet long by 20 broad built by John Nicholson in 1728 with a grant of £50 from the Irish Linen Board.[24]

John Christy (spelt also Christie) was the youngest of three brothers who became prominent bleachers in Scotland. Their grandfather, Alexander Christy, born in Scotland in 1642, came to Moyallen on

[18] *Precedents and abstracts*, p. 15; H.D. Gribbon, *The history of water power in Ulster* (Newton Abbot, 1969), p. 82.

[19] *Precedents and abstracts*, pp. 31, 93.

[20] *Precedents and abstracts*, pp. 92–3.

[21] National Library of Scotland, Saltoun MSS, box 329, 'Observations on Dr Cullen's remarks on the art of bleaching or whitening linen by John Christy [*c.* 1752–3], p. 8. I am indebted to Dr Alastair J. Durie for this reference and advice about the Scottish linen industry: see his *Scottish Linen Industry in the Eighteenth Century* (Edinburgh, 1979).

[22] Gribbon, op. cit., 83; A. McCutcheon, *Wheel and spindle* (Belfast, 1977), p. 68; Registry of Deeds, Dublin (hereafter RDD), Book 63, p. 449, Number 44351, Nicholson to Jenney.

[23] A.J. Durie, 'Saltoun bleachfield 1746–73', *Transactions of the East Lothian Antiquarian and Field Naturalists' Society* 15 (1976), 52.

[24] *Precedents and abstracts*, p. 93.

the river Bann in 1675 and is said to have introduced the linen trade into that district. His son John (1673–1763) had five sons: Alexander (1699–1764), Joseph (1703–54), John (1707–62), James (1709–?), and Thomas (1712–80).[25] Alexander went to Scotland and set up a bleachgreen in 1731 at Ormiston near Edinburgh on the property of John Cockburn, the noted agricultural improver, who put up part of the capital. John assisted him and took over the Ormiston green when Alexander moved to set up another field at Perth in 1733: he himself moved on to Kinchey in 1741. Joseph sold his interest in property at Moyallen in 1744: he does not appear to have arrived in Scotland until the late 1740s when he took possession of a new bleachgreen at Saltoun Barley-mill field on Lord Milton's estate. All three ran successful ventures with the assistance of skilled tradesmen from Ireland. They taught the Scots the Irish method of finishing linens. Although the traditional Dutch method produced a quality finish to the linens, its cost proved too expensive for any but the fine linens. Much of the linen woven in Scotland was cheap and coarse and did not require high whitening; so the Scottish bleachers availed themselves of the wash mills, the rubbing boards and the beetling engines that the Irish had devised.[26] In time Irish bleachers and tradesmen came to be resented in Scotland and the comment made about the Irish in 1748 by the then secretary of the Scottish Board of Trustees ('multitudes of such are coming yearly and none of them have the skill wanted') really marks the coming of age of the Scottish linen bleaching industry: by that date Scotland was training its own managers and believed that it had nothing new to learn from the Irish industry.[27]

It is not easy to account for the great advances made in Irish bleaching methods in the first half of the eighteenth century, but a comparison between the evolution of Irish and Scottish developments in that

[25] Quaker records, T1062/37/71.

[26] See Appendix 2. That the new Irish methods were not imported from Lancashire but were indeed exported to Manchester by 1752 is illustrated by an advertisement for a new bleachgreen where the 'Dutch and Irish methods' were to be employed: see A.P Wadsworth,. and J. de L. Mann, *The Cotton Trade and Industrial Lancashire 1600–1780* (Manchester, 1931), p. 306. I am indebted to Dr Durie for much of the information about the activities of the Christy brothers in Scotland and to Mrs Brenda Collins of Edinburgh University for enabling me to fill in details about their careers.

[27] A.J. Durie, 'The Scottish linen industry in the eighteenth century; some aspects of expansion' in L.M. Cullen, and T.C. Smout, (eds), *Comparative aspects of Scottish and Irish economic and social history 1600–1900* (Edinburgh, 1977), p. 93.

period does suggest several points of interest. The rapid expansion of the linen industry in both countries owed much to the imposition by the Westminster parliament of high duties on continental linens while it removed duties on Irish linens in 1696 and permitted their direct export to the colonies after 1704, before it admitted the Scots to the same privileges by the Act of Union in 1707. The increasing demands of the English market provided the catalyst for the expansion of both the Scottish and Irish linen industries: in 1738 the London agent of the Scottish Board claimed that the Scottish and the Irish could sell three times the quantity they were selling if they could manufacture it.[28] Yet how can we explain why Scottish bleachers tended to concentrate on traditional methods of bleaching while at least some of the Irish bleachers were devising and adopting new methods? Part of the answer may lie in the lapse of time between the creation of the Irish Board of Trustees in 1711 and the Scottish Board in 1727. Both boards in their desire to promote the industry were ready to countenance claims put forward by innovators and to give rewards and grants towards expenses incurred in developing new processes, but the Irish had a lead of sixteen years. There men like Thomas Turner and James Bradshaw were encouraged to experiment, to study contemporary developments outside as well as inside Ireland, and to propagate their ideas. Entries in *Precedents and Abstracts* demonstrate that the Irish Board countenanced even proposals from individuals who had not the skill to translate them into practice. In defence of the Irish Board it should be added that at a time when bleachers could still refer to their trade as a 'mystery or art' and relied overmuch on experience when handling raw materials like potash and lime or using apparatus like rubbing boards, the only standards of judgement for laymen were the finished products. It also has to be admitted that the attitude of the boards in both countries did create a climate for innovations with a premium on efficiency and costcutting. The response went further than the Irish Board, for its part, was prepared to tolerate and it is a moot point whether their regulations on several matters did hinder progress in certain fields. Between 1736

---

[28] N.B. Harte, 'The rise of protection and the English linen trade, 1690–1790' in N.B. Harte, and K.G. Ponting, (eds), *Textile History and Economic History* (Manchester, 1973), pp. 91–6; A.J. Durie, 'The markets for Scottish linen, 1730–1775', *Scottish Historical Review*, iii (1973), 35–8.

and 1749 rubbing boards were banned by the Irish Parliament while the use of lime for bleaching was actively but never completely suppressed by prosecutions in the courts.[29] In the use of chemicals it should not be overlooked that Irish bleachers were among the first to experiment with oil of vitriol (sulphuric acid) for bleaching and that in 1764 Thomas Greg and Waddell Cunningham, two prominent Belfast merchants, were sufficiently confident of a local market to open their Vitriol Island works at Lisburn; another vitriol works in operation at Moyallen by 1786 had a Christy as its shareholder.[30]

The other great incentive to the introduction of mechanisation into bleaching in Ulster may have been an accident of historical geography. The heart of the linen industry in the early part of the eighteenth century lay in north Down and north Armagh and the bleachers who served it used water wherever it was available in rivers, streams, ponds or lakes. It is probable that, as we have seen in the case of Christy and Nicholson, the bleachers along the river Bann began to adapt the machinery of their tuck mills for linen bleaching whenever they realised the advantages provided by a regular, strong, plentiful supply of water of good quality for washing linen. Soon a stretch of some ten miles along the river around Gilford and Banbridge became a nest of bleachgreens. This development of water power rang the knell for those earlier establishments that lacked adequate water supplies and was responsible for the erection of some thirty-six bleachgreens on the river Callan in mid Armagh between 1743 and 1771.[31] Both districts were well supplied by water transport with coal from the Coalisland collieries or turf.

The capital to develop these sites does not appear to have been in short supply. Even a cursory examination of the mortgages and sales memorialised in the Registry of Deeds (established in Dublin in 1708) reveals that many local individuals prominent in the industry were negotiating with Dublin merchants, landowners, or clergy for their capital needs. Of special interest are two series of transactions

---

[29] Gribbon, op. cit., 83–4; Gill, op. cit., pp. 63, 208–10.

[30] A.J. Durie, 'Textile bleaching: a note on the Scottish experience', *Business History Review*, xlix (1975), 340; *JHCI* (1765–72) part 1, 181, 196; *Post Chaise Companion* (Dublin, 1784), p. 642. When sulphuric acid replaced buttermilk in the bleaching process, the buttermilk would have been used to feed pigs.

[31] PRONI, Foster–Massereene MS D562/1270, Robert Stevenson's view of County Armagh, 1795.

involving John Nicholson. Between 1715 and 1726 he leased, bought, or secured on mortgage, titles to a variety of properties in nine transactions. In 1725 he mortgaged most of these properties for £1,000 to Rev. Henry Jenny, the then Archdeacon of Dromore. He mortgaged more property to Jenny in 1726 for an additional £500 and yet more in 1730 for an undisclosed sum. The awards by the Linen Board made early in 1728 of a sum of £100, plus £50 towards the construction of a drying house, and a further provision of two large coppers, eight kieves, a wringing-engine, and a cold press, suggest that Nicholson had mortgaged his property to develop the bleachgreen. Even as late as the 1730 deed John Nicholson was described as 'merchant of Lurgan' but when the mortgage of all the property was renewed in 1739 to another clergyman, Archdeacon William Usher, John Nicholson had become 'gent of Nicholson's Hall, County Down'; his bleachgreen at Hall's Mill was the only green on the river to be noticed by Walter Harris in his 1744 survey of County Down.[32]

Nicholson's apparent transformation from draper or merchant to bleacher is not surprising when we learn that he had served his apprenticeship in the linen trade. It does, however, call attention to the real distinction between bleachers and drapers in the early years of the industry.[33] Bleaching was not a business to be entered upon

---

[32] RDD, Book 15, 130, Number 6964 (1715) Reilly to Nicholson;
27/409/17586 (1720) Robson to Nicholson;
28/109/16769 and 16770 (1720) Brownlow to Nicholson;
31/371/19482 (1721) Finlow to Nicholson;
34/97/20717 (1721) Thompson to Nicholson;
39/155/24730 (1723) Thompson to Nicholson;
40/152/24727 (1723) Moore to Nicholson;
40/153/24729 (1723) Thompson to Nicholson;
46/188/38249 (1724) Moore to Nicholson;
47/272/30549 (1725) Nicholson to Jenney;
49/99/31050 (1725) Tuft to Nicholson;
52/139/33927 (1726) Nicholson to Jenney;
63/449/44351 (1730) Nicholson to Jenney;
97/92/67454 (1739) Nicholson to Usher;
[W. Harris] *The ancient and present state of the county of Down* (Dublin, 1744), p. 106.

[33] This paragraph reflects a slight change in the interpretation of evidence presented on page 14, as a result of the evidence about John Nicholson and the Christys considered above. The bleachyards in and around Lurgan town were very small in scale and not to be compared with the greens being developed by individuals like Turner, Bradshaw, and Nicholson. The fact that bleachers always referred to themselves as drapers indicates both that bleachers would purchase webs as well as bleaching on commission, and that drapers had had more social standing than bleachers in the early years of the century.

lightly because lack of skill and errors of judgement could prove costly. Anyone, however, could set himself up as a linendraper if he had
the capital to purchase webs. Indeed, Arthur Brownlow, the owner of
a large estate in north Armagh, claimed in 1708 that he had established a linen market in Lurgan at an earlier date by purchasing all the
webs that were brought to the market.[34] Conrad Gill in *The Rise of
the Irish Linen Industry* assumed for want of 'definite evidence of the
origin of the drapers' class ... that drapers were becoming a distinct
class about 1720, at the time when specialised bleaching was developing, for the presence of bleachers implied the existence of drapers'.[35] Evidence that as many as nineteen individuals on the Brownlow
estate were named in leases to property as linendrapers before 1720 –
the earliest in 1696 – indicates an earlier date for their appearance.
The very number indicates that they were merchants and shopkeepers, as Gill surmised, who were prepared to deal in linens as a profitable trading line, rather than specialists concentrating their whole
attention and capital on the purchase of linens. That they would be
prepared to switch their activities from linen to any other commodity can be inferred from another comment on the Lurgan area as late
as 1745, 'that the breaking of so many factors in London has so discouraged this [linen] manufacture of late in this place where I best
know it, that many substantial dealers are turning their money to
other business; and the great plenty of the hides of the cattle of the
poor which died this spring has induced them to turn tanners ...'[36]
The linendraper who bought the web in the market or in his shop
would contract with a bleacher to finish it according to his specifica-
tions and then carry it to Dublin or ship it to London for factors to
market. As the century passed, more bleachers and their agents
appeared in the linen markets to purchase linen for their greens: until
the business careers of these individuals have been investigated it will
not be possible to determine the relative proportions of merchants
and of bleachers who claimed to be linendrapers, nor to reckon the
rate of capital investment and accumulation by the bleachers.

It has been possible to collect sufficient evidence for analysis about

34 From Dr Thomas Molyneux, 'Journey to the north in 1708' printed in R.M. Young,
   Historical notices of old Belfast (Belfast, 1896), p. 154.
35 Gill, op. cit., pp. 51–2.
36 Richard Barton to Walter Harris, 27 May 1745 (Armagh Public Library, Harris MSS).

Robert Hoope, the earliest man on the Brownlow estate to be described as linendraper in 1696, and his son John who succeeded him in business. Robert Hoope had come to Ireland in 1660 from Yorkshire as a tailor and had become a Quaker about seven years later. By 1696 he was the wealthiest member of the Quaker community in Lurgan and had subscribed £40 of the £208 raised to complete a new meeting house there. According to a eulogy of him preserved by John Rutty in his 1751 revised edition of *A History of the rise and progress of the people called Quakers,* Robert had retired about 1700 to concentrate on his religious life and he left his business to his son John.[37] In 1706 John demonstrated his wealth when he became a partner of his landlord, Arthur Brownlow, in the purchase of another estate in north Armagh, the Richmount estate, for £13,000: John Hoope's contribution was three thousand pounds, for which he received a proportion of the lands.[38] He did not retire to enjoy his new rural estate but remained a merchant of Lurgan until his death in 1740 at the age of 74. In his will made in the previous year Hoope described himself as a merchant and mentioned his stocks of iron, lead, linen cloth, linen yarn, cashub (potash for bleaching) and kelp (also for bleaching): unfortunately no inventory of them survives and so the value of his stock cannot be assessed. Hoope referred also to the post-office which he had administered in Lurgan for about forty years. He also held a two-thirds share in a bleachgreen at Ballymacateer: this he had taken in partnership with John Turner and John Nicholson in 1717 and leased to Thomas Turner for his experiments in 1728.[39] There is no doubt that Hoope was deeply involved in the linen trade although he had other business interests.

John Hoope was highly regarded not only by his local Quaker meeting but also by the Friends in Dublin. In general, links between the Northern and the Dublin Quakers were not strong and they met only when representatives of the Northern meetings attended the

[37] Quaker records, T1062/37/66; J. Rutty, *A history of the rise and progress of the people called Quakers in Ireland* (fourth edition, London, 1811), pp. 262–3; Quaker records, Lurgan men's meeting, T1062/47.

[38] PRONI, Brownlow MS T3300, Conveyance of townlands in manor of Richmount from Arthur Brownlow to John Hoope, 1706.

[39] RDD 100/33/69469 (1740), Will of John Hoope, Lurgan, County Armagh, merchant; a summary of the will is published in P.B. Eustace, (ed.), *Registry of Deeds Dublin: Abstract of Wills, I (1708–1745)* (Dublin, 1956), pp. 272–4. Also RDD 36/517/23896.

national half-yearly meeting in Dublin.[40] Yet the marriages made by John Hoope's children reveal a much more intimate relationship with the Dublin Quakers and indicate that Hoope's social standing and reputation matched theirs. His first daughter, Abigail (to whom he left £600), married the third son of Amos Strettell, one of the leading Dublin linendrapers. Hannah, the second daughter (to whom he left £400), married John Petticrew, another Dublin merchant, and Sarah, the third daughter (to whom he left £300), married John Clibborn of Moate in County Westmeath, by then the head of a very influential Quaker family. John's first three sons had all died young. The fourth, Edward, married Sarah Willcocks, daughter of another Dublin merchant, Joshua Willcocks, but Edward died in 1738 leaving children. Robert, the fifth son, married Sarah Lark, daughter of James Lark of London, but he died in 1737. John Hoope himself, after the death of his first wife in 1714, married Elizabeth Willcocks, the widow of Thomas Willcocks of Dublin. She bore him two sons, James and Joshua, before her death in 1721. James was apprenticed to Robert Clibborn, a Dublin merchant, and married a daughter of Timothy Forbes, another Dublin merchant who had held letters of attorney from Robert Hoope, young James's grandfather.[41]

This marriage network may have been the product not so much of Hoope's religious connexions as of his financial links. In an account book kept by John Hoope with William Brownlow, the owner of the estate in which Hoope lived, several of the names of Hoope's Dublin kin regularly appear, notably Amos, Abell, and Thomas Strettell, James and John Petticrew, and Timothy Forbes.[42] While Brownlow lived in the capital each winter season he drew on Hoope's accounts with these merchants: until 1720 he drew mainly on the Strettells but after that time James Petticrew had the business. Hoope received cash from several of Brownlow's servants and in return he transmitted cash

---

[40] John 'Hoop' was one of the sixteen signatories of 'The humble address of the people called Quakers, from their national half-year's meeting held in Dublin, the 10th of the ninth month, 1715' to the Dublin government: see Rutty, op. cit., p. 220. Amos Strettell was another signatory.

[41] Compiled from John Hoope's will and the Hoope family entry in the Quaker records; see also Eustace, *RDD: Abstract of Wills, I (1708–1745)* and P. B. Eustace, and O.C. Goodbody, (eds), *Quaker Records Dublin: Abstracts of Wills* (Dublin, 1957) for reference to the other families.

[42] PRONI, Brownlow MS D2667/5/2, John Hoope's account book with William Brownlow 1711–39.

or bills to Dublin, serviced interest charges and annuities, met any bills drawn on him, and paid local accounts. Each year in October on the eve of Brownlow's return to Dublin the account was settled but occasionally it ran for as long as two years and there was no hurry to settle although the average annual account reached £1,300. The arrangement clearly suited both men because Hoope could obtain cash (the linen trade was conducted only in cash transactions and rents were taken only in cash and not in banknotes or bills of exchange) while Brownlow was provided with ready access to money in the capital. Brownlow dealt with regular banks also: in 1731–2 it was Messrs Swift and Company, in 1733–6 Hugh Henry's, and from 1737 until Brownlow's death in 1739, Richard Dawson's. When he visited England Brownlow was able to draw on Hoope's running account with Jonathan Gurnell and Company or Robert Hales in London. Elsewhere in England Hoope had three other correspondents: James Bolt of Bristol and Jonathan Patton and Robert Fielding of Manchester.

The structure and detail of the account book suggest that it is unlikely that John Hoope ever operated as a correspondent for one of the Dublin banks of the period. It does suggest that he did discount bills for cash for his fellow merchants and linendrapers. In this context it is surprising that his will does not mention any significant sums of money lent by him either to them or to innovators such as Thomas Turner or John Nicholson. An entry in the account book suggests a reason. It records that on 24 July 1733 John Hoope purchased from William Brownlow for £600 the townlands of Derrykeevan and Derrykeeran close to his other property in the manor of Richmount, County Armagh. Hoope's family commitments and his age (66 years) may have forced him to invest in land rather than in ventures.

The approach used in this study may not find favour with those economic historians who rely on statistics to determine norms of human and mechanical activity. Yet in the absence of reliable statistics or any other source materials capable of providing a comprehensive account of developments, it is still necessary to construct a model. We have to piece together and to probe even fragments of evidence in order to determine the parameters of problems. We have to test and discipline our speculations. From the records of the Scottish Board of

Trustees Dr Durie has provided a coherent picture of the development of the linen industry in Scotland and if we can appreciate the comparisons and contrasts between the Scottish and Irish industries we should be able to apply some of his findings to improving our model of the development of the Irish linen industry and the commercial structure in which it evolved.

NOTE: *The case of the linen manufacture of Ireland, relative to the bleaching and the whitening the same* published in Dublin in 1750 and reprinted here as Appendix 2, provides some corroboration for the interpretation advanced in this study.

4

The market book of Thomas Greer, a Dungannon linendraper 1758–9[1]

PLATE 4
The common method of Beetling, Scutching and hackling the Flax . . .
WILLIAM HINCKS 1783

WHENEVER THE ORIGINS of Ulster's prosperity are discussed the linen industry is bound to be mentioned. The actual scale of the industry has been somewhat exaggerated yet it did stimulate economic growth which converted Ulster from the most backward province in Ireland in 1650 to the most prosperous in 1800. The higher standard of living it ensured was a key factor in the tremendous increase in population, so that by 1789 it was observed: 'In many parts of the great manufacturing counties of Ulster, the people are so numerous as not to be able to procure milk for their families, or flax ground and depend almost entirely on markets for their oatmeal and other provisions.'[2] The linen industry in Ireland depended for its prosperity on the fact that Irish linens entered England duty free while foreign linens were subject to high tariffs. Because of the low cost of living and low wages in Ulster it was possible for the industry to compete in the English market[3] while its continental competitors were regularly excluded by frequent continental wars.

The growing demand for linen in England greatly boosted Ulster's economy but the wealth it generated subsidised and bolstered up inefficient and unprofitable practices in agriculture: farming and the linen industry went hand in hand and the income from the linen industry enabled many tenants to take more expensive leases, forcing up the price of land through the free competition of the market.[4] By the mid-eighteenth century there were many weavers in Ulster who spent most of their time at the loom, especially in the Lagan valley and north Armagh.[5] In the more remote areas, however, earnings from spinning and weaving supplemented the poor returns from farming so that in such provincial centres of the industry as Ballymena, Coleraine, and Dungannon, professional weavers rubbed shoulders in the markets with the casual weavers, the farmers who wove in their spare time. Since bleaching at this time was confined to the summer months the drapers purchased most of their cloth in the spring. This meant the weaver had to concentrate on his loom just when his small-holding required much attention: small wonder that

[1] First published in *Ulster Folklife* 13, 1967, pp. 54–60.
[2] Stephenson, Robert, *A letter to the Right Honourable and Honourable the Trustees of the Linen Manufacture* (Dublin, 1789), p. 19.
[3] *The Dublin Society's weekly observations*, 1 (1737), 181, 233.
[4] Ibid., 1 (1737), 181, 188.
[5] Ibid., 1 (1737), 192. Confirmed by letter from Rev. Richard Barton, Lurgan, to Walter Harris, 27 May 1745 (Harris MSS, Armagh Public Library).

many contemporaries complained of the very low standards of arable farming[6] and that the industry flourished most in the Lagan valley where dairy farming was the concern of the women folk. The implications of this domestic system and its effects on the rural community still require to be studied. One source for such an examination is a market book kept by a Dungannon linendraper, Thomas Greer, between October 1758 and September 1759.[7]

From the collection of Greer letters in the Public Record Office of Northern Ireland,[8] Thomas Greer emerges as an able but headstrong Quaker patriarch whose business prospered but at the expense of his fraternal relations with other Quakers. He was the great-grandson of an immigrant who had come to Ireland from Northumberland in 1653 and settled at Redford, near Grange, County Tyrone. He was born in 1724 so that he was in his thirty-fifth year when this market book was compiled. He was even then in a considerable way of business, as reflected in his total outlay in the period covered by the book of £2,054 for the purchase of linens (see Table 4.1). Although the total number of webs purchased, 1,061, was only a fraction of the 'vast quantity' of 3,000 pieces bleached by Barclay of Lisburn in 1766,[9] it should be noted that 746 of these were double webs so that he bought the equivalent of 1,807 single pieces.[10] At this time Greer did not possess his own bleachgreen and he sent his brown linens for bleaching to several other greens. There is evidence, too, that he dealt directly with Quaker merchants in London, Warrington, and Manchester, and from their letters it appears probable that he acted as their agent in selling North American flax seed, in buying linen yarn for the English market and brown linens for bleachers, and in providing cargoes of finished cloth for sale overseas.[11] He became one of

---

[6] Ibid., 1 (1737), 181–8. Repeated by Arthur Young in 1776: see *A Tour in Ireland* (ed. A.W. Hutton,) (2 vols, London, 1892), vol. 1, 113, 116, and especially his famous diatribe, vol. 2, 214–17.

[7] Transcript in the Public Record Office of N. Ireland: T1127/4. Copied from an original in the possession of Miss Sheila Greer, Tullaghoge, Co. Tyrone.

[8] Greer MS: D1044.

[9] McCall, H., *Ireland and her Staple Manufactures* (Belfast, 1870, 3rd edn), p. 87.

[10] Double webs were not made in the Belfast–Lisburn neighbourhood: *Observations upon the Linen Trade humbly submitted to the consideration of the Right Honourable and Honourable The Trustees of the Linen Manufacture by the Drapers of Belfast* (Belfast, 1763), p. 29.

[11] Greer MS: D1044/16, 21, 45, 46.

the foremost drapers in county Tyrone, for in 1782 he was chosen at an assembly of 437 linendrapers to be one of the two Tyrone representatives on the committee of Drapers for Ulster Province who opposed the new measures introduced by the Linen Board to regulate the industry.[12]

The market book is a record of the cloth purchased by Thomas Greer in the markets of Dungannon, Stewartstown, Coagh and Caledon (all in County Tyrone), Moneymore (County Londonderry), and in Armagh, Monaghan, and Cootehill (in County Cavan); all these markets except Monaghan and Cootehill lay within a radius of ten miles from Dungannon. In the book were noted the number of each web purchased with the name of the seller, the length claimed by the seller and the length measured by the draper, with the price per yard or, in the case of cheaper linens, per score of yards, and the price paid. It does not mention the quality or the kind of cloth he purchased although seven-eighth yard-wide linens were distinguished from the more common yard-wides. In the left-hand margin the webs were ticked off when checked and the total cash outlay was noted in the right-hand margin. It is clear that the book was written up at the office and not at the market; the entry for Stewartstown on 1st May followed the entry for Dungannon on 3rd May and the entries for both Caledon and Moneymore were made on 21st May. Indeed, attendance at several markets tended to produce some confusion in the numbering of the webs and from 21st February to 22nd March parallel columns of numbers record such adjustments. At least two people were concerned in compiling the market book, Thomas Greer and his younger brother, James (whose name or initials appear several times in the margin against his entries), and occasionally one of them finished the lists for a market after it had been commenced by the other. It is not completely accurate for, in reckoning the total amount spent, the figure for the sixth page (numbers 139–166) was omitted while that for the third page contains a slight inaccuracy.

Thomas Greer's activities were dictated each spring by his need to purchase a sufficient number of webs for the summer bleaching. According to the market book, less than one tenth of his total requirements for the seasonal bleaching were bought before January since

12 *Belfast News-Letter* account of a meeting held at Armagh on Monday, 5 August 1782.

money laid out at this time was dormant. Serious activity commenced early in the new year when Greer and his other buyer or buyers began regularly to attend the weekly markets on Wednesdays in Stewartstown and on Thursdays in Dungannon. He depended on Dungannon for 60 per cent of all his purchases of yard-wide linen and for one third of all his seven-eighth yard-wide linens and on Stewartstown for another 40 per cent of narrow linens. About the 21st of each month Moneymore monthly market was visited instead of Stewartstown; it is not clear why he preferred to attend Moneymore instead of Stewartstown for he did not buy a large number of webs and their price was, if anything, a little higher on average. By the end of March there was a notable drop in the number of narrow (seven-eighth) linens purchased, from 62 in February and 89 in March to 19 in April and 30 in May. At the same time there was a corresponding increase in the purchase of yard-wide linens from an average of 78 per month in the first quarter of the year to 151 in the second quarter. This seasonal increase in demand alone would have forced up the price but it is clear that Greer, moreover, was concentrating on the purchase of better quality linens than in the early months of the year, for several visits were paid to a very good monthly market at Caledon, to the regular weekly markets of Armagh and Monaghan, and even one to Cootehill in County Cavan, about 30 miles away. Only 35 webs were bought in four visits to Armagh but 98 in Caledon and 86 in Monaghan. A rather surprising point is that Armagh market was never visited on the day following Caledon market and there is no evidence to suggest a regular circuit of markets except for the June visit to Cootehill and Monaghan. For Greer the buying season ended at the end of June; he attended only two markets in Dungannon in July and another single market there in September.

It was in March 1759 that a movement began among the linen-drapers to withdraw from the country fairs, especially in Counties Tyrone and Monaghan. So many new markets were being established in the towns and villages that they were no longer prepared to suffer 'the inconveniences and loss for want of accommodation in country fairs' which they condemned as 'highly inconvenient and troublesome by means of the hurry and confusion to which they are liable several kinds of fraud and roguery have often been successfully prac-tised'.[13] It would appear from Greer's market book that he was already pursuing such a policy except in the isolated instance of a visit to Coagh on Friday 9th March to purchase seven webs. Such a decision by the linendrapers, however, would have entailed a certain amount of contraction for the industry in the outlying areas unless dealers there were numerous and wealthy enough to assume the role aban-doned by the drapers. These dealers or jobbers were disliked by authority in the shape of the Linen Board, because they were so often guilty of shady practices, but individual drapers were quite prepared to do business with them in the markets. It was against such a back-ground of change that Robert Stephenson, the chief adviser to the Linen Board, urged that the expansion of the linen industry depend-ed on regular visits by linendrapers to the outlying provincial towns in order to stimulate spinning and weaving. For this reason he thought that premiums should be offered by the Linen Board to those who would buy the largest quantities of linens in those markets where the industry was under-developed.[14] Such a policy was adopted on local initiative in 1759 in Ballymoney, Broughshane, and even Coleraine. The impetus to trade that resulted from the payment of premiums is also reflected in the establishment of new markets, par-ticularly that of Keady in south Armagh by Letters Patent granted to Trinity College, Dublin, on 13th March 1759 to hold a Friday mar-ket, and in the creation of three new fairs at Dungannon on the first Thursday in February, April and July.[15]

It is not possible from this market book alone to estimate how many people attended these markets, but an analysis of the lists of people who sold cloth to Greer has produced some rather surprising conclusions. In a region where weaving was extensively practised we might reasonably expect to find Greer dealing with a considerable body of regular clients, a number of whom might be dependent on him for regular employment; this latter phenomenon was widespread in the industry and had been noted in the North as early as 1737.[16]

13 *Belfast News-Letter*, 24 March 1759 and 23 March 1762.
14 Stephenson, Robert, *A letter to the Right Honourable and Honourable the Trustees of the Linen Manufacture* (Dublin, 1759), pp. 22–4.
15 *Belfast News-Letter*. Many advertisements in the first half of 1759.
16 *The Dublin Society's weekly observations*, 1 (1737), 192.

Instead it was found that in Dungannon Greer bought a total of 559 pieces from 329 weavers, of whom 233 sold to him on only one occasion and 64 on only two occasions. Three men sold him 12 webs each and seven more a total of 48 webs; these were his regular customers. In Stewartstown and Caledon the situation was similar: 137 individuals sold him 169 webs in Stewartstown, and in Caledon he bought 92 webs from 72 persons. A certain number of individuals sold to him in more than one market; of those with whom he dealt in Dungannon, 14 turned up in Stewartstown, 3 in Moneymore, 9 in Caledon, 6 in Armagh, and 2 in Monaghan. Some of them may have lived convenient to two market towns but it is probable that some of them were dealers who purchased throughout the country: there were in fact four people whom he met in three separate markets. The pattern of purchases from individuals also indicates that some of them were either employers or dealers. Some of them sold several webs in a market while others appeared frequently within the period of three or four weeks required to weave a web of fifty yards.

It appears, therefore, that in the Dungannon area in 1759 the majority of the weavers were independent producers. Their independent status may have been secured by their ability to make a sufficient livelihood from farming or at least to provide their own flax.[17] Moreover, the linen industry was booming (although 1758–9 did see the beginning of a temporary recession caused by the outbreak of the Seven Years' War) and, by reason of the continuing strong demand for linens, independent weavers were in a relatively strong position. We have no contemporary evidence of the numbers of weavers or drapers that attended the markets nor of the amount of business done in them, but there must have been considerably more than the number of weavers who dealt with Greer because even in the final weeks of the season the majority of those who sold to him in the regular markets were new faces. It was estimated, however, in 1784 that the Dungannon market produced £1,500 per week and Stewartstown £800.[18]

[17] Arthur Young (op. cit., vol. 1, 122) was told in Armagh that 30 stone of flax, the produce of an acre, would make 20 pieces of linen, 25 yards long and a yard wide. A single piece was woven in ten to twelve days.

[18] McCall, H., op. cit., p. 95, quoting from John Greer's *Report on the State of the Linen Markets of Ulster*, 1784.

The conduct of these markets did not differ substantially from any of the other Ulster markets. Weavers crowded around the stand of the draper where after a brief altercation the price was struck and the draper's clerk initialled the web and noted the bargain in his book. Payment was traditionally made in cash as the weavers would not take bank notes. Greer's book, however, provides an exception to the rule, for on a spare page he noted:

6 mo (June) 12 Thomas Brunhert drawn to my draft on John Barclay No. ( ) received.	£15 0 0
To cash	4 5 5
	£19 5 5
By sundry Linnens see Entry if stands measure	19 5 5

On 12 June Thomas Brunhert had sold Greer eight webs in Monaghan for £19 5s. 5d. and been paid partly in cash and partly by a promissory note. The other interesting point in this transaction is the phrase 'if stands measure'. When Greer bought the eight webs from Brunhert he obviously did not measure them on the spot but paid Brunhert for the lengths specified minus the customary deduction of 'yards' or 'half yards'. There was obviously an agreement that if the webs were deficient in length Brunhert would repay Greer for the deficiency or give him an allowance on a future purchase.

The measurement of webs in markets had always provoked 'idle disputes between buyer and seller', mainly because some of the drapers insisted on taking final yards and fractions of yards for nothing while others used their own systems of measurement. In a series of resolutions passed by linendrapers on 1st September 1758 and published in the *Belfast News-Letter*, they stated: 'we are determined to have one yard to the single piece [of 25 yards] and two yards to the double piece [of 50 yards] on all brown linens bought by us in any of the aforesaid markets. And in order to make a sufficient recompense to the sellers of brown linens for said yards, and to prevent the many idle disputes arising between buyer and seller, at the time of measuring, we recommend to the Magistrates of said towns, to have all brown cloth yards cut to thirty six inches.'[19] According to the market

19 *Belfast News-Letter* advertisement of resolutions passed at the drapers' meeting on
   1 September 1758. See also *Observations on the several Matters offered to the Linen Board as
   Materials for a Linen Bill ... by the Linen Weavers and Manufacturers of the Towns of Belfast,
   Lisburn, Hillsborough, and Country adjacent* (1763), pp. 30–39.

book Greer's practice was to deduct one yard from a double piece and half a yard from a single piece. He did often take two yards from the double pieces and in a handful of cases he deducted three yards but his maximum deduction from the single pieces rarely exceeded half a yard. It is worth noting that he paid for the half yard, which was not by any means a universal practice among drapers at this period. Of course it would be dangerous to use this evidence to praise the standard of Greer's business ethics for we do not know what his conception of a yard was or whether he had idiosyncrasies in his technique of measuring.

Webs were valued according to their fineness but we have no details of the quality of those bought by Greer. Stephenson noted in 1760 that 'the south-east part of the county [of Tyrone] joining Armagh is entirely engaged in the manufacture of low-priced yard-wides from ninepence to thirteen pence per yard';[20] he had overlooked the considerable manufacture in this region of seven-eighth yard-wides which composed about 30 per cent of all the linens Greer purchased. In the markets linens were assessed by the draper in pence per yard or, in the case of linens worth less than one shilling per yard, in scores of yards. The latter practice meant that distinctions in quality could be made to a twentieth of a penny per yard whereas with linen worth more than a shilling, one farthing and very occasionally an eighth of a penny was the minimum difference. It is not surprising therefore that there was 'a little altercation whether the price should be one halfpenny or a penny a yard, more or less' which appeared so useless to Arthur Young when he noted it in Lurgan market.[21]

The market book is a valuable piece of evidence about the prices paid to weavers around the middle of the eighteenth century and will be useful in any future survey of the standards of living they enjoyed. In 1763 even the drapers admitted that the weavers were poorly paid but they blamed foreign competition for the low price of webs and did not see any prospects of improvement. Robert Stephenson on the other hand does not appear to have shown a similar concern but

[20] Stephenson, Robert, *The Reports and Observations of Robert Stephenson made to the Right Honourable and Honourable The Trustees of the Linen Manufacture for the years 1760 and 1761* (Dublin, 1762), p. 90.
[21] Young, Arthur, op. cit., vol. 1, 128.

Market	When held	How often attended	Type of cloth	Price in pence/yard	No. of pieces	No. from whom	Total yards purchased	Total cost (£ s. d.)	Average price/yard (d.)
Dungannon	weekly – Thursday	35	yard and 7/8 yard	8–17	559	329	21,811	1,045.18. 0½	11½
Stewartstown	weekly – Wednesday	12	yard and 7/8 yard	9–11	169	139	7,318	308. 8. 4	10
Moneymore	monthly – 21st	5	yard and 7/8 yard	9¼–11¼	87	73	3,751	160.14. 0½	10¼
Coagh	Friday, 9 March 1759	1	7/8 yard	9½–11	7	6	306	12.11. 2	9¾
Caledon	weekly – Monday	4	yard	10½–15	98	72	4,019	206. 4. 4½	12¼
Armagh	weekly – Tuesday	4	yard	10½–15¾	35	30	1,281	67.13. 1½	12¾
Monaghan	weekly – Monday/ Tuesday	3	yard	10–17	86	63	3,493	198. 1. 9	13½
Cootehill	weekly – Saturday, 9 June 1759	1	yard	11–16 ¾	20	15	919	54. 9. 2½	14¼
TOTAL	–	–	–	–	1,061	*	42,898	£2,054. 0. 0½	11½

* No total appears for this column because some individuals sold to Thomas Greer at more than one of the markets listed.

TABLE 4.1
An analysis of the market book of Thomas Greer to show his attendance at the markets and the extent of his purchases in each

bitterly attacked the growth of combinations among workmen; he laid on them the blame for the failure of the *doulass*, or coarse sheeting, industry in Dublin.[22] It would appear however that a period of comparative prosperity for the weavers was beginning about this time and it probably lasted until the 1780s. But it depended so completely on the linen industry that, when the latter was challenged by cotton manufacturing, the spinners and weavers in the outlying areas were the first to be affected. Soon a very large population had no other means of dependence than the underdeveloped and under-capitalised farming industry. Irish agriculture failed to carry this huge burden and crashed in the Great Famine with terrible consequences.

.

---

[22] Stephenson, Robert, *Letter to the Trustees of the Linen Manufacture* (1789), p. 27; but see also *The Reports and Observations … for the years 1760 and 1761* (Dublin, 1762), pp. 101–3.

5

The linen industry portrayed in the Hincks prints of 1783[1]

PLATE 5

A perspective view of a Scutch Mill, with the Method of Breaking the Flax with groved Rollers, and Scutching it with Blades fixt on a shaft, both turn'd by the main Wheel. Great Improvements in the Method of Breaking and Scutching of Flax . . .

WILLIAM HINCKS 1783

A SUPERB INTRODUCTION to the industry as it evolved in the late eighteenth century is provided in the twelve engravings published by William Hincks in 1783 to illustrate the several stages in the preparation of linen from sowing the flax crop to the sale of the bleached cloth.[2] Hincks portrayed not only contemporary methods but also some of the earlier skills that they had displaced.

PLATE 1

'Taken near Scarva in the County of Downe, representing Ploughing, Sowing the Flax Seed and Harrowing …'

Because flax needs strong well-prepared ground it was usually grown after a potato crop which opened up the soil and cleansed the land of weeds, especially redshank, charlock and scutch grass. The land might require up to four ploughings and then harrowing to render it fine enough for the young shoots. The seed was sown broadcast in mid-April. Much of the seed was imported. It came in hogsheads (large barrels) from Holland and the Baltic countries but at the time of this picture much of it was being imported from New York and Connecticut. (See page 1)

PLATE 2

'Taken near Hillsborough in the County of Down, representing pulling the Flax when grown, Stooking or putting it up to dry, Ripling or saving the Seed, and Boging or Burying it in Water …'

After about three months the flax was about three feet high and ready for pulling. It had to be pulled rather than cut because the fibre went down into the roots.

If the seed was to be saved for the next crop, the flax would be left for another fortnight or so to mature: this would produce a coarser yarn from the flax. During years when foreign seed was scarce, farmers were encouraged to save seed but in years of plenty foreign seed was preferred. The seeds were removed by drawing it through a ripple resembling a huge metal comb.

---

[1] First published in an illustrated brochure, *The Irish Linen Industry*, prepared for the 'Our Linen Industry' exhibition in the Ulster Folk and Transport Museum, 1987.

[2] W.G. Strickland, *Dictionary of Irish Artists* (Dublin and London, 1913), vol. 1, 485–7.

Flax had to be retted (soaked in water) for about ten to fourteen days so that the woody core could be softened and removed. (See page 7)

PLATE 3

'Taken in the County of Louth representing taking the Flax out of the Bog when it has laid a sufficient time to separate the Rind, (which is the Flax) from the Stem, and strengthen it, spreading it to dry, stoving, beetling, and breaking it …'

After the flax was removed from the 'lint dam' it had to be dried. Because in Ireland drying in the open was difficult in damp weather, flax was often dried over a hot kiln. There was a risk that too much heat would harden the gum that had previously bound the fibre and the woody stem, thus making the flax difficult to scutch (separate the fibre from the stem). Once dried, the 'beets' or sheaves of flax were beaten by a long mallet or put through a flax breaker to fragment the woody stem in preparation for scutching. (See page 23)

PLATE 4

'The common method of Beetling, Scutching and hackling the Flax …'

After the flax straw was pounded with a beetle, women scutched it with a long wooden blade over a scutching block to strike off most of the 'shous', or woody stem. The fibre was then drawn through a series of blocks containing different sizes of hackle pins in order to remove remaining pieces of straw as well as 'tow' (short fibres), and to comb out the long fibres for the spinner. Shows was burned on domestic fires and its acrid smell was said to identify the neighbourhood of a scutch mill. (See page 38)

PLATE 5

'A perspective view of a Scutch Mill, with the Method of Breaking the Flax with groved Rollers, and Scutching it with Blades fixt on a shaft, both turn'd by the main Wheel. Great Improvements in the Method of Breaking and Scutching of Flax …'

Although the scutch mill was invented in Scotland and introduced into Ireland about 1725, it was not popular: the Irish model appeared about 1760. Water power was used to turn the scutching blades to imitate hand scutching over the stock (as in Plate 4). Scutching was carried out in the autumn after the flax was retted so that the scutched flax could be sold by November, when rents were due. When scutching was in full swing the air in the mills was full of dust called 'pouce', which workers inhaled into their lungs. (See page 49)

PLATE 6

'Taken on the spot in the County of Downe, Representing Spinning, reeling with the Clock reel, and Boiling the yarn …'

Throughout the eighteenth century the spinning of yarn was done by women in their cottages. Spinning was done on the Dutch wheel, kept in motion by a treadle. By two separate cords the wheel turned both the bobbin on which the spun yarn collected and the flyer which spins and distributes that yarn along the bobbin. A flax wheel is distinguishable from those used to spin other fibres by its rock or distaff on which the lint hangs for the spinner's convenience.

The bobbins of yarn were then passed to another woman for winding on the clock (or click) reel. One hundred and twenty revolutions of the wheel wound three hundred yards of yarn equal to one cutt; twelve cutts made a hank and four hanks a spangle. These standards were imposed and enforced by the Linen Board. When the hank was wound it was taken off the reel by twisting a movable head on one of the arms. The yarn was then boiled in a pot on the fire and dried. Then it was ready for weaving. Yarn was graded according to the number of hanks that would weigh one pound: sixteen hank yarn, for example, would weigh one sixteenth of a pound or one ounce per hank. (See page 58)

PLATE 7

'Winding, Warping, with a new improved Warping Mill, and Weaving …'

The weaver needed both warp yarn and weft yarn. The warp yarn had to be strong enough to stand the tension of the loom for it stretched from the warp beam at the back of the loom forward to the cloth beam. On this new type of warping mill, or machine, the warp yarn was wound off a rack of bobbins on to the warp frame by employing a pulley.

In the background the boy had hung cutts of yarn on a swift and was busy winding pirns (bobbins of weft to fit into the shuttle) on a pirn winder which bears a superficial resemblance to a spinningwheel.

The loom is a simple treadle loom for weaving plain cloth. The weaver is using the traditional curved shuttle because the flying-shuttle, already in use in cotton and woollen weaving, was not adapted for linenweaving in Ireland until the turn of the century. This delay is surprising because the weaver with the hand-shuttle could not sit while he was weaving but had to crouch over the web so that he could 'pitch each shot of weft across the loom'. Yet many experienced weavers were loath to use the flying shuttle. (See page 86)

PLATE 8

'The brown Linen market at Banbridge in the County of Downe, the weavers holding up their pieces of Linen to View, the Bleachers elevated on Forms examining its Quality'

The weavers brought their webs to the weekly 'brown linen' markets where dealers known as linendrapers purchased them for bleaching and finishing. In the street these drapers agreed a price with individual weavers and later under cover measured the webs and paid for them. Although webs were checked for quality before sale and then stamped by seal-masters appointed by the Linen Board, there were continual complaints about dishonest practices.

Banbridge was one of the new towns that had arisen on the prosperity of the linen industry. At the beginning of the century it had been no more than a cluster of houses around a wooden bridge over the River Bann. A stone bridge was built in 1712 to carry the main road from Dublin to Belfast. The settlement grew rapidly in importance because of the bleach-greens in the district. Under a patent of 1726 Solomon White secured for the village of Ballyvally a weekly market and four threeday fairs each year. These linen fairs attracted merchants even from England to buy bleached linens. In 1750 the settlement was acquired by the Hill family of Hillsborough (later the Downshires) who laid it out in its present pattern and built the market-house. In 1766 a new patent for Banbridge took over the rights of the Ballyvally market and fairs.

Brown linen markets declined during the first half of the nineteenth century with the putting out of fine yarns to the weavers from the spinning mills. (See page 105)

PLATE 9

'A complete Perspective View of all the machinery of a Bleach Mill, upon the Newest and Most approved Constructions, Consisting of the Wash Mill, Rubbing Boards moved by a Crank, and Beetling Engine for Glazing the Cloth, with a View of the Boiling House'

In the early years of the eighteenth century the Dutch method of bleaching required up to five months to produce white cloth. All the work was done by hand and the bleaching materials were potash (obtained from wood ashes) for the alkali ley (bleaching liquid) and buttermilk or bran sour for the acids to neutralise them. Much time was spent then in boiling the pieces over great turf fires and then rinsing them in clear cold water. The annual output of the largest bleachgreens would not have exceeded one thousand pieces.

In the 1730s bleachers began to adapt the heavy wooden machinery of the local 'tuck' mills (for finishing woollens) to prepare their linen cloth: although the Linen Board was anything but enthusiastic, wash mills and rubbing boards came into general use. The beetling engine for finishing off the quality linens with a glaze appeared about the same time. All this machinery has survived in use into the twenty-first century. (See Appendix 2)

More important even than machinery in increasing the output of the bleachgreens was the chemical revolution that greatly reduced the time required for bleaching. For neutralising the alkalis based on potash, dilute sulphuric acid (known then as 'oil of vitriol') replaced buttermilk in the 1760s and by the close of the century a new bleaching liquor derived from chlorine reduced the time required for souring from several weeks to a single day. By the end of the century some greens could turn over ten thousand pieces each year, and this output continued to increase. (See page 116)

PLATE 10

'Perspective View of a Bleach Green taken in the County of Downe, Shewing the methods of Wet and Dry Bleaching, and the outside View of a Bleach Mill on the most approved Construction ...'

Until the end of the eighteenth century bleaching was restricted to the period from March to October. Because bleachgreens operated in the summertime only, their owners had to acquire reliable and inexhaustible supplies of water. The consequence was that the major greens were soon to be found along the banks of those rivers that continued to provide a good flow of water in summertime. When this linen was watered regularly as it lay on the green, the process was termed 'wet bleaching'. It was considered superior to 'dry bleaching' by the Cootehill method.

The number of bleachgreens reached a maximum of 357 in 1787, but after this the number fell rapidly as bleaching methods continued to improve. By the 1850s there were only forty coping with many times the quantity of cloth finished in an eighteenth-century green. (See page 127)

PLATE 11

'Perspective View of a Lapping room, with the Measuring, Crisping or Folding the Cloth in Lengths, picking the laps or lengths, tying in the Clips, acting by the mechanic power of the Laver [*sic*] to press the Cloth round and firm, and Sealing it preparatory to its going to the Linen hall ...'

Throughout the first half of the eighteenth century the most important men in the linen trade were the linendrapers or merchants who purchased brown linens from the weavers in the markets and had them bleached on commission before taking them to Dublin to sell in the White Linen Hall. By the time of this engraving, however, the bleachers were beginning to displace the drapers: some drapers took up bleaching as well while many bleachers employed their own buyers in the brown linen markets. They invested the profits of their bleachgreens in linen that they exported direct to London and Chester rather than through Dublin. It was estimated that more than two-thirds of all the linen woven in Ireland was exported and that ninety per cent of all exports in the eighteenth century went to Britain. The success of the bleachers in gaining control over the trade was responsible for much of its future success. As buyers of the linen the bleachers were able to reward the best weavers and attack mal-practices; they benefited directly from the improvements they intro-duced in bleaching methods; and they were able to respond to changing market demands. In the long term it was the bleachers who organised the response of the industry to the challenge of new tech-nology. (See page 132)

PLATE 12

'Perspective View of the Linen Hall in Dublin, with the Boxes and Bales of Linen ready for Exportation, the Emblems of their Industry ...'

The White Linen Hall had been built in 1728 by the Linen Board with the assistance of the Dublin government to accommodate those linen merchants and factors who dealt in the finished linens. Administered by the Board, it was 'a plain brick building, consisting of six large courts, surrounded by stores, which communicate below by piazzas and above by galleries, and a yarn hall. The Linen Hall con-tains five hundred and fifty-seven rooms, an elegant coffee-room, and a board room for the trustees ...' Because Dublin finance and com-merce was essential to the subsequent development of the industry, the Linen Hall had been frequented by Northerners to such an extent that three neighbouring streets were named after Ulster towns: Lisburn, Lurgan and Coleraine.

In 1782, the year before this view was drawn, a violent argument broke out between the Northerners and the Linen Board over the reg-ulation of the trade. The result was that the Northerners resolved to build a white linen hall in Ulster. Since they could not agree on a site, white linen halls were erected in both Belfast and Newry, resembling that in Dublin. This turn of events, however, was not unexpected since the percentage of finished linen shipped direct to England from both Belfast and Newry had been increasing steadily since at least 1750. The Dublin hall continued to operate as the headquarters of the Linen Board until its dissolution in 1828. (See page 157)

6

Ulster landowners and the linen industry[1]

PLATE 6

*Taken on the spot in the County of Downe, Representing Spinning,
reeling with the Clock reel, and Boiling the yarn . . .*

WILLIAM HINCKS 1783

IT IS SURPRISING THAT IRELAND has not attracted the attention of more economic and social historians in Great Britain. Content to accept what Dr Cullen has described as 'facile generalisations about the Irish economy to which we have become accustomed',[2] based all too often on studies of the nineteenth century, they have not seriously examined Ireland within the larger framework of the British Isles. In American history the grafting of British civilisation on an alien culture, the influence on the colonists of their early struggle to establish themselves, and the effect of mercantilism on the colonial economy have been studied, but in Irish history the surface has only been scratched. In the context of contemporary discussions about the origins of the Industrial Revolution the sudden appearance and rapid growth of an important linen industry in Ireland must attract serious attention.[3] The Irish Sea separated two different worlds and so the factors in the rise and development of the linen industry in such a colonial atmosphere, where its promotion with government support and under the aegis of the Linen Board was designed originally to strengthen the Protestant interest, differ in degree from those of a comparable industry in Britain. As Professor Charles Wilson has said: 'The ... expansion of the Irish linen trade forms a remarkable chapter in the economic history of the eighteenth century.'[4]

When William Hincks in 1783 published a set of twelve engravings depicting the various processes in the manufacture of Irish linen, he dedicated the first to the Lord Lieutenant, the second to the members of Parliament, the third to the trustees of the Linen Board and a further eight to various noblemen; only the twelfth and final engraving was inscribed to the linen merchants and manufacturers. Although Hincks was more concerned with potential patrons than with eulogies, any student of Irish life, aware of the influence of the landowner and the 'big house' in the community, would be inclined to accept

[1] First published in J.T Ward,. and R.G. Wilson, (eds), *Land and Industry: the Landed Estate and the Industrial Revolution* (Newton Abbot, 1971), 117–144.

[2] Cullen, L.M., 'The value of contemporary printed sources for Irish economic history in the eighteenth century', *Irish Historical Studies*, 14 (1964), 155.

[3] The only full-scale treatment of the industry in the eighteenth century is contained in Conrad Gill, *The Rise of the Irish Linen Industry* (Oxford, 1925, reprinted 1964). See also E.R.R Green., *The Lagan Valley, 1800–1850* (London, 1949) and *The Industrial Archaeology of County Down* (Belfast, 1963).

[4] Wilson, C., *England's Apprenticeship, 1603–1763* (London, 1965), p. 198.

these dedications at their face value: to him they are evidence of the authoritative role played by the landlord in the development of the linen industry. This view, however, would be an over-simplification, especially of social conditions in the province of Ulster, which was recognised as the home of the industry. It is time therefore to attempt an assessment of the influence of Ulster landowners in the rise of the linen industry; but the evidence has revealed that its rise seriously affected the influence of these landowners by encouraging the growth of an energetic and independent middle class, while it increasingly weakened the power of the landowners to control the development of their estates.

The birth of this industry lay in the Restoration period. Although previously the Irish had produced linen cloth for home consumption, they had exported considerable quantities of yarn only.[5] Indeed this yarn surplus was one of the most important factors in attracting the immigration of skilled weavers from Britain into northern Ireland. In 1682 Colonel Richard Lawrence, who had managed a linen manu-factory for the Duke of Ormonde at Chapelizod near Dublin, wrote:

> the Scotch and Irish in that province [Ulster] addicting themselves to spinning of linen yarn, attained to vast quantities of that commodi-ty, which they transported to their great profit. The conveniency of which drew thither multitudes of linen weavers, that my opinion is, there is not a greater quantity of linen produced in like circuit in Europe: and although the generality of their cloth fourteen years since was sleisie and thin, yet of late it is much improved to a good fineness and strength.[6]

Settlement in Ireland was an attractive prospect to many British tradesmen; according to the English House of Lords in their petition of 1698 against the Irish woollen manufacture, 'the growing manu-facture of cloth in Ireland, both by the cheapness of all sorts of nec-essaries for life, and goodness of material for making of all manner of cloth doth invite your subjects of England, with their families and

---

[5] Rawlinson MSS (Bodleian Library, Oxford) D 921, fo. 147 (transcript in PRONI T545/8) 'Proposals for the cultivation of flax and hemp in Ireland' (undated, but Dr Cullen believes that internal evidence points to a date early in the 1680s), 3.

[6] Lawrence, Richard, *The Interest of Ireland in its trade and wealth stated* (Dublin, 1682), vol. 2, 189–90.

servants, to leave their habitations to settle there.'[7] Land was very cheap in Ireland: on the Brownlow estate in north Armagh, where many immigrants from northern England settled, lands outside the town parks were let in the 1660s for 18d per acre and did not double in value until the first decade of the eighteenth century.[8] At the same time religious persecution drove many Scottish Covenanters into Ireland and it was probably responsible for the large number of Quakers among the immigrants from the North of England who settled in the Lagan valley.[9] These people found themselves at home in the Nonconformist atmosphere and in the exercise of their trades were untrammelled by English guild restrictions. Into this energetic and enterprising community was injected a Huguenot contribution of capital, new equipment and new techniques, with the official approval and support of the Dublin government. [10]

At least some of the Ulster landowners recognised the opportunities which had been presented to them. As early as the 1680s it had been forecast that by the linen manufacture 'Ireland will soon be so enriched that in probability the price of land will bear double the value that it doth at present so that the nobility and gentry will be great gainers in particular.'[11] The weakness of the landlords' position was their lack of capital to invest in the industry. William Molyneux wrote to John Locke in 1696 that the noblemen and gentry had been admitted into a joint-stock corporation to promote the linen industry 'more for their countenance and favour than for any great help that could be expected either from their purses or their heads'.[12] If they had any spare capital he did not expect them to invest it in linen. Yet some of the landowners did offer the immigrant tradesmen encouragement and leases on favourable terms. In the town of Lurgan, County Armagh, which was described in 1682 as the

---

[7] House of Lords' address to King William III, 9 June 1698. published in A. Young, *Tour in Ireland* (Hutton, A.W., 1892), vol. 2, 193.

[8] Brownlow MSS (PRONI) T970, Arthur Brownlow's lease book.

[9] There were strong Quaker communities in Lisburn and Lurgan: their first meeting in Ireland was formed in 1653 at Lurgan by William Edmundson, a Cromwellian soldier. See Quaker meeting records (PRONI T1062 and Mic/16).

[10] Gill, op. cit., pp. 16–20.

[11] 'Proposals for the cultivation of flax and hemp in Ireland', p. 10.

[12] Quoted in W.R. Scott, 'The King's and Queen's Corporation for the linen manufacture in Ireland', *JRS Antiq. Ire.*, 5S, p. 11 (1901), 371.

greatest centre of the linen manufacture in the north,[13] Arthur Brownlow granted beneficial leases to tradesmen[14] and deliberately stimulated the industry on his estate. He founded a linen market and until it was soundly established he bought up all the webs which were brought to it: at first he had lost money but later he made great profits.[15] As a result Lurgan recovered very rapidly from the effects of the Williamite wars, with an increasing population, reflected in the building of more houses in and around the market place and in the extension of both the Anglican and Quaker houses of worship, so that in 1708 it was 'the greatest mart of linen manufactories in the North, being almost entirely peopled with linen weavers'.[16] A few miles away, Brownlow's young neighbour, Samuel Waring, who had taken a tour through Flanders and the Low Countries about 1688, brought over a number of Flemish weavers from the Low Countries and settled them in Waringstown.[17] Crommelin's Huguenot colony in Lisburn was established with the support of Lord Conway who granted the French the site for their church: Lisburn was probably chosen by them because of its location in the heart of the linen-manufacturing area.[18] Its destruction by fire in 1707 checked its progress, so that some of the weavers went to Crommelin's brother's settlement at Kilkenny and others 'lodged themselves in Lurgan'.[19] Yet the town was very soon rebuilt and in a short time regained its position as one of the chief markets in Ulster. The landlords of Counties Cavan and Monaghan were responsible for planting the industry in those counties. Dean Richardson, writing in 1740 to the famous scholar and antiquarian Walter Harris, referred to the success of the industry about Cootehill in County Cavan:

[13] William Brooke to Dr William Molyneaux, published in 'An account of the Barony of O'Neiland, Co Armagh, in 1682', *Ulster Journal Arch.*, 2S, 4 (1898), 241.

[14] Arthur Brownlow's lease book, 87. Lurgan Quaker Records note a 1695 lease of a tenement in their account of the rebuilding of the meeting-house. Both the Quakers and Brownlow regarded these leases as copyholds: they were not fee-farm grants but leases for three lives renewable on the fall of each life with fixed rents and renewal fines and subject to the usual duties of the manor, especially suit to courts and mills.

[15] Thomas Molyneux, 'Journey to the North, August 7th 1708', in *Historical Notices of Old Belfast and its Vicinity* (ed. R.M. Young, Belfast, 1896), p. 154.

[16] Molyneux, op. cit., p. 154.

[17] Atkinson, E.D., *An Ulster Parish* (Dublin, 1898), p. 49.

[18] McCall, H., *Ireland and her Staple Manufactures* (3rd edn, Belfast, 1870), p. 40.

[19] Louis Crommelin to Duke of Ormonde, 24 May 1707, *Ormonde Calendar*, ns, no. 4, 299.

a good market house, a large market kept on Fridays in which there is plenty of provisions and abundance of good yarn and green cloth sold. There is a great number of weavers and bleachers in this town and neighbourhood and no less than ten bleach yards the least of which bleaches a thousand pieces of cloth every year. All which was brought about by means of a colony of Protestant linen-manufacturers who settled here on the encouragement given them by the Honble. Mr Justice Coote, who with a great deal of good management took care to have this new town so tenderly nursed and cherished in its infancy that many of its inhabitants soon grew rich and brought it to the perfection which it is now at; to which if we add the great pains that he took and the expense he was at in propagating this profitable branch of our trade thro' other parts of the kingdom he may justly be called the Father of the Linen Manufacture in Ireland.[20]

The success of the industry in County Monaghan was attributed to several gentlemen:

The linen manufacture has made great progress in this county since the year 1703 by the industry and care of several gentlemen and particularly of Edward Lucas of Castleshane, Esq., who first introduced it, and for many years employed workmen and kept them under his own inspection.

Lucas is said to have introduced French and Dutch looms for his workers. Afterwards William Cairnes of Monaghan followed this example and settled this manufacture in the town of Monaghan.[21]

About this period the industry seems to have established itself throughout the rest of the province. There is evidence of a linen exhibition in Strabane in 1700, when local people were awarded prizes for their skill.[22] In Coleraine the London-based Irish Society in 1709 had declined to encourage the manufacture of linen cloth,[23] and yet by an Act of 1711 the name 'Coleraines' was applied to linens seven-eighths

---

[20] Lodge MSS (Armagh Public Library) Bundle no. 35, 'Cavan' in bundle of Topographical and Statistical returns from various respondents sent to Walter Harris and the Physico-Historical Society of Ireland *circa* 1745.

[21] Lodge MSS, Bundle no. 35, 'Monaghan'. Mr William Cairnes, a Dublin merchant, bought the Blaney estate in County Monaghan in 1696; two of his brothers were London merchants. See H.C. Lawlor, *A History of the Family of Cairnes or Cairns* (1906), pp. 82, 83.

[22] Abercorn MSS (PRONI) D623/47; this is confirmed by Molyneux, op. cit., p. 159.

[23] A. Marmion, *The Ancient and Modern History of the Maritime Ports of Ireland* (1855), p. 383.

yard wide.[24] In 1708 Antrim was 'enjoying a considerable linen trade'.[25] In the Ballymena and Cullybackey area the first bleachgreens date back to about 1705.[26] The introduction of the weaving of diapers and damasks into north Down is ascribed to James Bradshaw, a Quaker from Lurgan who was persuaded by Robert Colville, the squire of Newtownards, to settle in that town in 1726.[27] The linen industry was also given credit for signs of prosperity in Larne where it was reported that 'a piece of forty hundred cloth manufactured in this town was made a present of to her Royal Highness the Princess of Orange at her wedding [in 1734][28] by the Trustees of the Linen and Hempen Manufactures being the finest then ever made in this Kingdom'.[29]

The success of these ventures induced the belief among landowners that any region could be improved by the introduction and expansion of the linen industry. Dean Henry, writing in 1739, noted that there was considerable trade in the linen manufacture throughout County Fermanagh, although Belturbet in County Cavan and not Enniskillen, the county town, was the chief market for counties Fermanagh and Cavan. He added, however:

> these places might with a little encouragement be made rich by
> the linen-manufacture. Enniskillen might be a chief mart for it,
> the soil and flats about it being very good and convenient for
> bleachyards and the waters of Lough Erne having hereabouts a
> particular softness and sliminess that waters the flax and bleach-
> es the linen in half the time that it can generally be done in
> other waters. It is not to be doubted but the happy national
> spirit for carrying on this manufacture and other useful branch-
> es of trade will in process of time exert itself properly along this
> lake as it has already done in other places.[30]

[24] 9 Anne c. p. 3.
[25] Molyneux, op. cit., p. 156.
[26] Lawlor, H.C., 'Rise of the Linen Merchants in the Eighteenth Century', *Irish and International Fibres and Fabrics Journal*, 7 (1941) p. 11; 8 (1942) 44.
[27] Harris, W. and Smith, C., *The Antient and Present State of the County of Down* (Dublin, 1744), p. 56; Green, County Down, 29; Londonderry Estate MSS (PRONI) D654/LE36A/10 and D654/LE31/1.
[28] In 1734 Anne, Princess Royal as eldest daughter of King George II, married the Prince of Orange.
[29] Henry William 'Henry's Topographical Descriptions' (a bound manuscript in APL), 142.
[30] Henry, op. cit., 96.

Unfortunately his dream never materialised.

About this time a number of serious attempts were made by landowners to sponsor the foundation of large manufactories. The most impressive to contemporaries was Lord Limerick's project at Dundalk, where in 1736 the Huguenot de Joncourt established a factory for making cambric;[31] it was probably in connection with this scheme that Harris noted in 1744 that a colony of fine diaper weavers had 'lately' been transplanted from Waringstown to Dundalk.[32] The Archbishop of Armagh,

> Primate Boulter … aided them materially by corresponding on their behalf with the government, as also in his office as one of the Trustees of the Linen Board; and, in addition to these efforts, he assisted in raising a subscription of £30,000 for the benefit of the settlement, which Lord Limerick encouraged in every way, by promising houses for the workmen, ground for the factory and a grant of ten acres for the sowing of flax.

It was later claimed that in a few years they had produced £40,000 worth of cambrics and lawns and that with the Board's help they had started a manufactory of black soap for the bleaching industry.[33] Although the factory was in operation in 1755, it had failed by 1776.[34] It was probably the initial and much discussed success of the Dundalk venture which impelled Sir Robert Adair of Ballymena to write to John Reilly in Dublin in 1741:

> I entreat you may if by any means possible to send me down by next post or the post following at farthest a proper draft of a subscription paper for establishing here a linen manufactory which can be done to great advantage in this place considering the many engines I have now fully fixed for that purpose which I am sure at present exceeds any in the Kingdom that is yet done.[35]

A linen manufactory was built in Hillsborough, County Down, by Lord Hillsborough, who later tried without success to encourage

[31] Gill, op. cit., p. 154.
[32] Smith and Harris, op. cit., p. 104.
[33] Purdon, D.C., communication to *Journal of the Historical and Archaeological Association of Ireland*, 3rd S, 1 (1868), 17–20.
[34] Young, op. cit., vol. 1, 115.
[35] Adair MSS (PRONI) D929/F4/1/15.

William Coulson of Lisburn to set up a damask factory there.[36] The most famous of these schemes were not established in Ulster, however, although Ulster experts and weavers were settled on the lands: they were Sir Richard Cox's great enterprise in Dunmanaway, County Cork[37] and Lord Shelburne's costly project at Ballymote in County Sligo.[38]

In contrast with the failure of these enterprises, sophisticated in their organisation and supported by substantial amounts of capital, was the growing success of the industry in Ulster where it had developed mainly on domestic lines. To the Lagan and upper Bann valleys the development of the industry brought increasing wealth, and competition forced up the value of land steeply. The conditions which the industry in this region required were explained by an agent in 1764 when advocating a scheme for the improvement of the estate and town of Rathfriland in County Down. In the first place, he pointed out, it was essential for the landlord to provide adequate market facilities. Then in order to persuade linendrapers to settle in the town and to build good houses, leases in perpetuity needed to be given for building plots, while the town parks could be let for profit for fixed periods; manufacturers of brown linens should be preferred when land was being let, not only because their competition would push up rents but also because they would stimulate the local markets for food, clothing and candles. As the whole tenantry paid their rents by some branch of the linen trade and were therefore not dependent on the land for their livelihood, only small areas needed to be leased to each individual at their full value, and so there would be no profit from subletting. On this point the agent noted:

> The manufacturers of brown linen in the neighbourhoods of Waringstown and Lurgan, whose stock is barely sufficient to keep their looms in work and support their families, will give twenty shillings or a guinea per acre for a small farm with a convenient house thereon, and even at that price find it difficult to get proper accommodation ...[39]

---

36 Smith and Harris, op. cit., p. 95; McCall, op. cit., p. 126.
37 *A Letter from Sir Richard Cox, Bart, to Thomas Prior, Esq, showing a sure method to establish the Linen Manufacture* (Dublin, 1749) (Hanson 6242).
38 Young, op. cit., vol. 1, 223–30; Greer MSS (PRONI) D1044/52.
39 PRONI T1181/1.

Since the closing years of the seventeenth century the houses in the town of Lurgan had been set in leases renewable for ever, but country leases to Protestants were for the term of three lives (the Penal Laws prevented Catholics from holding leases of more than thirty-one years). With the appearance of the bleach-mills requiring a more substantial investment of capital, linendrapers demanded much better terms. Harris attributed the success of the industry around Waringstown to the encouragement of long tenures:[40] in Waringstown five leases made to linendrapers in 1720 and 1730 were for sixty-one years, but after 1736 leases were freeholds.[41] Because of a minority between 1739 and 1747, it was not until 1748 that a spate of freeholds was granted to linendrapers in the Lurgan area: these took the form of three life leases renewable for a peppercorn, and the linendrapers paid substantial fines for them.[42]

Some landowners found at this time that their estate entails or marriage settlements prevented them from leasing land in freehold: both Lord Donegall in Belfast and Lord Hillsborough in north Down could grant leases of no more than three lives or forty-one years.[43] It was therefore the landowners who successfully passed through Parliament two bills, which became Acts in 1764 and 1766, to enable

[40] Smith and Harris, op. cit., p. 105.
[41] Leases made by Samuel Waring and recorded in the Registry of Deeds, Dublin:

BOOK	PAGE	NUMBER	LESSEE	TERM	YEAR
62	4	41615	Thomas Waring	61 years	1729
62	4	41616	Henry Close	61 years	1729
64	504	44915	John Murray	61 years	1730
69	321	48537	Mark Gwyn	61 years	1732
72	43	49626	Thomas Factor	61 years	1730
84	356	60015	Thomas Waring	For ever	1737
87	174	61151	John Houlden	For ever	1736
114	340	79161	Robert Paterson		1744
121	98	82221	Samuel Paterson	For ever	1745

[42] Brownlow estate papers (PRONI):
Brownlow to David Maziere for land in Derrymacash and Derryadd (1755)
Brownlow to James Bradshaw for land in Drumnakelly (1750)
Brownlow to Henry Greer for land in Dougher (1759)
Registry of Deeds Book 139, p. 68, no. 92984 to Henry Greer (1749)
Registry of Deeds Book 135, p. 452, no. 92216 to James Greer (1749)
Registry of Deeds Book 143, p. 208, no. 96608 to David Ruddell (1750)
Registry of Deeds Book 143, p 209, no. 96611 to James Forde (1750)
Registry of Deeds Book 193, p 106, no. 127135 to Ben Hone (1757)
[43] Donegall MSS (PRONI) D509/129; Downshire MSS (PRONI) D607/259A, John Slade to Lord Hillsborough 20 Feb. 1786.

themselves to break estate entails in order to grant leases of land not exceeding fifteen acres 'for one or more lives renewable for ever or for any terms of years' for the purpose of making or preserving a bleach-green.[44] The substance of this provision was quoted by the agent John Slade to his master, Lord Hillsborough, in 1786, in an attempt to persuade him to grant a freehold lease to Messrs William and John Orr for a large cotton manufactory at Hillsborough to employ from two hundred to four hundred weavers and three times that number of women and children in spinning. However, although they proposed 'to expend in building for their manufactory only at least £600, and if it succeeds to build handsome houses for their own habitation', and although they did in fact purchase a house, they soon left the area because they had no lease.[45]

Landlords were stimulated, however, by the success of the industry and the attendant prosperity of the province, to indulge in schemes for town building, which produced important changes in the character of towns in this area. Harris recorded in 1740 that in the villages of Greyabbey and Saintfield in County Down proprietors had specifically built good houses 'for the habitation of manufacturers'.[46] Yet the finest achievements were the creation of the modern towns of Hillsborough in County Down about 1740 and Cookstown in County Tyrone about 1750. Lord Hillsborough gave:

> great encouragement ... to linen manufacturers. His Lordship has already erected two ranges of commodious houses, to each of which are annexed a garden and park of five acres, with ground for bleach greens at a convenient distance, and plenty of firing in the adjacent mosses.[47]

William Stewart of Killymoon Castle executed in Cookstown what has been described as 'one of the boldest attempts at town building during the whole of Ulster's history':[48] the magnificent main street, 130 feet in width and beautified with trees, runs in a straight line for a mile and a quarter. To provide water for the linen bleachers, he

[44] 3 Geo. III, c. 34 and 5 Geo. III, c. 9, s. 4.
[45] Green, op. cit., p. 26.
[46] Smith and Harris, op. cit., pp. 49, 71.
[47] Ibid, p. 95.
[48] Camblin, G., *The Town in Ulster* (Belfast, 1951), p. 81.

dammed a ravine above the town and so harnessed the river which was taken by a race to drive both cornmills and bleach-mills.[49] Although the scheme was never completely realised, Cookstown and Dungannon, in which Lord Ranfurly had encouraged enterprise, were, with eight bleachyards apiece, the chief centres of the industry in County Tyrone in 1802.[50]

While many of these improvements remain as memorials to the efforts of the landlords, the most symbolic of all was the market house or linen hall. In Lurgan, 'the greatest market for fine linens' in the north, a market house built soon after the Restoration served until its destruction by fire in 1776 and was subsequently replaced by a linen hall.[51] In 1728 Dublin White Linen Hall was built on the same lines as Blackwell Hall, the London centre of the woollen industry, suggesting that it was designed to fill a similar role in the Irish industry.[52] The first linen hall (for brown or unbleached linens) in Belfast was built in 1738 with the help of Lord Donegall, who granted £1,500 towards its construction.[53] By 1755 Lisburn (built by the Marquess of Hertford), Downpatrick (the de Clifford family), Strabane (the Earl of Abercorn), and Cookstown (Stewart) had their own halls or at least special facilities provided in the market house.[54] Coleraine had two linen halls (one on each side of the River Bann) built in the last decade of the century, but because of the rivalry between their respective sponsors neither was used and the linen market was held in the street: the Marquess of Waterford had sponsored the erection of one, while a minor local landlord named Stirling built the other.[55] In Londonderry the Hamilton family built a linen hall, but the Inspector-General in 1817 frowned on the Hamilton charge of 2d per web.[56] Ballymena, Armagh, Newry, Limavady, Banbridge, Kircubbin, Ballynahinch, Rathfriland and Dungannon all had linen halls before

---

[49] Article in *MidUlster Mail*, 12 Sept. 1925 (PRONI T1659).

[50] McEvoy, J., *Statistical Survey of the County of Tyrone* (Dublin, 1802), pp. 138–9, 158.

[51] Lurgan town lease no. 103. It is surprising that Arthur Young, who visited the linen market a month after the fire, did not comment on it.

[52] Gill, op. cit., pp. 79–81.

[53] Young, R.M. (ed.), *Town Book of Belfast, 1613–1816* (Belfast, 1892), p. xii.

[54] Pococke, R., *Tour in Ireland in 1752* (ed. G.T. Stokes, Dublin, 1891), p. 13 (Downpatrick); Abercorn MSS T2541/1A1/2/31 and p. 34.

[55] Corry, James, *Report of a tour of inspection through the province of Ulster* (Dublin, 1817), App. 94. PRONI D699/5. Will of Robert Rice, 6 Oct. 1800.

[56] Corry, op. cit., App. 91.

1810, most of which had been provided by the proprietor of the town.[57]

Resident landlords often displayed an intelligent interest in their markets and some landlords gave premiums to tenants for the production of high-quality flax, yarn and cloth. It was said of Lord Hillsborough and William Brownlow:

> Both these landowners were well-known as being the most liberal patrons of flax-culture, flax-spinning and linen-weaving, as these industries existed among the tenantry of their respective estates. They gave liberal premiums for the largest and finest growths of flax produced by their tenants ... Once a year three different classes of prizes were given, on the market day preceding Christmas, for the best 'bunches' of linen-yarn, and the prizes consisted not of money but of dress patterns, as well for maids as for matrons.[58]

Such interest in the trade was remarked on in 1817 by the Inspector-General appointed by the Linen Board for Ulster, James Corry: in Ballygawley, County Tyrone, he found that the proprietor of the town, Sir John Stewart, distributed premiums every market day 'among the weavers who bring webs to the market of the best quality and in the greatest number – those premiums generally amount to £3, half of which is paid by the shopkeepers of the place, and the remainder by himself.'[59] These demonstrations of enthusiasm tended to be confined to those landowners who believed that their encouragement would be reflected in their rentals and often evaporated if this object was not speedily realised.

It was not only landlords who were genuinely interested in the welfare of the industry on their estates that applied regularly to the Linen Board for allocation of spinning wheels and reels: some felt it incumbent on themselves to get as many as possible, even if it was only to demonstrate the extent of their influence in high places. In an amusing letter about the profits of office in Dublin, Charles Coote of County Cavan commented in 1748:

---

[57] Ibid., Apps 12 (Dungannon), 59 (Banbridge), 71 (Ballynahinch), 75 (Kircubbin), 83 (Ballymena); Marmion, *Maritime Ports of Ireland* (Newry), p. 314; Boyle, E.M., *Records of the town of Limavady, 1609–1808* (Londonderry, 1912), p. 98; Lewis, S., *A Topographical Dictionary of Ireland* (1837), vol. 1, 68; vol. 2, 498.

[58] Green, W.J., *A Concise History of Lisburn and Neighbourhood* (Belfast, 1906), p. 30.

[59] Corry, op. cit., p. 76. See also his references to Monaghan (p. 75) and Enniskillen (p. 84).

the business as usual is a series of jobs, the pleasure ends in awkward minuets and romping country dances; we begin to scramble for wheels and reels tomorrow and as soon as it is over I return to my much better business or more agreeable idleness in the country ... if I get a tolerable harvest of wheels and reels I shall go home rejoicing.[60]

His cynicism was justified, because the Linen Board did not trouble even to keep track of the wheels. Robert Stephenson, the most able critic of the Board's undertakings, exposed this abuse when he heartily condemned the Linen Board's foolishness

to bestow money as cheerfully as we do, for spinning wheels, thousands of which lie idle and are spoiling for want of use in the garrets and outhouses of gentlemen, because they have neither material nor proper persons to employ them; and here we may reasonably enquire after spinning wheels, there being about 7,000 of them given away annually in three afore-mentioned provinces [Munster, Leinster and Connaught]; how are they employed?[61]

In the areas where the industry was increasing many landowners took full advantage of the grants. William Brownlow's account books show that between 1771 and 1792 he received from the Linen Board at least £200 towards the purchase of wheels and looms: he was allowed £1 15s. 0d. each for thirty-three looms in the years 1775–7 and his rentals note more than twenty looms given to tenants. Five shillings was the grant for each wheel. In 1754 the absentee Earl of Abercorn's agent asked him, 'Will your Lordship be pleased to direct me how I shall dispose of the wheels [fifty wheels and ten reels], whether your Lordship would have them spun for, or divided amongst the poorer sort of tenant?'[62] In a countryside where the linen industry flourished such gifts were considered as an investment in the estate, since they enabled poor tenants to pay their rents and reduced the number dependent on the parish.[63]

60 Charles Coote to Earl of Abercorn, 31 March 1748 (Abercorn MSS, T2541/1A1/1D/13).
61 [R. Stephenson] *Remarks on the present state of the linen manufacture of this Kingdom* (Dublin, 1745), 13. Stephenson's career and his influence over the policies of the Linen Board are examined in some detail in Gill, op. cit. pp. 96–7.
62 Abercorn MSS, T2541/1A1/2/44/175.
63 Stephenson, R., *Considerations on the present state of the linen manufacture* (Dublin, 1754), p. 21.

In the train of the linen industry came a revolution in communications in the north which seems to have got under way in the 1730s. The landlords were the foremost sponsors of this revolution and were active in presenting schemes for constructing roads and canals to open up the undeveloped countryside to trade and industry. They forced through an active policy of road construction, putting pressure on the parish vestries to improve local roads, submitting presentments to the grand juries for county roads, or promoting turnpike trusts. Harris commented on County Down in 1744: 'As these roads cannot be well-repaired by the statute or day labour of the welders [*sic*] only, so the gentlemen of the county, who wish well to the commerce of it, now think it worth their attention to repair them by a county charge, which has been done to good advantage in other places.'[64]

The system of statutory labour was finally abolished in 1765. The roads from Dundalk to Banbridge and from Banbridge to Belfast had been placed under turnpike trusts by Acts of 1733, and two years later trusts were created for the roads from Newry to Armagh, Lisburn to Armagh, and Banbridge to Randalstown. For lack of sufficient revenue to pay interest on debentures and wages to officials even before the consideration of repairs, the turnpike roads tended to deteriorate more rapidly than the new county roads.[65] Arthur Young commented in 1776 that the turnpikes were as bad as the by-roads were admirable.[66]

As early as 1699 the idea of a canal from Lough Neagh to Newry was seriously examined by a group of landowners which included Arthur Brownlow and Samuel Waring,[67] and the region was mapped for the purpose in 1703 at the instance of several members of the House of Commons;[68] again in 1709 Thomas Knox of Dungannon petitioned Parliament for its construction but without any success.[69] The increasing exploitation of coal deposits in east Tyrone added much more weight to their arguments and with the foundation of the 'Commission of Inland Navigation for Ireland' in 1729 official

[64] Smith and Harris, op. cit., p. 77.
[65] *Commons' Journal Ire.*, VII, *pp.* 51, 112, 113, 192; VIII, 468, 495, 501–2 (dealing with the problems of the Lisburn to Armagh turnpike).
[66] Young, op. cit., vol. 2, 7. See also vol. 1, 116.
[67] Waring MSS (PRONI), D695/51, Arthur Brownlow to Samuel Waring, 27 August 1699.
[68] Waring MSS D695/M/1.
[69] McCutcheon, W.A., *The Canals of the North of Ireland* (Newton Abbot, 1965), p. 63.

approval was given to the scheme. Work commenced in 1731 but the first cargoes of coal from Coalisland in County Tyrone did not arrive in Dublin until 1742: even so it was the first major inland canal in the British Isles.[70] The section of the Lagan canal from Sprucefield near Lisburn to Lough Neagh was completed in 1794, cost £62,000 and was constructed almost entirely at the Marquess of Donegall's expense.[71] The Strabane canal, first suggested to the Earl of Abercorn in the early 1750s,[72] was not constructed until 1796: the then Marquess bore the total cost of £11,858.[73] Although these eighteenth-century canals did play an important role in promoting the growth of the regions they served, they were eclipsed by the rapid expansion of the railway network in the mid-nineteenth century.[74] It is significant, however, that Ulster landowners were prepared to advance so much for improvements in Ireland.

Some of the Ulster landowners were among the most active members of the Board of the Trustees of the Linen and Hempen Manufactures which had been established in 1711 to regulate the industry, to spread the knowledge of methods and technique throughout the country and to subsidise worthwhile projects. The Board tackled these tasks with enthusiasm but without sufficient knowledge of the trade; it did not ensure that the terms of its grants were fulfilled and so money was wasted; and in spite of its measures to encourage the industry in the south, the slump of the early 1770s almost obliterated the industry outside Ulster. Yet if the Linen Board had been more effective and able to regulate the industry as it pleased, there was a serious danger that its inexperience and lack of knowledge combined with an increasingly inflexible and bureaucratic approach to problems, would have imposed a strait-jacket on the industry. It was, for instance, fortunate for the industry that the Board was unable to enforce such of its regulations as concerned the reeling of yarn, the dimensions of cloth and the time and method of bleaching.[75] The trade carried on by 'jobbers'[76] and 'keelmen' on the fringe

70 Ibid., pp. 11, 20.
71 Ibid., p. 45.
72 Abercorn MSS, T2541/1A1/2/149.
73 McCutcheon, op. cit., p. 86.
74 Ibid., p. 16.
75 Gill, op. cit., pp. 150–51.
76 'Jobbers' bought webs in outlying markets to sell them in the chief centre of trade: their existence was vital to the small markets. Gill, op. cit., pp. 170–2.

of the industry was impossible to regulate and regularly condemned as illegal and yet it played an important role in serving the remoter districts and encouraged enterprise among the smaller dealers: it was reckoned in 1821 that in Armagh market, then one of the most considerable in the north, more than one-third of the dealers were 'keelmen'.[77]

The Linen Board enjoyed great authority in its early years, especially when the Ulster landowners were most busily engaged in its support. They were very active in the House of Commons, particularly on committees which discussed the linen trade and relevant matters.[78] Only through the landlords could the rising class of drapers make its demands heard. It was Brownlow of Lurgan who introduced the Linen bill of 1762 to regulate both the bleachers and the brown linen markets[79] and in 1766 Thomas Knox of Dungannon (later Lord Ranfurly) wrote to Thomas Greer:

> I ... think myself much honoured by the respectable body of Linen Drapers, that thought proper to fix on me to present their memorial to my Lord Lieutenant. I beg you will assure them from me that I did with pleasure this day deliver it, and had the strongest assurance from his Excellency that he would recommend it to the Linen Board with all his power, which gives me reason to hope we shall succeed.[80]

John Williamson, an eminent linendraper from Lisburn, resented the condescending attitude adopted by the trustees when Henry Betty of Lisburn and himself tried to salvage the Linen bill of 1762 when it was dropped by the Commons:

> We have carried everything we wished for. Very full boards of the trustees have sat nearly every day and tomorrow there is to be a final settlement. It is, however, my opinion that we would never have got a patient hearing, but would have been condemned and abused, had it not been for Lord Hillsborough, who has been our patron, our friend and adviser, in all cases. He received us as his children and since we came here he has laboured for us night and day, the effect of

---

[77] 'Keelmen' were dealers who bought cheap coarse cloths in the local markets and retailed them in Britain. J. Corry, *Report on the measuring and stamping of brown linen sold in public markets* (Dublin, 1822), App., pp. 174–5. See Appendix 5.

[78] *Commons' Journal Ire.*, III, 31, 251; IV, 13, 337; V, 228.

[79] McCall, op. cit., p. 74.

[80] Greer MSS, D1044/92.

which has been that we are now treated with the highest respect by people who, when we came here, were ready to insult us … Many of the noble lords here would not vouchsafe to look on us, even though we worshipped them; they would suffer our cause to fail even though their own estates and the whole kingdom were equally involved in the same.[81]

Williamson, who was presented by the merchants of Dublin and London and by the linendrapers with a piece of engraved silver plate in recognition of his work on the 1764 Linen Act, was punished for his presumption by the Linen Board, who refused to grant him a white seal although every other bleacher in the kingdom had been furnished with one: the Board did not reply to a memorial submitted by the drapers on Williamson's behalf and after a further petty insult Williamson went to live in London.[82]

Yet the landowners in Ulster were themselves well aware of the growing importance and influence of the linendrapers. On the Brownlow estate in north Armagh the most important men in the community were the wealthy linen-merchants and they were independent enough for Brownlow to cultivate their friendship and regard. During the 1761 election he had to quieten the fears of his partner Sir Archibald Acheson that their opponents, the Caulfields, were sounding out possible support among the Lurgan merchants and linen drapers: Brownlow's local agent, the linendraper Jemmy Forde, had to make it clear to Maziere and Ruddle, two fellow linendrapers who were disposed to listen to the Caulfields, that Brownlow was engaged to support Acheson and would have to share the expenses of the poll if one was necessary. Brownlow himself warned Acheson:

the people of substance here would, to be sure, wish to be conversed and to appear of consequence, which they cannot be without an opposition, and on that account grumble a little at your going on so smoothly but I shall take all the care in my power to make that ferment subside, and so strengthen your interest.[83]

In 1783 Thomas Knox of Dungannon professed friendship in his

81 McCall, op. cit., pp. 74, 75.
82 Ibid., pp. 84–7.
83 Gosford MSS (PRONI), D1606/1/21 March 1761.

letters to the draper Thomas Greer, while apologising for being unable at the time to repay a loan of £1,000.[84] In Strabane an even more powerful landowner, the Earl of Abercorn, had during the 1760s the greatest difficulty in his attempts to secure control of the corporation of Strabane, the chief town within his estates.[85] The increasing authority of the drapers may have been responsible for the initial collapse of the 1762 bill over the clauses designed to regulate bleachers,[86] but the real clash between the Linen Board and the drapers came twenty years later in 1782 over 'Mr Foster's' Act.[87] The bleachers and drapers had been consulted by a parliamentary committee before the bill was drafted and they expected a renewed campaign to tighten up the administration of the 1764 Act against the frauds of the brown-sealmasters (who examined unbleached linen), but they found that the whole burden of the Act was directed against them: although their trading reputation as responsible merchants should have guaranteed their products, they were to be held liable and punished for dealing in poor-quality cloth. As white-sealmasters they were to be strictly regulated: they would have to take an oath to obey all the Board's rules and each man would have to provide not only bonds of £200 for his conduct but also two sureties who would guarantee him and bind themselves for similar sums. Although these clauses provoked angry reactions, the most serious of all was the Linen Board's demand that each sealmaster had to perfect a warrant of attorney confessing judgement on the bond. This step would enable the Linen Board to adopt the simplest, quickest, and most economical method of securing all fines it might levy on the sealmasters: it would not be necessary to sue the sealmasters as by their warrant they had already admitted their liability to pay. The white-sealmasters objected that both the oath and the warrant bound them to obey without question any Act which the Board might introduce in the future no matter if they faced thereby the loss of their trade and the destruction of their livelihood, and several petitions on these lines

---

[84] Greer MSS, D1044/692. See also D1044/677A.
[85] Abercorn MSS. The correspondence for 1764 contains many references to this struggle since it lasted throughout the year.
[86] McCall, op. cit., p. 74.
[87] Gill, op. cit., p. 206.

were laid before Parliament. [88]

The drapers were angry when they learned that their memorials, supported by their testimony before the Board, had been rejected out of hand and that instead a meeting of only five trustees on 23 July 1782 had decided to enforce the Act imposing a fine of £5 for each illegally sealed web; so they decided at meetings held in Lisburn, Lurgan and Newry that they would buy no more brown linens. At a meeting held by the Ulster drapers in Armagh on 5 August following, 437 drapers decided not to carry on trade until they obtained an assurance from the Linen Board that they would not be required to take the new oath or give any other than the usual simple bonds for their conduct. They further resolved 'That whoever acts contrary to the general sense of the trade ought never to be considered as one of our body, or a friend to the linen manufacture of Ireland; nor will we on any pretence whatsoever bleach any linen for such persons who will not strictly and uniformly adhere to this our general determination.'[89]

In face of this opposition fifteen trustees (including only one of the original five and not John Foster, the real author of the measure) met two days later in Dublin, took into consideration the resolution at Armagh and revoked the order of 23 July on the grounds that no words appeared in the Act authorising or requiring the administering of the oath: if this was the case, however, it was a loop-hole in the Act.[90] A meeting at Newry three days later refused still to resume trade, on the grounds 'that the Linen Board have not yet given the trade satisfaction sufficient to enable them to proceed to business with safety'.[91]

At the same time, however, the drapers had found their own loop-hole in the Act and were trying 'to procure five trustees who will join in issuing seals without putting the sealmaster to the severe qualifications required by the present Act of Parliament'. Five was the minimum number of trustees required by the Act to authorise

[88] Massereene MSS (PRONI) D207/28/3, 99, 100, 101; Greer MSS, D1044/899. The row is discussed in detail in Nevill, John, *Seasonable remarks on the linen trade of Ireland* (Dublin, 1783).

[89] Massereene MSS, D207/28/3.

[90] Ibid., D207/28/99.

[91] Ibid., D207/28/100.

appointments.[92] Brownlow and Sir Richard Johnston were joined first by Lords Hillsborough and Moira and then by John O'Neill of Shane's Castle (all Ulster landlords) as the five trustees.[93] The Board had been forced to surrender. There is no doubt that, like the Irish Volunteers, the northern drapers had adopted the language and attitudes of the American rebels with success. The lesson had not been lost on John Nevill, the self-appointed advocate of the drapers' cause: 'the stubborn perseverance of enforcing an Act of Parliament lost Britain the greater part of her dominions; there is no reason to believe that the experiment will be attempted on the trade of Ireland.'[94]

From this time the independence of the northern drapers became more pronounced. Later in the same year it was decided to build a white-linen hall in Ulster to sell white linens in the heart of the manufacture: it was unnecessary to send linens to Dublin when they could be shipped from Belfast or Newry.[95] Underlying these valid arguments was a certain resentment felt by the Ulster drapers against the authority of the Dublin factors and this was expressed in the grumble that the government in Dublin paid more attention to the views of the Dublin factors than to those of 'the most eminent drapers in the country'.[96] By 1785 white-linen halls were open in Belfast and Newry: although the Newry hall soon failed that in Belfast grew steadily at the expense of Dublin.[97]

The Act of Union (1800) saw the end of the Irish Parliament and a subsequent decline in the influence of the Board of Trustees: Dublin was no longer the centre of government which attracted active personalities and it became more and more divorced from the industry. The Board was still the guardian of the linen trade but now its meetings were very sparsely attended and in some years there was not a quorum of twelve.[98] It was run by John Foster (now Lord Oriel) and its secretary James Corry, both of whom showed energy and initiative in making grants for the erection of scutch mills to prepare flax for

[92] 21 & 22 Geo. III, c. 35, s. 9.
[93] Massereene MSS, D207/28/100; Greer MSS, D1044/899.
[94] Nevill, op. cit., p. 39.
[95] Ibid., pp. 68, 69; Greer MSS, D1044/900.
[96] Nevill, op. cit., p. 52.
[97] Gill, op. cit., pp. 189–91.
[98] Massereene MSS, D207/28/272.

the spinners.[99] Yet they could only subsidise, not initiate, changes in the industry. One of the arguments used by an English manufacturer to dissuade an Irishman thinking of establishing a spinning mill at Dundalk in 1801 was that 'the premium to be expected from the Linen Board would be of little importance compared with the eligibility of the scheme':[100] the optimism of the mid-eighteenth century had submitted to the realistic assessment of the nineteenth. The Board itself was increasingly under fire for inefficiency, jobbery and ostentation;[101] even Foster was forced to recognise the justice of these criticisms when he complained in 1819: 'It strikes me that the flax seed inspectors ought not to take advantage of the two Acts of 1802 and 1804 to do an act to put money in their own pockets without any advantage to the trade or any additional security against the sale of bad seed to the grower.'[102]

It is not surprising that one of the fiercest diatribes against the Board came after its decease from the Lisburn historian of the industry, Henry McCall (1805–97):

> The Board of Trustees – the supreme authority on all questions – issued their decrees with the pomposity of three-tailed bashawism. Their dogmas dare not be disputed; and the secretary of that formidable cabinet, Mr James Corry, made his tour of the provinces in semi-regal state, the county inspectors, the deputies, and sealmasters forming his body-guard in every market town which he honoured with a visit. All this complicated and cumbrous machinery was kept in motion at great cost, and it was only when forward men arose and stood against such mischievous meddling, that the trade was emancipated from its trammels.[103]

The forward men had their reward in 1828, when the government withdrew its grants from the trustees and the Linen Board ceased to function.

Yet early in the nineteenth century the domestic linen industry reached its peak and played a very important role in the economy of the Ulster countryside. The rapidly increasing population was already

[99] Ibid., D207/28/249A.
[100] Ibid., D207/28/113.
[101] Ibid., D207/28/249A.
[102] Ibid., D207/28/214.
[103] McCall, op. cit., p. 243.

pressing hard on the resources of the land in Ireland; emigration had eased the pressure on Ulster but modern industry had scarcely made its appearance and natural controls had not yet operated to check the growing numbers. As a result many small farmers and their families were forced to take up the linen industry to make a living, although as contemporary observers noted, weavers might earn no more than day labourers.[104] The organisation of the industry in Ulster had become so efficient that it was able to cope with the increasing production of the remoter areas and to give the North the relative appearance of prosperity which so impressed travellers after their experiences in the south of the country.[105]

How the linen industry and changing conditions on the land interacted may best be learned from an examination of four distinct regions. Around Belfast by 1800 the majority of handloom weavers relied on manufacturers for regular employment and the supply of raw materials, so that the cotton industry was replacing the linen industry and encouraging many men to break their final ties with the land.[106] Away from the coast, however, in north Armagh and west Down observers were surprised to find that highly skilled linen weavers were often independent of the manufacturers and still farmed smallholdings. Further south in Cavan and Monaghan such smallholdings were usually leased directly from landlords by weavers of coarser linens and were the prevalent features of the rural scene. In the rest of the linen country in Counties Antrim, Londonderry, and Tyrone, the weavers were usually cottiers dependent on weaving to supplement their earnings on the land. On the verge of poverty lived the weavers in mountainous districts, compelled to rely on the markets for their supplies of flax and thread which they themselves could not produce.[107]

The heart of the industry lay in the triangle between Lisburn, Armagh and Dungannon and there the independent craftsmen secured small parcels of land in the vicinity of a good market town as they were able to pay a higher rent than any farmer who was prepared to earn his living by farming alone. A study of estate rentals and

[104] Wakefield, E., *An Account of Ireland* (London, 1812), 700.
[105] Beckett, J.C., *The making of modern Ireland*, 1603–1923 (London, 1966), p. 180.
[106] Green, *Lagan Valley*, p. 99.
[107] McEvoy, op. cit., p. 200.

leases on Brownlow's manor of Derry shows that when leases expired the previous sub-tenants had been taken on as full tenants because they were able individually to offer a higher rent than a middle-man.[108] In this way Brownlow and landlords who adopted a similar policy had been able to take advantage of the rising value of rents but they were prepared in turn to grant to good tenants long secure leas-es instead of mere tenancies at will. The landlords' readiness to lease holdings direct to sub-tenants forced out the middleman or the orig-inal holder of the grand lease who was thus deprived of what had been a valuable and easy source of income. As a result there were in this region by 1800 very few substantial farmers and even fewer minor gentry: most of the gentry owed their prosperity to wealth acquired from trade or the professions or indirectly from the profits of the linen industry.

Although observers like Arthur Young and Sir Charles Coote were convinced that in such circumstances agriculture must suffer as the skills of weaving and farming could not be combined,[109] the weaver took a different view. If he grew his own flax he could employ the skill of his womenfolk to spin the very fine threads needed for his cambrics and lawns while he had turbary rights and enough grass for one or two cows: on a farm of ten acres two cows would supply a family with milk for a year and one hundredweight of butter to sell in the mar-ket. It is not surprising then that the linen country was noted for its dairy farming and supplied the Lagan valley and Belfast.[110] Here the weaver knew too that he could turn to farming during slumps in the industry which occurred more frequently as the market for expensive

---

[108] Table based on PRONI D1928/R/1/ Rentals, the rentals of the Brownlow estate (1755–94) to show changes in the size of holdings in statute acres:

	0–5	5–10	10–20	20–50	50–100	100+	Total
1755	10	31	55	55	34	14	199
1765	14	34	75	49	35	13	220
1775	27	52	83	42	19	11	234
1785	56	114	113	53	12	5	353
1794	70	153	115	49	12	5	404

Note: Of the leases in 1785 eight were perpetuities, 196 were for terms of three lives, 78 for thirty-one years and 9 for twenty-one years while 60 had no lease. In 1765 and 1775 the number of tenants without a lease had been 10.

[109] Young, op. cit., vol. 2, 215–17; Coote, Sir C., *Statistical survey of the county of Armagh* (Dublin, 1804), pp. 261–7.

[110] Green, *Lagan Valley*, p. 142.

fine linens was more liable to saturation than that for coarse linens; he was also able to cushion himself against the fluctuating price of oatmeal, his chief article of diet, especially during bad seasons. Coote himself did admit that he believed 'that the people would rather have nothing to do with agricultural pursuits if the markets were more numerous and constantly supplied with provisions'; besides, too much farming rendered their hands unfit for weaving fine linens.[111]

In south Armagh, Cavan and Monaghan, the southern counties of Ulster, where the population density often exceeded four hundred persons to the square mile, the lot of the farmer-weavers was harder. The weavers manufactured the cheaper coarse linens while their farming was very poor and reflected none of the more modern techniques. Of the barony of Tullaghonoho in County Cavan Coote reported: 'Here there is no market for grain ... They breed but very few horses here, and less of black cattle; tillage is their principal pursuit, and they cultivate now no more of provisions than they require for themselves, their great concern is flax-husbandry and the linen-manufacture', and complained: 'In so many thousand acres now occupied by very poor weavers we rarely see better than black oats, of an impoverished grain, which are capable of yielding the finest wheat, or could certainly be converted to the best sheep-walk.' Pressure of population had reduced the weavers to subsistence level and the standard of agriculture to such a condition that the landlords did not attempt to introduce improvements and often did not even trouble to renew leases but permitted them to continue as tenancies at will after they had lapsed.[112] The tenants, on the other hand, feared that improvements would only mean increased rents and tithes.[113]

In this region there were also many cottiers; but cottiers were much more numerous in the northern counties of Antrim, Londonderry and Tyrone, where they were employed by farmers and manufacturers. These counties contained a larger percentage of more substantial farmers than anywhere else in the province and in the Bann and Foyle valleys they farmed some of its best agricultural lands. Young noticed in 1776 that the farmers in north Londonderry concentrated on farming and gave out to weavers the yarn their womenfolk had

[111] Young, op. cit., vol. 1, 134.
[112] Coote, Sir C., *Statistical survey of the county of Cavan* (Dublin, 1802), pp. 108–9, 151, 157.
[113] Hall, Rev. J., *Tour through Ireland* (London, 1813), pp. 116–17.

spun.[114] Dependent on such farmers or on linen manufacturers for employment, the cottier tenants secured scraps of land on which to graze a cow and grow potatoes and although they were given no title to the land they paid exorbitant sums for it or worked for their land-lord.[115] Whether their employer was a manufacturer or a farmer the cottiers were at his mercy in their pursuit of a livelihood and they were exploited; of County Londonderry in 1802 it was reported:

> In many districts the cottier could not hold out but for the liberal wages of linen merchants and other gentlemen ... I assure the read-er that the grass of a cow, which three or four years ago was valued at 20s is now raised to two guineas even on the bare moors where the poor animal is tethered and where she has better opportunity of grinding her teeth on the sand than of filling her belly with pas-ture.[116]

Often they owed arrears of rent to their employers. When farmers wanted to consolidate and improve their farms it was easy for them to remove cottiers since they had no rights to their land. One observ-er noticed in 1813 that the population of Omagh was increasing 'not only on account of the linen and other manufactures there carried on, but also by reason of the people here, as almost everywhere, being driven from their farms into towns by monopolizing farmers'.[117] But the small provincial towns could not absorb such large-scale immi-gration.

Such was the condition of the industry throughout Ulster on the eve of the introduction of machinery. The first dry-spinning mills had appeared in Ulster soon after 1800 but for twenty years they made lit-tle progress because of the low cost of labour in Ireland: indeed the spinning women were often forced to cut their losses by disposing 'of the worked article for less than the raw material cost them', and it was said that the women regarded it as 'an alternative to idleness' rather than a paying pursuit.[118] When the more efficient process of wet-spinning displaced dry-spinning the domestic industry soon

---

[114] Young, op. cit., vol. 1, 165.
[115] McEvoy, op. cit., pp. 99–100; Dubourdieu, Rev. J., *Statistical survey of the county of Antrim* (Dublin, 1812), p. 147.
[116] Sampson, Rev. G.V., *Statistical survey of the county of Londonderry* (Dublin, 1802), p. 298.
[117] Hall, op. cit., p. 118.
[118] Wakefield, op. cit., p. 684; Green, *Lagan Valley*, p. 116.

vanished, with a consequent decline in the rural standard of living. Soon after 1850 the introduction of the power-loom finally destroyed the livelihood of the handloom weavers.[119] Their numbers declined so rapidly that by the early twentieth century only the finest damask tablecloths were still woven by hand.

Irish landlords had promoted the linen industry to improve their estates: that they succeeded in Ulster their substantial rentals will testify. This does not mean that the tenants on their estates benefited to the same extent. To the region bounded by the triangle of Belfast, Armagh and Dungannon where skilled weavers from England, Scotland and France had congregated, the industry brought increasing wealth but in the surrounding counties it had become by 1800 a means of supplementing farming incomes and with the rapidly increasing population had artificially inflated the value of lands where improved methods of farming had never been adopted: there it depressed the standards of agriculture and the subsequent decay of the domestic linen industry left these remoter districts in comparative poverty. It may be true also that the spread of the industry had hastened the collapse of the manorial system originally introduced into Ulster by the English government and the planters early in the seventeenth century, but before we can make a judgement, much more detailed investigation of estate records will be required: linked with this is the problem of land tenure and the evergreen topic of Ulster tenant right and its origins. There is no doubt, however, that the rise of the linen industry produced from the descendants of yeoman and tradesmen a new wealthy class which in 1782 successfully challenged the authority of the Linen Board to dictate the conditions under which the industry should operate. It would be interesting to find out the extent to which linendrapers were involved in the United Irishmen as their successful opposition to government interference in industry may have been reflected in a radical approach to politics. To the Ulster linen industry must be attributed the creation of conditions in which the cotton industry flourished for a time, and indeed it played an important part in laying the foundations for Belfast's rise to eminence in the nineteenth century. With the subsequent

[119] Johnson, J.H., 'The population of Londonderry during the great Irish famine', *Econ. Hist. Rev.*, 2S, 10 (1957), 272.

establishment of the factory system in the linen industry, however, the landlord's interest in it faded.

7

The political economy of linen:
Ulster in the eighteenth century[1]

PLATE 7

Winding, Warping, with a new improved warping Mill, and Weaving . . .
WILLIAM HINCKS 1783

ULSTER, THE MOST NORTHERLY PROVINCE of Ireland, is surrounded on three sides by sea and separated from Scotland by only some twenty miles. Half of its surface lies more than three hundred feet above sea level while there are also extensive lakelands and bog. Little of the land is naturally fertile. Yet during the eighteenth century much land was reclaimed and brought under cultivation by an increasing population, and pasture gave way to tillage. By 1800 Ulster was the most densely peopled of the four provinces of Ireland so that its population of two million in 1821 almost equalled that of the whole of Scotland. Contemporaries believed that Ulster had also become the most prosperous province. So much economic expansion could not have been achieved by agricultural improvements alone, in spite of a major transfer from pasture to tillage. The real responsibility lay with the success of a single industry, the domestic linen industry. Its very prosperity had far-reaching consequences for the future of the province. It created a merchant class and financed industrial development. It was responsible for the initial creation and subsequent development of many market towns. Throughout the countryside the fact that the industry depended on yarn handspun from flax cultivated by local people, disseminated cash right down to the bottom of the social structure so that even small farmers could rely on a supplementary source of income to maintain the viability of their holdings: this was to prove a not unmixed blessing to Ulster society. Yet the relative prosperity of the poorer classes in Ulster was evident to every traveller.

In 1700 Ireland exported one million yards of cloth, and by 1800 the figure was 40 million yards (36.6 million metres), in addition to supplying an expanded home market. Why was the linen industry so successful in Ulster in 1800? Much of the answer lies in the timing of the industry's development in Ulster on commercial lines. Whereas Irish society outside Ulster evolved along traditional lines so that local craftsmen could continue to meet the demand for textiles in Ireland, Ulster society was unstable and disorganised but enterprising and ready to experiment. The sudden influx of population into Ulster in

1 First published in Ciaran Brady, Mary O'Dowd, and Brian Walker, (eds), *Ulster: an Illustrated History* (London, 1989), pp. 134–57.

the second half of the seventeenth century had compelled the immigrants to engage in a variety of occupations to earn their living. Their
landlords had encouraged such enterprise in the hope of securing
their rents. The new linen industry developed on the basis of local
production of linen yarn that had been exported to Lancashire for
very many years, and from the arrival among the immigrants of
weavers experienced in producing for the commercial market. The
new industry appeared at a time when the demand for cheap textiles
was growing fast in Britain.[2] Dublin merchants, in their search for
goods to sell, provided capital and skill to promote Ulster linens until
the Ulstermen were able in the long run to make their own capital
and business contacts.

When the industry needed to expand production, especially in the
1730s and 1740s, it was able to obtain extra supplies of yarn from
counties such as Roscommon and Sligo. Its own entrepreneurs adapted the technology of woollen tuck mills to mechanise the mills on
their bleachgreens with rubbing boards, wash mills and beetling
engines all driven by waterpower: their technology was introduced to
Scotland in the mid-1730s.[3] In the second half of the century the finishers of the linens were quick to adopt new bleaching materials and
methods so that the output of a major bleachgreen was increased by
a factor of ten.[4] Throughout Ulster many landlords organised their
market towns to attract both drapers and weavers. As demand
increased throughout the century the industry expanded in its search
for weavers as far as County Mayo. Farmers took up weaving in their
spare time while the women of the family spun the yarn; farmers also
employed journeymen to weave for them by providing them with the
necessities of life. Agriculture became an adjunct of the domestic
linen industry.

It is difficult to conceive what eighteenth-century Ulster would
have been like without the linen industry. Much of the province was
still in its primeval state, mountain or bog, while the climate, especially in the west, could rarely ripen crops like wheat, peas and beans.
It would have been able to support an increasing population at no

[2] See pages 9–12, 60–66.
[3] See pages 31, 54 and 55.
[4] L'Amie, A., 'Chemicals in the eighteenth-century Irish linen industry', MSc Thesis, Queen's
University, Belfast, 1984, p. 174.

more than bare subsistence level, vulnerable to years of shortage. The first half of the eighteenth century reads like a catalogue of woe with tales of famine and food shortage and epidemics among both men and cattle: fear of the future and resentment against rents and tithes too high to be paid from farming drove many to listen to tales of a promised land across the Atlantic and induced some to uproot themselves. A pamphleteer in 1740, writing on the eve of the worst decade in the century, recorded:

> But the scarcity of bread (especially in the North) by the badness of the seasons and crops for several years past, and the loss in two years, viz. '28 and '33 by shaking winds has reduced the case of multitudes very mournful before the present year, and contributed much of the distress in it. Nay, for above a dozen years past, we could scarcely be said to have plenty ...[5]

In contrast to this pessimism was the optimism displayed by contemporary commentators about the districts where the linen industry was flourishing. One pamphleteer in 1732 reckoned that 'the lands of Ulster, though naturally very coarse and for the most part the worst in the kingdom, yet by help of this manufacture are come to be valued almost equal with the best.'[6] Walter Harris, in *The Antient and Present State of the County of Down* (1744), a volume designed to be the model for a series on all the Irish counties, decided 'the staple commodity of the country is linen, a due care of which manufacture has brought great wealth among the people. The Northern inhabitants already feel the benefit of it, and are freed from much of that poverty and wretchedness too visible among the lower class of people in other parts of the Kingdom, where this valuable branch of trade has not been improved to advantage.'[7]

In the early years of the industry weavers had prospered under the patronage of landlords: most of them were craftsmen weaving finer linens and living in those towns and villages that administered and serviced the compact estates created by the plantation scheme. Because the structure of linen marketing was primitive in the early

[5] Royal Irish Academy, Haliday Collection, vol. 151, no. 5, *The distressed state of Ireland considered, more particularly with respect to the North, in a letter to a friend* (1740), p. 4.
[6] Slater, L., *The advantages which may arise to the people of Ireland by raising of flax and flaxseed* (Dublin, 1732).
[7] Harris, W., *The Antient and Present State of the County of Down* (Dublin, 1744), p. 108.

years of the eighteenth century many weavers' families supplemented their incomes from farming and their success attracted farmers to weaving to improve their economic status. Landlords were anxious to accommodate these weavers on their estates by offering them long leases of smallholdings convenient to the major market towns. In 1739 a commentator had remarked on 'the happy success which this method of dividing the land into small partitions and encouraging the cottager and the manufacturer has had in enriching both land-lords and tenant'.[8] On the expiry of leases of lands held by middle-men or by substantial farmers who had profited by subletting their land to weavers, landlords in the major linen-weaving districts seized the initiative by leasing farms directly to those weavers who occupied the land. The result was that by the closing decade of the eighteenth century on several estates in the 'linen triangle' (the district lying between Belfast, Dungannon and Newry that specialised in the weav-ing of fine linens) thousands of weaver-farmers leased land directly from the owners of the estates. Leases to Protestants lasted for three lives while those for Catholics ran for 31 years; although this distinc-tion did not disappear until the 1793 Catholic Relief Act, it had never been of much significance because landlords readily renewed leases to such weavers on the termination of the leases.[9]

The security of tenure that these weavers enjoyed was coveted by many occupiers of land in other parts of the province but their hopes were often disappointed. Outside the linen triangle earnings from the coarser linens were lower so that landlords were not tempted quite so much to take weavers on as direct tenants instead of leaving them as subtenants to the farmers. Even landlords who tried to obtain securi-ty of tenure for subtenants were outmanoeuvred by the tenants. On the Abercorn estate in north-west Ulster, for example, the landlord in 1771 instructed his agent to pressure the tenants into giving subtenants a form of lease that might be renewed to them directly when the main lease expired. The agent reported later the same year after only one success:

---

[8] Public Record Office of Northern Ireland (hereafter PRONI), Mic. 198, 'Hints towards natural and topographical history of the counties of Sligo, Donegal, Fermanagh and Lough Erne by Rev. William Henry … 1739'.

[9] Crawford, W.H., 'Landlord–tenant relations in Ulster 1609–1820', *Irish Economic and Social History*, ii, 1975, 5–21.

It is plain by all their agreements that they guard against that, for they set five or six years short of the tenure they have. Besides they bind them under a penalty, and sometimes by oath, to give up peaceably when their term is expired and that they are not to petition or otherwise apply for any tenant right. Was I to lean to either side it would be to that of the under tenant who generally labours with great industry, and pays exorbitantly, for his earnings and improves much more land I am sure than the immediate tenant, and if he was found on the land at the end of the lease I would wish him to be continued. But if he bargains and obliges himself to give it up, I think his pretension [i.e. claim] is the less. The case of such is certainly hard; they must, if not by the merest chance they become tenants themselves, go on with much hardship and lose the fruits of their labour.[10]

During an economic depression two years later the same agent was forced to report that tenants were more reliable in paying rents than the subtenants. In the long term the tenants solved the problem in their own favour by refusing to grant subleases, while permitting their undertenants to remain. This solution amounted to the creation of a specific 'cottier' status where the undertenant obtained, in return for his labour, no more than a yearly occupancy of a 'dry cot-take' on which crops, especially potatoes and perhaps flax, were planted, or a 'wet cot-take' which included also feeding for a cow or two. He was to have no security of tenure against the very tenant farmer who insisted on his claim to tenant-right against his landlord.

It was the struggle for holdings that was responsible for both subletting and subdivision. In a rural society characterised by family farms, subdivision was the commonest strategy for transmitting property to posterity. In certain sections of the Ulster community partible inheritance was practised among the males of a family while in others all the children shared in their father's property. It was the involvement of all the members of a family in different processes in the domestic linen industry that encouraged families to hold together into adulthood. Then, however, all the individuals would have had to be provided with portions. Subdivision of a farm by successive generations would soon have reduced the family group to beggary if participation in the domestic linen industry had not provided a

---

[10] PRONI, Abercorn papers, James Hamilton to the Earl of Abercorn, August 1771, D623/A/39/135.

supplementary source of income. It is likely therefore that subdivision was both a consequence of the prosperity of the linen industry and a pressure on individuals to take up spinning or weaving to make ends meet. Dependence on the domestic linen industry to maintain such tiny farms was dangerous for the future of the society because any reversal of the process was bound to be painful. Emigration to the American colonies provided a potential safety valve, but until the later decades of the century it attracted mainly single men rather than families.[11]

A related phenomenon was the colonisation of the marginal lands. This provided an opportunity to land-hungry families to carve out holdings for themselves instead of remaining undertenants. Estate rentals and leasebooks indicate that rents of marginal land began to rise from a very low base only after 1750 when arable land was becoming scarce. Attention to the potential of the more sparsely populated districts had been drawn by the new technology of the bleaching industry based on the use of water to power wash-mills and beetling-mills. In search of water supplies men moved into the marginal lands. This was especially true of the Callan valley south of Armagh city. According to a document dated 1795:

> The manufacture gaining strength, about fifty years ago they began to push their improvements into the mountains which separate the low country from Louth, and by the assistance of turf fuel being convenient, and good constant rivers for feeding bleachyards and working machinery, they were enabled to extend their improvements into the mountains. And many wealthy farmers and manufacturers were induced by the low price of them – about a shilling to half a crown an acre – to take farms, lime and burn them although the limestone quarries were distant from the centre of the mountains, measuring from the quarries at Armagh or those on the Louth side towards Dundalk, at least eight or nine miles either way ...[12]

The successful colonisation of the marginal lands in south Armagh encouraged families elsewhere to move to the uplands so that new townlands were marked out on the mountainside, divided among

---

[11] A summary of the argument in Crawford, 'Landlord–tenant relations'.
[12] PRONI, Massereene–Foster MSS, D562/1270, 'Scheme of R. Stevenson 1795'.

tenants, and converted into farms by hard labour.[13] The crop that made feasible the cultivation of marginal land was the potato. Whereas land for grain, crops and flax had to be well prepared, rough 'scraw' or top sods could be levered up and turned over with the native 'loy' into 'lazy beds' resembling broad drills. The potato not only produced a better crop than grain on poor land but it also broke up lea ground and cleansed it of weeds. The other attraction of marginal land was an unlimited supply of turf to provide cheap fuel. As land became more scarce and expensive in the lowlands, more of the poorer people migrated to the mountain valleys and the shores and islands of the loughs and converted them into the farmsteads seen across much of Ulster today.

Capital for the development of marginal land came from the linen industry in the form of increasing demand for food and linen yarn for the linen triangle. As early as the 1720s northerners were buying yarn in County Sligo and it was recorded that 'about the year 1735 the inhabitants of the North growing too numerous for its produce, in their visits for yarn bought wool in this country, soon after beef and mutton, and corn was sometimes exported from Sligo.'[14] By 1770 Sligo was part of the Ulster economy and many Ulster people had moved there in search of land. An agricultural revolution from pasture to tillage was recorded for County Monaghan in 1739 so that it was supplying 'some of the neighbouring counties with bere [cereal resembling barley], barley, and oatmeal'.[15] Later in the century it was said that absentee landlords from Connacht found that their rent remittances were sent to them in bills of exchange drawn on London merchants by Ulster linendrapers and used by them to purchase ponies from Connacht for their businesses.[16] Oatmeal was

---

[13] McCourt, D., 'The decline of rundale, 1750–1850', in Roebuck, P. (ed.), *Plantation to Partition* (Belfast, 1981), pp. 122–6.

[14] National Library of Ireland, O'Hara Papers, Charles O'Hara's account of Sligo in the eighteenth century.

[15] Armagh Public Library, Lodge MSS, 'County Monaghan by Archdeacon Cranston and Mr Lucas, January 8th, 1738–9'.

[16] Blackhall, J., *Some Observations and reflections on the state of the Linen Manufacture in Ireland* (Dublin, 1780).

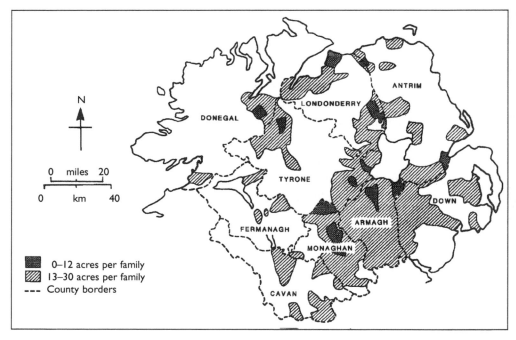

FIGURE 7.1
1766 census – population density

transported to Ulster from many other parts of Ireland: during periods of scarcity this led to local outcries.[17]

The tremendous explosion in the population of Ulster was in its relatively early stages when a census was taken for the Irish House of Lords in the mid-1760s as part of an inquiry 'into the state of Popery' in Ireland.[18] The project was entrusted to the local gaugers, or excise men, in 1764 but the results seemed so defective that it was given in 1766 to the clergy of the Church of Ireland. However defective these returns may be, they do distinguish between Protestants and Catholics. They can be used to map both population density (Figure 7.1) and religious affiliation (Figure 7.2) throughout the province.

To focus attention on the practical implications of population density it is more effective to measure not the number of people per square mile but the number of acres of land per family. This reveals that as early as 1766 the size of family farms was already less than 30 acres (*c.* 12 hectares) and in a few parishes was smaller than 12 acres

[17] Cullen, L.M., *An Economic History of Ireland since 1660* (London, 1972), pp. 67–72; J. Fitzgerald, 'The organisation of the Drogheda economy 1780–1820', MA Thesis, University College, Dublin, 1972, p. 25.

[18] PRONI, T808/14900, 15261, 15264, 15266, 15267, 'Religious returns of 1766'.

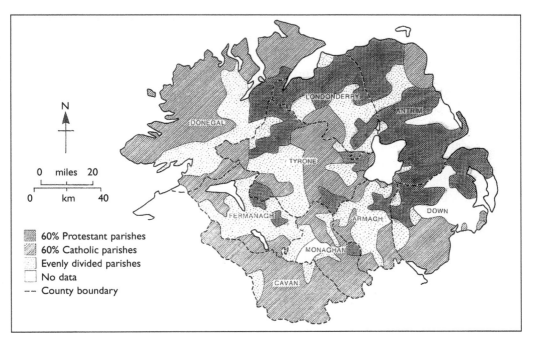

FIGURE 7.2
1766 census – religious affiliation

(4.9 ha.). At this time, therefore, there still existed a balance between the linen manufacture and agriculture since 30 acres of land could provide a decent living by contemporary standards, farmed by traditional methods. An increasing population after this date was compelled to turn to the linen industry to supplement its income. The marginal lands – mountains and bogs – are clearly distinguished: in the west, Donegal, and in the north-east, the Antrim plateau; the Sperrins running south through the centre of the province to Monaghan; and the heavy soils of Fermanagh and Cavan. Cavan was to become much more densely populated, with hosts of cottiers working and weaving for the weaver-farmers: it became part of the linen country. Fermanagh, on the other hand, never became a significant weaving county although it produced much yarn for weavers elsewhere. Notable at this time was the relatively low population of west Donegal, especially in comparison with the eastern side of Inishowen whose economy was linked with that of north Londonderry and Antrim around the ferry at Magilligan, for sales of both yarn and barley. The major problem for those colonising the mountains was that they could not share in the prosperity of the linen industry because they could not produce crops of quality flax on their poor lands. They

95

were forced to concentrate on rearing young stock to sell to the low-landers and their major cash crop became barley that was always in demand by distillers.[19]

One of the most important factors in opening up the marginal lands for colonisation was the development of communications. Even in the first half of the eigheenth century Ulster benefited from two major projects. The most spectacular and one of the earliest feats of its kind was the construction of the Newry Navigation linking Lough Neagh with the sea at Newry by 1742. Although Parliament was disappointed in its intention that the canal would provide cheap Irish coal for Dublin, mid-Ulster was opened up to the influence of Dublin while the canal saved many thousand lives by enabling great quantities of grain to be carried into the heart of the province during the hungry Forties.[20] About this time too the linen country benefited from the construction of many miles of turnpike roads under the sponsorship of the local landlords.[21] These roads were essential to cope with the traffic generated by the linen industry but until the 1765 Road Act permitted grand juries to tax the occupiers of land to provide for the construction of roads and bridges, county funds could not be used to meet the challenge. The 1765 Act itself was the government response to the Hearts of Oak agitation against the earlier system that had required every landholding to supply six days of free labour to mend the roads in each parish. Yet so radical and far-reaching was the 1765 act in its implications for society that it encountered severe opposition, culminating in the Hearts of Steel agitation in the early 1770s. In essence, it placed responsibility for the construction and maintenance of major roads and bridges on the county grand juries and provided capital from a county cess or tax. As the collection of this tax became more efficient and the prosperity of the province increased, the funds available to the grand juries enabled them to execute a great programme of road- and bridge-building. Most impressive was the series of three timber bridges thrown across the Lower Bann (Toome, Portneil, and Agivey) and the great timber

[19] McEvoy, J., *Statistical Survey of the County of Tyrone* (Dublin, 1802), p. 32.
[20] Barton, R., *A Dialogue Concerning Some Things of Importance to Ireland, particularly to the County of Ardmagh* [*sic*] (Dublin, 1751), p. 14.
[21] Crawford, W.H., 'Economy and society in eighteenth century Ulster', PhD Thesis, Queen's University, Belfast, 1982, pp. 110–12.

bridge built across the Foyle at Londonderry by the American firm of Lemuel Cox of Boston in 1791.

In Ulster road projectors were encouraged by two acts passed in the 1771–2 session, the first permitting Ulster parishes to raise an extra parish cess to maintain minor public roads and the second enabling grand juries to raise money 'for the making of narrow roads through the mountainous un-improved parts of this Kingdom'.[22] New roads opened up land for development and increased its value while they made possible the transport of lime and other commodities essential for its exploitation. Too little notice has been taken of the great expansion of the road network in this period. Because the law ensured that roads could be made only between market towns or between market towns and the seacoast, road building stimulated the development of the whole urban network and diffused prosperity through the byways.

It was said of County Tyrone, for example, at the end of the eighteenth century that it was as well supplied with market towns as any county in the kingdom,[23] and yet many of these towns had been created, or revived, only in the eighteenth century. They owed their creation to energetic landlords anxious to secure some of the prosperity generated by the linen industry. Although neither linen nor cloth paid tolls, these markets and fairs attracted buyers and sellers of other goods as well, especially oatmeal for food and candles for light. As early as the 1740s linendrapers were making it known that they would attend regular well-organised weekly markets in preference to the haphazard seasonal country fairs.[24] In response landlords provided markethouses and tried to ensure that markets were properly conducted while some offered premiums or inducements to attract buyers and sellers. Such concern could make all the difference between the success or failure of a market. The whole atmosphere of this period is caught in a letter from Nathaniel Nisbitt of Lifford in County Donegal reporting in his capacity as agent to the Earl of Abercorn in April 1758:

We had the 17th inst at St Johnstown a very fine market for the first;

---

[22] Ibid., pp. 121–7.
[23] See McEvoy, op. cit., pp. 53, 158–60, 207–9.
[24] *Belfast News-Letter*, 11 November 1746.

there was about £100 worth of green [unbleached] linen bought, a large quantity of yarn; there were also several other sorts of goods, such as suit the markets of this country; our next is the 15th of May for we were obliged to make it the third Monday in the month, to steer clear of other markets; I would allow neither cockfight, nor horse race, though the people of the town were for it, as all towns are indeed, but I satisfied them by saying that an inch gained by honest industry was worth a yard otherwise, and that we did not want to gather idle folk at all.[25]

This letter contains one of the earliest references to a monthly market in Ulster – later to be known as the 'fair day' – and illustrates how the date in the month was selected. St Johnstown (or Altacaskine) had been granted a patent in 1618 for a Monday market and two fairs in the year on Easter Tuesday and the Tuesday after Michaelmas respectively. By the time this letter was written the fairs had increased to four, a common occurrence in Ulster at that time. Although St Johnstown had been incorporated as a borough, it had not been able to sustain a weekly market and this letter records the efforts of the Abercorns to found a monthly market that would take advantage of the increasing prosperity of the district. To create a reputation for the conduct of the markets, the agent had refused to permit either cock-fighting or horse-racing, both of which sports were associated with the traditional fairs. These monthly markets got their greatest fillip from the expansion of the cattle trade after 1760 and they extended rapidly through the bleaker countryside of Counties Tyrone and Donegal. Successful markets attracted shopkeepers and tradesmen while a professional class began to appear in many of the larger provincial towns. This was reflected in their domestic architecture, notably in Belfast, Newry, Armagh, Dungannon and Londonderry.[26]

Although the sudden flowering of towns and villages all over Ulster was one of the most notable characteristics of the late eighteenth century, it has to be admitted that in almost every instance they were no more than market towns with primitive organs of administration. Only the city of Londonderry appears to have had an effective corporation with wide-ranging powers that could be adapted to meet

[25] PRONI, Abercorn papers, D623/A/33/23, Nathaniel Nisbitt to Earl of Abercorn, 20 April 1758.
[26] See the publications of the Ulster Architectural Heritage Society.

changing economic and social circumstances. Even the corporations of the boroughs created in the seventeenth century had been neutered by the practice of packing corporations with non-residents who could be relied upon to maintain the landlords' control over the boroughs' parliamentary seats. The legality of this practice had been confirmed by the Newtown Act of 1747 and case law in the courts recognised the rights of these self-perpetuating oligarchies. For local administration, therefore, the boroughs had to rely on corporation grand juries which had no legal status, manor courts held by the landlords, or parish vestries, or a combination of all three.

The legal limitations of these courts rendered them a potential source of political trouble in the closing years of the century. In Belfast, for example, the sovereign was the nominee of the landlord but he had to act as clerk of the markets, chief magistrate and coroner, as well as superintending the paving, lighting, and cleansing of the town. The initiative in local government came from outside the corporation of Belfast: town meetings could be called by a public notice instituted by influential inhabitants and published in the newspapers. The parish vestry was the instrument used to assess and collect rates but when some people refused to pay, the legality of the rate was questioned. The problem was exacerbated when the economic crises of the 1790s caused an increase in crime and poverty, so that in 1800 Parliament was compelled to pass a special act for the reform of the government of Belfast. The other towns in the province had to await local government reform in the nineteenth century to give expression to the wishes of the townspeople and to free them from landlord domination.[27]

In fact landlord power in Ulster reached its peak in the late eighteenth century. Before that time very few of them had been titled but many were then ennobled and exercised considerable influence in the Dublin Parliament. The zenith of their power coincided with the success of the Irish Volunteers movement when they mobilised the Protestants for the defence of the country against French invasion and for the protection of property rights. Such an assertion, however, would greatly oversimplify the complexities of Ulster society. Although outside Dublin itself Ulster was the great stronghold of the

---

[27] Crawford, 'Economy and Society in Eighteenth Century Ulster', ch. 6.

Volunteering movement, it was not the landlords but the middle class of merchants and professional men who had created it. The landlords did manage to gain control of the leadership of the movement but only at the cost of recognising the strength, and representing the aspirations, of their supporters.[28] It was not a mere coincidence that in 1782, the same year that the Volunteers held their first great convention at Dungannon, the linendrapers of Ulster met at Armagh to compel the withdrawal of new regulations by the Linen Board in Dublin and secured their ends with the support of several great landlords who represented Ulster on the Linen Board.

These years introduced Ulstermen to the techniques of politics – public meetings, resolutions, lobbying – and some of them proved to be enthusiastic students. Even after the close of the American War of Independence when the majority of the Volunteers put away their equipment, some radical spirits continued to diagnose the ills of their own society. They resented the dominance of the landlord interest in politics and in the control of all the organs of government but they could not convince their fellow citizens to break what they viewed as the shackles of oppression.

This continuing movement for reform was consolidated and developed by the foundation of the Society of United Irishmen in Belfast in October 1791. (A similar association was established in the following month in Dublin.) Influenced by the more radical ideas of the French Revolution, the Society, which had initially endorsed a programme of moderate constitutional reform, moved steadily toward the advocacy of a republican constitution, to be established through revolutionary change. By 1796 it had experienced considerable success in establishing branches outside Belfast, particularly in Counties Antrim, Down and Londonderry. Moreover, its alliance with the Catholic agrarian movement had given it a popular base and contributed greatly to its potential force. Its gathering strength, however, convinced the government that Ulster was the centre where rebellion was most likely to begin. Therefore in 1797 General Lake was authorised to enforce a policy of severe repression throughout the province.

[28] Smyth, P.D.H., 'The Volunteers and parliament, 1779–84' in Bartlett, T. and Hayton, D.W. (eds), *Penal Era and Golden Age* (Belfast, 1979), pp. 113–36; Crawford, W.H., 'The influence of the landlord in eighteenth century Ulster', in Cullen, L.M. and Smout, T.C. (eds), *Comparative Aspects of Scottish and Irish Economic and Social History, 1600–1900* (Edinburgh, 1977), pp. 193–203.

Within a year political opposition in Ulster had been so weakened through Lake's campaign that when rebellion actually broke out elsewhere in the country, the attempts by Henry Joy McCracken and Henry Munro to raise the United Irishmen in Antrim and Down failed after brief campaigns.

Blame for the '98 rebellion was in large part laid upon the republican shopkeepers for misleading the countryfolk. Yet several Presbyterian clergymen also played a part. For political dissent in Ulster – even if it was tempered by the spirit of the French Revolution and couched in radical language – represented in essence a further expression of the ancient resentment nursed by certain elements in the Presbyterian congregations against the Anglican aristocratic ascendancy.[29]

Though it is clear that the rebellion of '98 did not impinge greatly upon general life in the province between the 1780s and the early 1800s,[30] it nonetheless convinced the London government of the need for a union between Britain and Ireland in 1800: they had lost confidence in the ability of the Anglican aristocracy to rule Ireland. The union concealed the developing political vacuum but, with hindsight, we realise that it was inevitable that in three provinces the Catholics would succeed to power whereas in Ulster they would not be in a position to challenge the Protestants.

In Ulster it was not just that Catholics were in a numerical minority. They were also at a severe social disadvantage. The sequence of wars in the seventeenth century had deprived not only the native landowners of their freehold property but also the farmers of their leaseholds. Over much of the province, wherever the British landlords were able to attract immigrants, the natives were reduced to the status of subtenants. In such a subservient position they posed no threat to the new social structure and were able to continue in their traditional lifestyle. Although many of them adapted to the expanding commercial economy by buying and selling around the country or taking up weaving for the linen export market, their lack of capital and business connections prevented them from securing a significant

29 Crawford, W.H., 'Change in Ulster in the late eighteenth century', in Bartlett and Hayton, op. cit., pp. 199–202.
30 Jupp, P., 'County Down elections 1783–1831', *Irish Historical Studies* 18, no. 70, Sept. 1972, 177–206.

share of the prosperity generated in the middle years of the century. They did benefit, however, from the readiness of the landlords to exploit the potential of their estates by negotiating leases with those who could afford to pay regular rents and many of them obtained leases for thirty-one years, placing them almost on a par with their Protestant neighbours. Especially in 'the linen triangle' many landlords pursued this policy of dividing up holdings among the original subtenants to such an extent that the class of substantial farmers that could have maintained order, was seriously weakened. In the egalitarian society that ensued, men were forced to band together to cultivate new group loyalties that would protect their local community interests.[31]

The most reliable guide we possess to the relative strength of Catholics and Protestants across the province is the previously mentioned 1766 census of religion by parishes. Contemporaries would have associated Protestantism with the descendants of British colonists and Catholicism with the native Irish even where they knew about exceptions to the rule. In order to emphasise the significance of the ratios, it is best to distinguish those districts that were predominantly (i.e. more than 60 per cent) Catholic from those that were predominantly Protestant, and those that were only marginally one or the other. (It might he objected that since the count was made by Anglican clergymen it would be biased either in favour of Protestants or against Catholics: if the census was taken during a period of a Catholic 'scare', then the numbers of Catholics would he inflated, but if it was taken during a period of Protestant confidence, Protestant numbers would be increased. It is likely, however, that Protestant numbers were overestimated simply because the clergy would be more able to identify Protestants than Catholics, especially in those areas where Protestants composed only a small minority.)

Very conspicuous on the map are two Protestant areas: the south Antrim/north Down region straddling the Lagan valley and the region stretching along the north coast from Lough Swilly in the west to the Giant's Causeway in the east and including the lower half of the Foyle basin: it was from these bases that British colonisation had

---

[31] For a fuller treatment of this theme see Crawford, W.H., 'The Ulster Irish in the eighteenth century', *Ulster Folklife* 28, 1982, pp. 24–32.

advanced in the seventeenth century. Just as striking is the broad Catholic strip running in depth all along the southern border of Ulster: this indicates that the colonisation thrust had been halted and contained before it reached either Leinster or Connacht. If the settlers had exerted serious pressure against Monaghan and Cavan it would have altered the religious balance and character of those two counties also. Pockets of colonisation around certain towns illustrate the success of certain landlords, such as the Abercorn and Brooke families, in promoting British tenants on their estates. In contrast is the apparent success of the Irish in the old O'Neill homelands around Dungannon on the Powerscourt, Ranfurly and Charlemont estates in County Tyrone.

Special attention should be paid to those districts such as the western shore of Lough Neagh where Catholics and Protestants occupied distinct neighbourhoods. In north Armagh, where faction-fighting (endemic in rural society throughout Ireland) first assumed a sectarian form, strong Catholic parishes faced Protestant parishes and the dense populations were well matched. Both parties were composed of weavers whose lifestyles differed little but they rarely intermarried. Throughout most of the century Catholics had been prepared to accept a subordinate role in society but by the 1780s they were confident enough to challenge this role and to assert their rights whenever necessary. These minor skirmishes were difficult to suppress. In the aftermath of the Volunteer period there were too many guns about the countryside and plenty of provocation to use them. Peace-keeping was in the hands of the local justices of the peace, but they could get little co-operation and in the absence of police or military aid had to depend on the local companies of Volunteers to keep the peace. Finally, the disbandment of the Volunteers in 1793 transferred the responsibility for keeping the peace from the hands of the landlords to government control.[32] As a result both Protestants and Catholics organised themselves more effectively, copying freemasonry lodge structures and emblems, and created respectively the Orange Boys and the Defenders. The skirmishes between them, especially at

---

[32] See Bartlett, T., 'An end to moral economy: the Irish Militia disturbances of 1793', *Past and Present* 99, May 1983, 41–64; as well as Miller, D.W., 'The Armagh Troubles, 1784–95', in Clark, S. and Donnelly, J.S. (eds), *Irish Peasants: Violence and Political Unrest 1780–1914* (Manchester, 1983), pp. 155–91.

fairs, continued until late in the nineteenth century.

In eighteenth-century Ulster the pace of change had been very rapid. So swift had been the increase of population that it was almost as large as that of all Scotland by 1821. The domestic linen industry had swept through the province dividing and subdividing the town-lands into myriad small farms, while cultivation had advanced settlements along the mountain valleys. The new farms were served by thousands of miles of new roads that linked a complex network of market towns and villages and imported the products of the new industrial culture. Urban life with its esteem for education and commercial progress introduced politics, organisation and administration that must serve as the hallmarks of nineteenth-century Ulster society. The Anglican ascendancy had been forced to share much of its power with the merchant classes in the towns and the more substantial farmers throughout the countryside, and it was they who set the tone for the new century.

8

The 'linen triangle' in the 1790s[1]

PLATE 8

*The brown Linen market at Banbridge in the County of Downe,
the weavers holding up their pieces of Linen to View, the Bleachers
elevated on Forms examining its Quality . . .*

WILLIAM HINCKS 1783

IN HIS PAPER Professor Louis Cullen has stressed that the causes of unrest in County Armagh in the 1790s were political in character rather than social or economic.[2] He believes that the government in Dublin had set out to undermine a county 'once solidly independent' and in the process had somehow created a hardline government party that provoked the Defenders and created the Orange Order. Professor David Miller, however, in a series of important studies attributes the unrest to a breakdown in the social order brought about by the development of the domestic linen industry and exacerbated by sectarianism.[3] In adopting these arguments both men make certain assumptions about the structure of society in County Armagh in the 1790s and their debate provides us with an opportunity to consider some aspects of their new interpretations in the light of local historical research.

In his study Cullen tries to go behind the obvious explanation of sectarianism because he believes that it has prevented historians from looking closely at the contemporary politics of the county. Although this observation will certainly focus more attention on the political aspect, it will need to be linked more closely to another phenomenon that had been undermining landlord control in north Armagh. This study will present evidence of the rise of a new political force among the farmer-weavers in the 'linen triangle'. It will set out to explain how and why this group materialised and why it split along sectarian lines into the Catholic Defenders and the Protestant Orange Order. The answers lies in an unusual combination of circumstances, some of which were peculiar to this district.

The 'linen triangle' is the term that I have applied to the region lying on the southern side of Lough Neagh between Lisburn, Dungannon, and Newry, in which the finest linens were woven. The social structure that had evolved there had its roots in the scheme for the Plantation of Ulster in the early seventeenth century. Although the character of the estates created by the London government was

[1] First published in *Ulster Local Studies* 18, no. 2, (spring 1997), 43–53.
[2] Cullen, L.M., 'The United Irishmen: problems and issues of the 1790s', *Ulster Local Studies* 18, no. 2 (1977), pp. 7–27.
[3] Miller, David W., 'The Armagh troubles, 1784–95', in Clark, S. and Donnelly, J.S. (eds), *Irish Peasants: Violence and Political Unrest 1780–1914* (Manchester, 1983), pp. 155–91; Miller, D.W., *Peep O'Day Boys and Defenders* (Belfast, 1990). Miller, 'Politicisation in revolutionary Ireland: the case of the Armagh troubles', *Irish Economic and Social History* 23 (1996), 1–17.

based on English models, its modification began almost immediately in order to cope with the realities of Irish life. London had allocated the several baronies that made up each of the six planted counties to distinct groups of potential landlords: either to English 'undertakers', Scottish 'undertakers', or 'native Irish' and English 'servitors' (soldiers and administrators), respectively. North Armagh, the core of this district, had been allocated to English undertakers and there were important servitors in both east Tyrone and west Down. While this may have determined the character of the landlords to some extent, their tenants were a much more motley and fickle crowd, moving about in search of the best bargains. Although this plantation was almost wiped out in the 1640s, the landlords retained their titles to their estates and those in the Lagan valley and in north Armagh were rewarded by an influx of new settlers from the North of England in the 1650s and 1660s. In this way the predominantly English character of the estates was maintained while elsewhere even the original English baronies were swamped by a huge influx from Scotland, especially during the great famine that devastated that country in the mid 1690s.

Although it is generally believed that the native Irish on the lands were driven out by the new settlers, the actual picture is much more complex. Because the initial influx of British settlers was insufficient to meet their needs, the new landlords managed to persuade the government in 1628 to allow them to retain Irish tenants on one quarter of the townlands on their estates, paying increased rents for the privilege.[4] Evidence for the Brownlow estate in north-east Armagh reveals that while most of the townlands allocated to Irish tenants did lie in the unprofitable fenlands on the Lough shore known as the Montiaghs, others lay on better land both east and west of the town of Lurgan, indicating that at least some Irishmen had been able to secure title to good land. The Hearth Money Rolls of the 1660s suggest that by then these Irish had managed to spread from these areas into neighbouring townlands. An examination of the leasebook used by Arthur Brownlow from 1667 to 1711 indicates, however, that the

[4] Moody, T.W., 'The treatment of the native population under the scheme for the Plantation of Ulster', *Irish Historical Studies* 1 (1938–9), 59–63; G. Hill, *An historical account of the Plantation of Ulster at the commencement of the seventeenth century 1608–20* (Belfast, 1877), pp. 447–8.

Williamite wars began a process of replacing the leases of these Irish on their expiry by newcomers with British names, even in the townlands of the Montiaghs.[5] For the first half of the eighteenth century a few Irish are noted in the estate records as leaseholders but the bulk of them were undertenants, paying rent to either Irish or English tenants.[6]

Many of these Irish surnames, however, reappeared as leaseholders in the second half of the eighteenth century. It is possible to identify these new 'popish leases', as they were commonly known, because the term for which they were granted was either twenty-one or thirty-one years whereas it was customary for British tenants to obtain leases for the term of three lives named in each lease (which made them freeholders with the right to vote in parliamentary elections).[7] The Catholic Relief Act of 1778 removed this distinction between Catholics and Protestants.[8] Although more Catholics became leaseholders as the eighteenth century drew to its close, the process was a slow one because it had to wait for old leases to expire. Nevertheless the process was ongoing and would have been perceived as a serious threat by the original Protestant leaseholders. It was haphazard in its effect but a potent cause of friction in the rural community.

Because three life leases took so long to run out, any analysis of leaseholders based on estate records would prove to be a very defective indicator of the relative strength of Catholics and Protestants. Yet there is a valuable source of quantitative evidence in a return of the relative numbers of Protestant and Catholic families, prepared for the Irish House of Lords by the clergy in each Church of Ireland parish in 1766. It would be interesting but not profitable to speculate on the accuracy of these returns, yet even as they stand they are very significant. In *Peep O'Day Boys and Defenders* Miller published a map based on these returns for County Armagh but since I have chosen to concentrate instead on the 'linen triangle', my table includes several parishes from west Down and east Tyrone (Table 8.1). These figures indicate that the region was already densely populated and that the

---

[5] Gillespie, R. (ed.), *Settlement and Survival on an Ulster estate: the Brownlow leasebook 1667–1711* (Belfast, 1988).

[6] Miller, 'Armagh Troubles', pp. 142–50; Public Record Office of Northern Ireland (hereafter PRONI), Brownlow Papers, D1928/L/1/1–4, leasebooks 1710–62.

[7] PRONI, D1928/R/1/27–8, rentals for Lurgan country 1775–8.

[8] 17 & 18 Geo. III (1778), c. 49, s. 1.

TABLE 8.1

Religious census returns of 1766 for the linen triangle (see page 95)

PARISH	TOWN	PROTESTANT %		CATHOLIC %	
County Down					
Moira		226	68	105	32
Magheralin		261	68	116	31
Donaghcloney	Waringstown	379	86	60	14
Tullylish		435	57	327	43
Seapatrick	Banbridge	481	88	67	12
Aghaderg		742	69	340	31
County Armagh					
Ballymore	Tandragee	615	68	286	32
Montiaghs		90	38	144	62
Seagoe		455	54	391	46
Shankill	Lurgan	759	70	319	30
Drumcree	Portadown	514	57	395	43
Tartaraghan		172	43	229	57
Loughgall		588	56	469	44
Kilmore	Richhill	791	66	410	34
Armagh		1,209	48	1,327	52
County Tyrone					
Clonfeacle	Moy	725	39	1,150	61
Killyman		204	38	332	63
Clonoe		72	16	382	84
Donaghenry	Stewartstown	268	80	69	20
Tullyniskan		114	50	116	50
Drumglass		76	36	133	64
Dungannon town		160	74	55	26
Donaghmore		540	37	930	63

proportion of Protestants to Catholics was no more than 55:45. While the west Down parishes display a 70:30 advantage for Protestants, that proportion falls to 57:43 in north Armagh and 40:60 in east Tyrone (this does not accord with the notion that the native population had been expelled from their lands at the time of the Plantation). The fulcrum, therefore, was around Loughgall in west Armagh, itself a small Protestant market town surrounded on three sides by parishes with a Catholic majority: there the major trial of strength was to take place in 1795. The figures indicate also that the strongest Protestant parishes had developed around the market towns containing the headquarters of the major estates: Loughgall was the centre of the Cope estate. A dense network of roads linking these towns strengthened their defensive position. The majority of townlands inhabited by Catholics were, in general, on the periphery of estates, linking them with their kinsmen on neighbouring estates and across the river Blackwater that marked the county boundary with Tyrone.

Such a demographic structure made this district very vulnerable to communal strife and it began to assume religious overtones in the 1780s. However, as Cullen has pointed out, the term 'sectarianism' is a blanket term that excuses historians from trying harder to discover the underlying causes of unrest. Because anything can be attributed to sectarianism, it is not a helpful explanation. It is important therefore not to jump to conclusions nor attempt to apportion blame but to record details about clashes so that the evidence can be scrutinised for other factors.

The social and demographic changes in this region described above were related to the great expansion of leaseholding that had taken place in Ulster over the previous two centuries. The written lease as a contract between landlord and tenant had been introduced as an integral part of the Plantation system which permitted landlords to retain a proportion of each estate as a personal demesne while insisting that they had to lease the remainder to tenants. Of course a wise landlord would grant leases only to those tenants who could and would pay their rents promptly, and would promise to develop the property and return it to the landlord at the expiry of the lease. For these reasons landlords granted leases in the seventeenth and early eighteenth centuries to only the more substantial farmers. By the 1750s, however, many of them could see that the farmers in their turn were subletting portions of their farms to linenweavers as smallholdings of from five to fifteen acres, knowing that the weavers could afford to pay high rents regularly from the sale of their webs. The landlords' response on the expiry of such old leases was to lease these smallholdings direct to the weaver-occupiers, cutting out the original tenants and charging the 'going rate' for land, to the great benefit of their rentals. The weavers, for their part, seized every opportunity to gain the security of a lease, knowing well that it could be mortgaged or sold to raise capital in the last resort. In this process it has to be recognised that while both Protestant and Catholic weavers were winners, the losers belonged to the substantial Protestant farming class and they had a lot to lose. Their attempts to claim 'tenant right' over the whole of the original holding were rejected as injurious to the rights of landlords.[9]

Because higher rents could be paid from money earned in the linen industry than from the profits of agriculture, the handloom weavers were able to obtain smallholdings convenient to the market towns.[10] A distinctive pattern of landholding and farming evolved in this region. Subsequent generations continued the practice of subdividing holdings with the result that the estates came to be filled with families concentrating on the domestic linen industry. By the eve of the Great Famine of the 1840s the 'linen triangle' was recognised as the most densely populated district in Ireland.

Although the rentals of the landlords were swollen by the growing number of farmer-weavers paying the 'going rate' for land, so too were the problems of managing their estates. Another landlord explained the complexity of the job:

> the management of estates requires much cleverness in their regulation to the mutual advantages of the landlord and the tenant. The parcels of ground, or farms, if I may so call them, being very small and numerous; rents being paid so irregularly, on account of the many divisions of these little plots; the attention necessary for proportioning turf bogs and approaches to each little farm; and the judicious laying out of new roads, are together fully adequate to employ the time of an active agent, who will also have no small trouble in his magisterial capacity to adjust disputes amongst the tenantry.[11]

By cutting out the farmer class the landlords were dispensing with its traditional role of maintaining discipline among the lower orders, thereby exposing themselves to the demands of the multitude. This problem manifested itself first in the early 1760s, both in the show of

9 Crawford, W.H., 'Landlord–tenant relations in Ulster 1609–1820', *Irish Economic and Social History* 2 (1975), 12–15.
10 Crawford, W.H. and Trainor, B. (eds), *Aspects of Irish Social History 1750–1800* (Belfast, 1969), 92–4.
11 Coote, Sir C., *A statistical survey of the County of Armagh* (Dublin, 1804), p. 117.

strength in Lisburn linen market in 1762 and in the Hearts of Oak disturbances that accompanied the agitation against the enforcement of the six days' labour on the roads. A decade later followed the Hearts of Steel, protesting against the efforts of the landlords and their agents in the grand jury to collect the county cess for the upkeep of roads. In both these episodes mobs threatened the persons and the homes of those gentry who incurred their displeasure. When, in 1772, Richard (later Sir Richard) Johnston of Gilford seized some of the ringleaders, his home was attacked and he was fortunate to escape with his life. Finally the army had to be sent in to break up the insurgents who formed large mobs roaming throughout the countryside.[12]

Miller has argued that the Hearts of Steel rising did shake the confidence of the landlords in their ability to control the artisan class and made them more wary in enforcing the law. Soon afterwards, however, their courage was restored by the institution of local Volunteer companies during the American War of Independence for they mobilised what was left of the 'armed property of the nation' in north Armagh along with the growing urban professional class. With their landlords as commanders they constituted the backbone of the independent interest in the Dublin Parliament and at the Dungannon convention. At that time they would not have been prepared to admit the farmer-weaver class to their ranks. Although landlords like William Brownlow of Lurgan had always been ready to welcome the popular support of the weavers with their music, drums and colours, they had long ago learned not to challenge the class of men who formed the 'petty juries' and gave judgments in favour of their friends and kin in the courts.[13] As long as the landlords in Armagh could rely on the loyalty of the Volunteers, they had the confidence to enforce law and order within their estates but when the government disbanded the Volunteers in 1793 the gentry were seriously weakened at a time of great crisis and had perforce to rely on the military in order to uphold their authority and control. It deprived them of their power and authority at the very time they needed them most, and placed them in the invidious position of having to rely for support on the military.

---

[12] Gill, C., *The rise of the Irish linen industry* (Oxford, 1925), pp. 108–13; Donnelly, J.S., 'Hearts of Oak, Hearts of Steel', *Studia Hibernica* 21 (1981), 773.

[13] *Belfast News-Letter*, 20 April 1753; Crawford, W.H., 'The significance of landed estates in Ulster, 1600–1820', *Irish Economic and Social History* 17 (1990), 55.

The excitement of Volunteering had its effect on the class of farmer-weavers. It could be argued that they had first flexed their muscles in the confrontation in 1762 at Lisburn over the new regulations introduced by the Linen Board for the certification of linens brought for sale to the public linen-markets. Although the Linen Board finally did achieve its long overdue aim to appoint 'brown-sealmasters' who would examine and stamp with their own seal (bearing their own name) every web before it was offered for sale in the market, it allowed these posts to be filled by farmer-weavers, thus recognising the influence of that group. Although brown-sealmasters were regularly disciplined and even dismissed for breaches of the regulations, weavers continued to administer the system that was fundamental to the success of the system of public markets until the abolition of the Linen Board itself in 1828. Even then some local markets continued to appoint brown-sealmasters.[14] It might be argued that the farmer-weavers had forced themselves into the polity of the linen industry, although the real power continued to be exercised by the bleachers and the linen-drapers who served them.

Professor Miller has provided such a valuable analysis of the circumstances that provoked sectarian confrontations that it is especially unfortunate that he has used the term 'minions' to describe the numerous class of farmer-weavers. It implies that they were merely tools of their lords and masters and would be prepared to do anything to retain their favour. This charge against the weavers, both Protestant and Catholic, is not borne out by the evidence. They were indeed 'citizens' – real democrats with all the virtues and failings that that term implies. On the expiry of old leases more weavers – both Protestants and Catholics – had acquired for the first time the security of leases and a sense of belonging to the body politic. They had gained the status of tenants because they were weavers or 'manufacturers' of fine linens, whose income was sufficient and regular enough to enable them to pay their rents half-yearly. They represented the pinnacle of the weaving industry for they wove the finest yarns that could be spun, into fine linen cloths such as calicoes and lawns. They had graduated to this standard over the years and attracted a regular trade in

[14] See pages 144 to 147.

the finest yarns from all over the province.

> In the north of Ireland ... the object of every person who has flax, is
> to have it of as fine quality as he can; and the spinners' object is to
> spin it as fine as they can, because it pays a better price; and the man-
> ufacturer's object is to weave the finest linen that he can, for which
> reason, the coarse article in the North of Ireland is made only of the
> refuse of the flax.[15]

In their concentration on fine linens they differed from those
weavers who lived outside the 'linen triangle', produced coarser
linens, and remained in the status of cottier-weavers dependent on
the tenant-farmers. Nor is it accurate to maintain the Gibbon thesis
that the weavers of the 'linen triangle' had been 'proletarianised'. The
structure of the industry did not change in the late eighteenth century. In Ulster the weavers continued to sell the vast bulk of linens in
the public markets to touring linendrapers, as well as purchasing the
several weights of yarns that they required from travelling yarn dealers. This practice lasted until the introduction of the wet-spinning
process to produce fine yarns in the late 1820s enabled the new class
of powerspinners to secure control of the raw material and 'put it out'
to weavers on their terms. Until then each master-weaver, or 'manufacturer', organised his own company of family, servants, and cottier-
weavers who could not afford to purchase the quantities of yarn they
needed. Both the 1816 and 1821 reports to the Linen Board show
that the master-weavers continued to attend the markets throughout
Ulster in large numbers, between ten thousand in slack times and
twenty thousand in busy times.[16] If we were to assume that there were
then as many as one hundred thousand weavers in the province (surely an over-estimate), each of these men at the markets would have
been representing an average of fewer than ten weavers. A generation
or so earlier the structure of the industry was much the same.

These farmer-weavers were the men, both Catholic and Protestant,
whose political demands caused the disturbances. They wanted to be
treated according to their new social status and expected to be allowed
the right to carry arms. Such a demand was complicated by the deter-

[15] *Report from the select committee on the laws which regulate the linen trade of Ireland,* British
Parliamentary Papers 1822 (560), 7, 486.
[16] See page 149.

mination of Protestants that the law against Catholics carrying arms should be enforced. This was manifested in the Peep o'Day Boys raids which forced the Catholics to organise lodges of Defenders that later united to co-ordinate action.[17] Their success in turn drove the Protestants to combine by affiliating their clubs or lodges to an association that they termed the Orange Society. The Protestant landlords, who had been left powerless by the recent abolition of the Volunteers, had to come to terms with the new dominant class among their tenants or risk letting them fall into the hands of more extreme elements.

A footnote can be added to another issue raised by Cullen: the strength of the United Irishmen in County Armagh on the eve of the rising. His suggestion that the United Irish movement in north Armagh carried a serious threat, however, runs counter to fresh evidence provided by a recent analysis by John Gray of the subscribers' lists of the *Belfast News-Letter* and the *Northern Star* newspapers respectively. The failure of the United Irishmen to secure a foothold in north Armagh is well illustrated by the success of the *Belfast News-Letter* in beating off the challenge of the *Northern Star*:

> the *News-Letter*'s greatest strength lay along the Lagan Valley and into Armagh. Thus Lisburn provided ninety-three subscribers, and Armagh with ninety-eight provided the greatest number of any single location. In between, the two relatively small villages of Tandragee and Richhill provided no less than seventy names ... As a whole this region provided 527 names or twenty-nine per cent of the total circulation.[18]

When Gray examined the numbers of subscribers to the *News-Letter* between November 1795 and April 1797 he found that while those in north and mid-Antrim almost halved, the Lagan valley and north Armagh remained virtually unscathed. If this transfer of newspaper readership can be used to demonstrate the rapidity of political polarisation in Ulster, it must also be an indicator of the steadfastness of the loyalist element in the linen triangle.

---

[17] McEvoy, B., 'The Peep of Day Boys and Defenders in the County Armagh', *Seanchas Ard Mhacha* 12.1 (1986), 147–51.

[18] J. Gray, 'A tale of two newspapers: the contest between the *Belfast News-Letter* and the *Northern Star* in the 1790s', in Gray, J. and McCann, W. (eds), *An uncommon bookman: essays in memory of J.R.R. Adams* (Belfast, 1996), p. 182.

9

Women in the domestic linen industry[1]

PLATE 9

*A complete Perspective View of all the machinery of a Bleach Mill,
upon the Newest and Most approved Constructions, Consisting of the Wash Mill,
Rubbing Boards moved by a Crank, and Beetling Engine for Glazing the Cloth,
with a View of the Boiling House . . .*

WILLIAM HINCKS 1783

OVER THE 17TH AND 18TH CENTURIES in Ireland the preparation and spinning of both woollen and linen yarns by women in their own homes provided a major source of employment and income for many families. Women processed raw materials not only for the weaving of clothes and household furnishings for the Irish market but also for profitable export as yarn to thriving English textile manufacturing regions. Just as English wool had been exported to Flanders in great quantities by the twelfth and thirteenth centuries to supply the thriving textile industry there,[2] so Irish linen and woollen yarns were being exported to several regions of England by the sixteenth century.[3] By the end of the seventeenth century exports of wool and woollen yarns accounted for more than half the value of Irish exports to England and linen yarn for one-eighth. Because England could not produce sufficient yarns to service its own textile industries it had to pay good prices to attract yarns from Ireland. Although wool declined to less than 20 per cent by the mid-1720s it was replaced as a money earner by linen: whereas exports of linen yarn as a percentage of total exports peaked with worsted yarn before 1720, linen cloth provided two-thirds of the value of Irish exports as late as 1788.[4] In spite of this export trade Ireland was still able to clothe its people, although it has to be admitted that most of the finer quality cloths were imported from England and the Continent. By the close of the eighteenth century, too, Ireland was producing at least one-third of all linens woven in the British Isles.

Although the woollen and linen trades in Ireland were both very important for Irish society and the economy, they developed in very different ways. The old nationalist tradition that the woollen industry suffered because the linen industry was promoted about 1700 by the London and Dublin governments at its expense, has been disproved. In general the home market continued to be dominated by Irish woollen cloth whereas the bulk of Irish linen was sold in the much more competitive English market along with large quantities of

---

[1] First published in Margaret MacCurtain, and Mary O'Dowd, (eds), *Women in Early Modern Ireland* (1991), pp. 255–64.

[2] Postan, M.M., *The Medieval Economy and Society* (London, 1972), pp. 190–2.

[3] Longfield, A.K., *Anglo-Irish Trade in the Sixteenth Century* (London, 1929), pp. 77–93; Wadsworth, A.P. and Mann, J. de L., *The Cotton Trade and Industrial Lancashire 1600–1780* (Manchester, 1931), pp. 5, 6, 11, 13, 46–7.

[4] Cullen, L.M., *Anglo-Irish Trade 1660–1800* (Manchester, 1968), p. 50.

Irish linen and woollen yarns. Towards the close of the eighteenth century, however, as the home market came under heavier pressure from English industrialists, the Irish woollen industry was severely affected and hand-spun yarns became a thing of the past while the linen industry only survived by itself industrialising.[5]

In Ireland, as elsewhere, the domestic woollen industry had readily adapted to a 'putting out' system because it was possible for middlemen to buy up the raw material and prepare it for wage or piece-workers. By contrast the structure of the linen trade in Ireland made it difficult for middlemen to secure and exercise similar domination. The basis of this structure was confirmed by a clause in an act of 1719 (6 Geo. I, c. 7) that declared:

> All linen-cloth and yarn shall be sold publicly in open markets or at lawful fairs, on the days such markets or fairs ought to be held, or within two days next preceding such fair-day; and all linen yarn shall be sold publicly at such markets or fairs without doors, between eight in the morning and eight in the evening; and if any person shall sell or expose to sale any such cloth or yarn except as aforesaid, all such cloth and yarn shall be forfeited.

Although this clause would have enabled middlemen to buy up flax for spinning into yarn, or yarn for weaving into linen, it acted as a strong encouragement both for those families who grew flax to convert it into yarn for sale in the public market, and for weavers to grow their own flax or purchase it in the yarn markets. Those weavers who could grow their own flax, have it prepared and spun by their own families, and weave it themselves, were liable to profit most in the public markets, especially if they were able, like those living in the 'linen triangle', to weave the finer quality linens. The system of public markets flourished and expanded with the support of the bleachers who had come to dominate the industry in the second half of the eighteenth century: they believed that if the linen markets were properly run with sealmasters to inspect the quality of the linens, they could obtain there for their bleachgreens the variety of linens that they needed to meet their orders from England.[6] The competition

5 Cullen, L.M., *An Economic History of Ireland since 1660* (London, 1972), pp. 39–42, 59–66, 105–6.
6 See pages 132 to 142.

engendered by this system of marketing promoted independence among the weavers and their families and constrained them to organise the resources of the family to produce webs of cloth for the market.

Flax has always required an abundance of cheap labour and provided work for the whole family. Even the preparation of land was labour intensive. Flax usually followed a well-manured potato crop that put the land into good heart and cleansed it of weeds. After the land was ploughed several times to produce a good tilth, women picked up any remaining clods of earth and stone and dumped them at the foot of the banks that enclosed the fields. They weeded the crop by hand and when it was ripe they worked with men to pull it, a job that was very sore on their hands. With men they rippled it to save the seed. It was, however, the men who placed it in the lint-dams for retting so that the woody core of the flax stems could be softened. Working in the lint-dams was not women's work, perhaps because it was a very heavy and dirty job where women's clothing would have rendered them ineffectual as well as immodest. After the removal of the flax from the dam by the men, it was the women who spread it to dry, a process known as 'grassing'. Then the flax was ready for scutching to extract the fibre from its casing. Women beat it with a wooden 'beetle' to fragment this casing and then other women hung the flax over a block of wood and struck away the broken straw with long wooden blades.[7] The remnants of the straw, known locally as 'shives' or 'shous', were removed by passing handfuls of the fibre through an implement known as a 'clove'.[8]

The economic value of this work was calculated by several respondents for Arthur Young when he was touring Ulster in the summer of 1776 (Table 9.1). About this table, drawn up for him near Armagh, Young was careful to note:

> If let to a man who should farm flax, the labour would be much higher, as it is here reckoned only at the earning, which they could make by the manufacture, and not the rate at which they work for others.

The essence of Young's argument is that flax was an expensive crop
TABLE 9.1

[7] See pages 50 and 51.
[8] Lucas, A.T., 'Flax cloves', *Ulster Folklife* 32 (1986), 16–36.

Expense of an acre of land under flax

	£ s. d.
Rent	0 14 0
Seed bought from 10s. to 13s. a bushel, average 12s.: 3 bushels	1 16 0
One ploughing	0 7 0
Carrying off the clods and stones by their wives and children, 6 women, an acre a day	0 2 2
Weeding, 10 women an acre in a day, 4d	0 3 4
Pulling by women and children, 12 at 4d	0 4 0
Rippling by men and women, say 4 men at 10d	0 3 4
Laying it in the water according to distance, say	0 5 0
Taking it out and spreading	0 5 0
Taking up, drying and beetling, 42 women a day at 4d	0 14 0
Scutching 30 stone at 1s. 1d.	1 12 6
TOTAL	6 6 4
30 stone at 4s. 2d.	6 5 0

Source: Hutton, A. W. (ed.), *Arthur Young's Tour in Ireland (1776–1779)* (2 vols, London, 1892), vol. 1, 122.

to grow if labour had to be paid for, because fieldwork costs had to compete against spinning wages.

In the second half of the eighteenth century the scutching of flax had been mechanised using water power to turn the scutching blades in scutch mills. As a result flax was taken to the scutch mills where men carried out all the scutching processes. The employment of men in mills was traditional, probably because the operation of corn mills and tuck mills (for finishing locally produced woollen goods) could require considerable physical strength to manage cumbersome machinery or move heavy weights and bags. Many men were available for employment after the end of the grain harvest whereas women would be busy spinning yarn. Although it was reckoned about 1800 that a scutch mill serviced by men and boys could do more work than a dozen women,[9] it is probable that flax intended for the making of fine linens was scutched and hackled at home. Young was told in Portadown:

In general they scutch it themselves and it is cheaper than the mills. Mr Workman has paid 1s. 6d. for it by hand, and 1s. 1d. to the mills,

[9] Coote, Sir C., *A Statistical Survey of the County of Monaghan* (Dublin, 1801), pp. 197–8.

and found the former cheaper; more flax from hand and much clean-er.[10]

This was said to be quite a common practice even as late as 1870.[11] Skilful hand scutching and hackling greatly reduced the amount of waste and best prepared the flax for spinning. For hackling it was reckoned worthwhile to employ a skilled craftsman and there were said to be many itinerant hacklers. One commentator remarked about the use of the hackling pins for combing out the fibres: 'The most experienced hands only attempt to work the finest hackle, which is very close, and a nice matter to perform well.' Spinning, however, was women's work. Many stories were told about the skill of famous women spinners and some of their achievements are recount-ed by McCall in the third edition of his book *Ireland and her Staple Manufactures* (Belfast, 1870): some specimens said to be much infe-rior to the finest yarns produced half a century earlier were awarded prizes at the Great Exhibition of 1851.[12]

Ireland had a long tradition of skill in spinning. In 1636 Lord Deputy Wentworth had observed that Irish women were 'naturally bred to spinning' and in 1673 Sir William Temple added: 'No women are apter to spin it well than the Irish'.[13] It was the task of successive governments to enforce standards that would guarantee the length of the yarn exposed for sale. By an act of 1705 (2 Anne, c. 2) flax yarn was to be reeled on a standard reel $2^{1}/2$ yards in circumference with 120 of these threads in a cut and 12 cuts in a hank so that each hank contained 3,600 yards; four hanks made up a spangle. The act proved very difficult to enforce. In 1723 even the possession of unstatutable yarn was made a punishable offence but as late as the 1780s the trans-gression persisted.[14] The Linen Board as early as 1717 had regulated and patronised spinning schools to propagate skills and precepts throughout the country[15] but as early as 1724 it was decided that no more schools should be allowed in Ulster, except for the county of Fermanagh only, because 'the art of spinning had made so great a

10 *Young's Tour*, vol. 1, 126.
11 McCall, H., *Ireland and her Staple Manufactures* (3rd edn, Belfast, 1870), p. 356.
12 Ibid., pp. 366–8.
13 Horner, J., *The Linen Trade of Europe during the Spinning-Wheel Period* (Belfast, 1920), pp. 16, 22.
14 Gill, C., *The Rise of the Irish Linen Industry* (Oxford, 1925), p. 68.
15 Ibid., pp. 75–6; Corry, J., *Precedents and Abstracts from the Journals of the Trustees of the Linen and Hempen Manufactures of Ireland* (Dublin, 1784), pp. 19–20.

progress in the province of Ulster'.[16] Nevertheless, spinning was carried on in the 'charter schools' provided by the Incorporated Society for Promoting English Protestant Schools in Ireland, and the sale of the yarn provided much of the finance required to maintain the children and their teachers.[17] In providing many families with an income or a supplement to it, the domestic spinning industry required them to meet government regulations and commercial standards. As women learned that they could earn more for quality yarns, output of them increased. Arthur Young noted that spinning and weaving for cambric (such as was used for making handkerchiefs) was being carried on around Lurgan.[18] Within thirty years it had spread to the surrounding towns of Lisburn, Banbridge, Tandragee and Dromore.[19] In 1822 the comment was made:

> In the north of Ireland … the object of every person who has flax, is to have it of as fine quality as he can; and the spinner's object is to spin it as fine as they can, because it pays a better price; and the manufacturer's object is to weave the finest linen that he can; for which reason, the coarse article in the north of Ireland is made only of the refuse of the flax.[20]

Of every stone of flax that emerged from the rough hackling process it was reckoned that about a quarter could be spun into the fine yarn needed for the finest webs whereas about a half was fit to be woven into a medium quality linen. The remainder of the yarn, known as tow, was hackled again and spun into tow yarn that was woven and made into work shirts.[21]

Although it was the family that was idealised in contemporary literature as the unit of production, it would have been more accurate to talk in terms of the household. Many families employed and lodged in their homes young men as weavers and unmarried women or widows as spinsters. They required them to carry out other duties in the house and around the farm. In his tour through the northern

[16] Corry, op. cit., p. 70.
[17] Harris, W., *The Antient and Present State of the County of Down* (Dublin, 1744), pp. 17, 77. Horner, op. cit., pp. 99–100 for a summary of a 1751 report on the spinning schools.
[18] *Young's Tour*, vol. 1, 128.
[19] See Appendix 4.
[20] *1822 Linen Laws Report*, p. 486.
[21] *Young's Tour*, vol. 1, 122, 126–7, 130, 139, 152, 161.

counties of Ireland in the summer of 1776 Arthur Young commented regularly on this phenomenon. South of Derry city he found: 'The
spinners in a little farm are the daughters and a couple of maid-ser-
vants that are paid 30s. a half year, and the common bargain is to do
a hank a day of 3 or 4 hank yarn.' Around Lisburn 'the spinners are
generally hired by the quarter, from 10s. to 12s. lodging and board
and engaged to spin 5 hanks of 8 hank yarn in a week.' For such fine
yarn a skilled spinster could earn up to 8d. per day but for the coarser yarns 4d. to 6d. was more likely, while a girl of 12 could earn 1½d.
or 2d. per day, and a girl of seven might get a penny. In these cases,
however, the spinster had to provide her own board and lodging.[22]

The relationship between 'the family' and 'the household' in this
context is worth further scrutiny. Those members of the household
who were not also members of the nuclear family were required to fill
an economic vacancy in the family, that is to undertake duties that
would have been carried out if the family had possessed someone with
the relevant skills and experience. Not only were women cheaper to
employ, they were also more versatile around the house and even the
farm as long as heavy work was not sustained or excessive. The ability of a family to provide and manage the work of its own members
depended much on its economic base. Poor families had to labour for
others who could provide them with work and so they were likely to
shed their children early. There were, however, considerable benefits
to be gained by those families that could organise themselves into an
effective production team. They were usually families that had managed to obtain a lease of their farm, no matter how small, because the
possession of a lease gave a family status and self-confidence as well as
an instrument for securing loans. As the lease aged, the fixed rent
became a smaller proportion of the family's expenditure because the
value of land rose steadily throughout the eighteenth century.[23] In
such circumstances a family might sublet part of its farm to pay for
the hire of a cottier at the loom or in the field. In many districts
throughout the north of Ireland women prepared and spun yarn
for sale in the market because their menfolk concentrated on their
farming duties and would not weave. As the century progressed, how-

---

22 Ibid., pp. 122–204, especially 133, 174.
23 Crawford, W.H., 'Landlord–tenant relations in Ulster 1609–1820', *Irish Economic and
Social History* 2 (1975), 12–18.

ever, more men took up the weaving of coarse linens when work on the farm was slack, or apprenticed their sons to the trade.[24] It is probable, too, that many women engaged at busy times in weaving. It was believed in the years before the fitting of the flying shuttle to looms about 1815 that the loom was too heavy for women, especially as the weaver was required to stand and stoop over the cloth.

It may be that the greater widths of cloth required for the commercial markets made the task of weaving too strenuous for women. Yet it had long been the practice for women to weave the woollens and linens needed by their own families. Or it may be that the introduction of the lighter cotton loom equipped with the flying shuttle and using mill-spun yarn encouraged women to take up weaving. The absence of direct evidence for weaving by women throughout the eighteenth century probably has much to do with the fact that men were responsible for selling the webs as well as purchasing yarn in the markets. In parallel situations in Lancashire and in the American colonies women were to be found among the weavers.[25] Indeed the American case is especially interesting because, although the introduction to a recent exhibition refers to both male and females working in New England, all the specimens attributable to individuals were woven by women: they were probably made for use in the weavers' homes.[26] In general, however, in the Irish industry women concentrated on spinning to keep the weavers supplied although they could have been required also to assist the weaver at the loom if a boy was not available.

In any consideration of the key role of the family and the family firm in the domestic linen industry, attention has to be paid to the family cycle. It has often been suggested that possession of skills in spinning and weaving enabled young people to marry early and set up home together. Their success, however, would depend to a great extent on the situation in their respective homes. It has to be remembered that these young people were in effect withdrawing from existing linen production units. If they had played their part at home

---

[24] McEvoy, J., *A Statistical Survey of the County of Tyrone* (Dublin, 1802), pp. 135–56.
[25] Wadsworth and Mann, op. cit., pp. 336–7.
[26] *All Sorts of Good Sufficient Cloth: Linen-Making in New England 1640–1860* (Merrimack Valley Textile Museum, North Andover, Massachusetts, 1980): a catalogue for an exhibition.

and the omens were propitious, they might not only count on the goodwill of their parents but might even be given at least a subdivision of a parent's holding on which to build a dwelling, as well as a dowry with the bride to establish the new family. With these essentials and the continuing support of their families they stood a good chance of establishing a new family. Without them they were very vulnerable to misfortune especially in the aftermath of the birth of their first children, when the woman's earning capacity was seriously reduced, so that many slipped easily into debt that brought them into the clutches of moneylenders and unscrupulous dealers. At the same time it was still possible for poor families to work themselves up the social ladder. A landmark in their success would be the purchase of an interest in a lease because its possession provided both status and security.[27]

It is important to point out that much of the evidence presented in this study relates to the eighteenth century when the domestic linen industry steadily increased until it came to dominate the economy of the north of Ireland and seriously altered its social structure. The process in County Sligo was described in 1766 by a local member of Parliament:

> the present great price of land is principally owing to the cottage tenants, who being mostly Papists, have long lived under the pressure of severe penal laws and have been enured to want and misery. The linen manufactory in its progress opened to these such means of industry as were only fitted to penurious economy. Three pence a day, the most that can be made by spinning, was an inducement fit only to be held out to women so educated. The earning was proportioned to their mode of living and became wealth to the family. In mountainous countries the grazier had formerly driven them [these people] to the unprofitable parts. Here they placed themselves at easy rents for the demand for cattle in these days was not more than the good lands could supply. The cottager, necessitated to try all means of drawing a support from his tenement, has in the course of his industry discovered that his mountain farm with the amelioration of limestone gravel, is productive both of corn and potatoes, and in succession afterwards of flax equal to the low grounds. But the labour of

---

[27] See the case argued in *Serious Considerations on the Present Alarming State of Agriculture and the Linen Trade, by a Farmer* (Dublin, 1773) in vol. 377 of the Haliday Pamphlets in the Royal Irish Academy, Dublin, published here as Appendix 3.

this is great and fit only for people so trained to hardship. The home consumption of cattle increasing with the wealth of the country, the markets of Great Britain open, and the colonies more extended and more populous, have multiplied the demand and given at last a value even to the mountains for pasture. But here the cottage tenant, abstemious and laborious, is enabled by the industry of his family to outbid the grazier. They cant each other and give to land the monstrous price it now bears. But from the inland countries where all the land is good the cottagers were early banished so that land only rises there in proportion to the additional demand for cattle. Besides that, most lands in such countries are fitter for pasture than for tillage. Thus we flourish and land continues to bear its present price and will do so till an increase of wealth shall create new desires in the cottager, and that small profit which now gives excitement to his industry shall cease to be an object. Then the factors must be content with smaller profits, some new manufacture must succeed, or we must return to pasture and land fall to a lower price.[28]

The scale of these changes makes it very difficult to generalise about the social characteristics of earlier centuries. Even the importance of the family cannot be taken for granted. The same member of Parliament had commented in 1760 that as a result of the economic changes, 'A family now has a better bottom than formerly: residence is more assured and families are more numerous as increase of industry keeps them more together.'[29] It was this cohesion of the family that gave the mother status and authority both at home and in society. Without this role a woman's value was dependent on her earning ability within the community. Women did many of the everyday jobs that their physical strength allowed. They were not allowed by men to undertake strenuous work that might injure them. That reality deprived them of equal status in a world where physical strength was esteemed.

[28] National Library of Ireland, O'Hara papers. Some of this collection has been photocopied by the Public Record Office of Northern Ireland and this important manuscript is T2812/19: 'Charles O'Hara's account of Sligo'.
[29] Ibid.

10

The introduction of the flying shuttle into the weaving of linen in Ulster

PLATE 10

*Perspective View of a Bleach Green taken in the County of Downe,
Shewing the methods of Wet and Dry Bleaching, and the outside
View of a Bleach Mill on the most approved Construction . . .*

WILLIAM HINCKS 1783

TRADITION GIVES THE CREDIT for the introduction of the flying shuttle into Ulster to the Moravian colony at Gracehill near Ballymena. The Moravians had established their colony in the townland of Ballykennedy on the O'Neill estate in 1759 and gained a reputation for their skill in textile crafts, especially needlework and later bone lacemaking.[1] In 1816 S.M. Stephenson in an anonymous article in *The Newry Magazine* wrote:

> The fly-shuttle was introduced from England into the Moravian settlement by Mr John McMullan, a member of that society. His object was to accommodate a linen weaver who had lost the use of his arm by a swelling in the joint. It was from thence transferred to Belfast, by the late Mr Robert Joy, of the house of Joys, McCabe and McCracken, about twenty-eight years ago [1788], and applied to the cotton loom. It by that means became generally known over Ulster.[2]

The *Belfast News-Letter* of 1 September 1778, however, ten years earlier than the date given by Stephenson, contains a letter addressed from Ballykennedy giving a detailed description of the technology involved in the flying shuttle:

> We are glad to communicate to the publick the following account of the Flying Shuttle, for weaving linen, which has been introduced with success among the Moravians at Ballykennedy. If it be found to work as well as the common shuttle, the use of it will be attended with many conveniencies; particularly, as by means of it the weaver sits upright, (which is a much more healthful posture than the usual one,) and as persons who have lost the use of one of their arms may work at it without the smallest inconvenience.
>
> *A Description of the FLYING SHUTTLE* [see Figure 10.1]
> A board [D] is fixed on the under ball of the slays, about three inches and a half in breadth, extending twelve inches longer on each end than the under ball; the under ball must be cut down the depth of the thickness of the board, so that the edge of the board forms the side of the rabbit in which the reed is fixed: the board must be so fixed as to be level with the under part of the shade, when open, and close to the shade, but not so close as to press against the yarn. This

---

[1] Boyle, Elizabeth, *The Irish Flowerers* (Belfast, 1971), pp. 13–14, 33–5.
[2] [Stephenson, S.M.,] 'On the Antiquity of the Linen Manufacture, with Account of its Progress and Establishment in Ireland', *Newry Magazine* 2, no. 9 (July and August 1816), 275, n.

board is of great use in the running of the shuttle, as it runs on it from one end to the other. On each end of the board is a box [E] about 14 inches long, from the middle of the slay-board until the end of the board: this box must be made just so wide that the shuttle can run in and out with ease, without having any room to spare. Over the middle of each box is an iron spindle, fastened at the extreme end of the box with a screw and at the other end fastened with a screw in the slay-board: on each of these spindles is a trigger [F] for driving the shuttle, the under end of which runs in a rabbit in the board or bottom of the box. To each of these triggers there is a cord, fastened to a piece of wood [B], which the weaver holds in his right hand, with which he pulls the trigger and drives the shuttle thro' the shade. The running of the shuttle into the box takes the trigger into the far end of the box, for it must move with the least touch. The yoke of the reed must be level with the split of the reed, as must the slay-board and backside of the box, other-wise the shuttle would not run true. The shuttle is quite straight; the quill wound like a broach, does not run round, the thread running off at the end, goes out of the shuttle at the end of the shuttle-box; the waft comes off the quill much easier, and does not break, even when the yarn is very weak.

Our weavers are coming more into the use of this method of weaving: some of them can do a third more work than usual, and with a great deal more ease. It however suits coarse work best, as weaving with one stroke goes exceedingly quick, and with great ease. But the greatest advantage is in weaving check;[3] for even where three shuttles are required, any of them can be brought to the shade as quick as the slays can fly.

No persons in this part of the country have yet tried this method, except our weavers. But I think it will by degrees come into general use.

BALLYKENNEDY,
AUG. 20, 1778.

As far as the weaver was concerned the most attractive feature about the flying shuttle was the consequent increase in the output of cloth. According to this account, production increased by a third. Yet in the long run the weavers must have been more grateful for being enabled

---

[3] The only surviving evidence about the manufacture of checks in Ulster about this period is to be found in the papers of the Adams family who lived at the appropriately named Chequer Hall at Ballyweaney in County Antrim: see Public Record Office of Northern Ireland D1518/2, Linen and general account book, c.1780–1830.

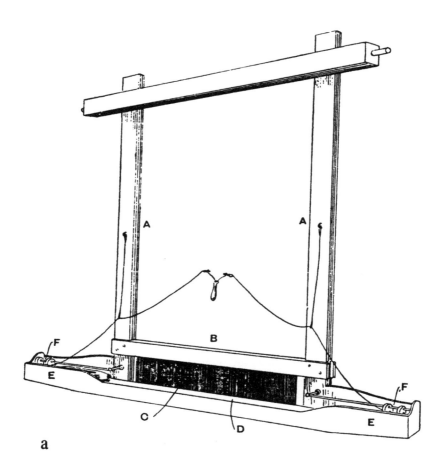

a

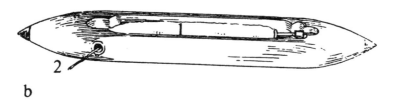

b

a. Front view of the batten of a loom showing the flying shuttle mounted as described in the letter: A, A, swords; B, hand-tree; C, reed; D, sley-sole or shuttle-race; E, E, shuttle-boxes; F, F, pickers.

b. Illustration of a shuttle as described in the letter: 1, quill; 2, yarn leaving the shuttle.

to sit at their work instead of stretching over the loom passing the curved shuttle from hand to hand through the 'shade'. This would have made it easier to work the treadles. It would also have eased the strain on the muscles of the lower back that must have resulted from weaving hunched forward over the older type of loom.

A postscript is provided by one of the early historians of the industry, Hugh McCall, in the third edition of his book *Ireland and her Staple Manufactures*:

> The improved shuttle (known as 'the shuttle with wheels') was brought out by Mr McMullan, a gentleman engaged in the educational department of the Moravian colony at Gracehill, near Ballymena. 'Mounted' shuttles rapidly rose in popularity, and from thence the progressive class of weavers threw aside the old ones, and by the addition of still further improvements, Mr McMullan caused the little machine to be much sought after. He also instructed several mechanics in that neighbourhood in the new mode of shuttle-making. An ingenious person named Kelly, residing in Lisburn, became much celebrated for his work. His shuttles cost 'five thirteens', as the Irish crown pieces were called ...[4]

---

[4] McCall, Hugh, *Ireland and her Staple Manufactures* (3rd edn, Belfast, 1870), p. 118.

11

The evolution of the linen trade in Ulster before industrialisation[1]

PLATE 11

Perspective View of a Lapping room, with the Measuring, Crisping or Folding the Cloth in Lengths, picking the laps or lengths, tying in the Clips, acting by the mechanic power of the Laver to press the Cloth round and firm, and Sealing it preparatory to its going to the Linen hall . . .

WILLIAM HINCKS 1783

THE CURRENT DEBATE on the merits of the concept of proto-industrialisation should make us re-examine the case of the Ulster linen industry. Leslie Clarkson referred to it often in *Proto-Industrialization: The First Phase of Industrialization?* (1985).[2] Reviewing his book, Pat Hudson urged us:

> to analyse the inter-related nature of factors in the environment of industrial regions. How manufacturing locked in with the agrarian base through the seasons and between regions; how the institutional environment of landholding, inheritance practices, the distribution of wealth, the nature of central and local government, and the role of urban centres were all crucially linked in providing the ether of expanding commerce and industry. Above all, the proto-industry debate has properly integrated the study of the family and households, gender and generational relationships, personal life, motivations and aspirations, demography, and work regimes ...[3]

There can be no doubt that such an approach to the study of the Ulster linen industry would illuminate many aspects of economic, social, cultural and political life, and make the history of the province more intelligible. The obstacle is that *The Rise of the Irish Linen Industry* (1925) by Conrad Gill is a classic of economic history.[4] Although its structure makes it difficult to comprehend, the authority of Gill's account has not been questioned. Yet Gill made a serious error in arguing that the 'cottage industry' of the first half of the eighteenth century evolved thereafter into a 'putting-out' system. He had fallen into the trap of believing 'in some progressive and linear evolution towards modern factory production'[5] and was searching for the factors that converted a system based on artisan production into one relying on a 'putting-out' structure.

This study attempts to provide a more accurate picture of the trade on the eve of its industrialisation, re-interpreting the evidence that was available in Gill's time. It will argue that a system of 'public markets' served by artisan weavers dominated the pre-industrial linen

---

1 First published in *Irish Economic and Social History* XV (1988), 32–53.
2 Clarkson, L.A., *Proto-Industrialization: The First Phase of Industrialization?* (London, 1985).
3 Hudson, P., review of Clarkson, op. cit., in *Economic History Review* XXXIX (1986), 308.
4 Gill, Conrad, *The Rise of the Irish Linen Industry* (Oxford, 1925), p. 138.
5 Hudson, P., 'Proto-industrialisation: the case of the West Riding wool textile industry in the 18th and early 19th centuries', *History Workshop* 11 (1981), 37.

trade in Ulster, whereas the cotton manufacture there was organised on a putting-out system. Relevant to this is an examination of regional differences in the kinds of linen produced and of how different regions reacted to the loss of many weavers to the cotton manufacture that was burgeoning in the Belfast region. Finally, the study will suggest how linen in Ulster was able to industrialise successfully (to the surprise of its competitors in England and Scotland), and why this development was confined to much narrower territorial limits than those of the domestic era.

The linen trade in Ulster had begun to develop on commercial lines in the late seventeenth century; a London-published pamphlet of 1682 notes 'Ulsters' in the Book of Rates, as well as imports of Irish yarn.[6] Stimulated by demand in the English market, Dublin factors purchased bleached webs of linen brought to the capital by northern linen drapers: for their benefit a Linen Hall was erected in 1728. Throughout the first half of the eighteenth century, trade in linen in the north was gradually concentrated in the hands of these drapers. In markets and fairs throughout the province they purchased unbleached webs from the weavers and organised the bleaching, sometimes in bleachgreens of their own but also by negotiating contracts with bleachers. For their part these bleachers began to reduce costs by introducing new bleaching methods and technology, and to increase the annual output of their greens.[7] The consequent cheapness of well-bleached good quality linens assured the Irish industry of success in the English market, so that exports surged from less than 2.5 million yards in the second decade of the century to almost 8 million in the 1740s and 17 million in the 1760s.

In the first half of the eighteenth century there was a strong emphasis on the promotion of colonies of weavers in manufactories where the supervisor provided the raw materials and managed production. This was the model introduced into Lisburn by Louis Crommelin in 1698.[8] None of these projects, except those involving the production of damasks on complex draw-looms, survived in Ulster into the second half of the century. Yet they appear to have left their mark on the

[6] Thirsk, J. and Cooper, J.P. (eds), *Seventeenth-Century Economic Documents* (Oxford, 1972), pp. 302, 303; see pages 9 to 13.
[7] See pages 24 to 48.
[8] See pages 65 to 66.

structure of the industry, for in the Lagan valley and north Armagh many weavers in the 1760s and 1770s continued to employ journeymen weavers, paying them their board and lodging and one-third of what they earned. Some weavers also took yarn for weaving from 'manufacturing drapers' (as they were termed).[9] Yet even in that district, as in the rest of the province, the emphasis was on independent farmer/weavers growing their own flax, having it processed into yarn by their womenfolk, and selling it in the public brown-linen markets to drapers who attended from neighbouring towns. When a weaver was not able to raise the price of the yarn he had either to work for hire for those who advanced him the yarn, or take credit with the yarn-jobber.[10]

It was the 1760s, a period of rapid expansion, that attracted the attention of Conrad Gill, interested as he was in the structure of the workforce employed in the industry. He decided that the rapid expansion of trade must have brought about important changes in organisation that were linked to a drift towards capitalism. He diagnosed in the circumstances of a famous riot in Lisburn in 1762 the symptoms of change: 'the old system of domestic manufacture and sale in open markets was gradually yielding to new methods'.[11] He decided that by the 1760s 'a class of permanent employees had appeared' and reckoned that in the year 1770, while rather more than 35,000 weavers in Ulster were still independent, as many as 7,000 or one-sixth of the weavers were employees working either for 'small manufacturers' (independent weavers) or for some 'manufacturing drapers' putting-out yarn. By 1784 he considered that probably 'rather more than 40 per cent of 40,000 weavers' (i.e. 16,000) would have been employees. According to Gill this trend continued:

> It seems probable, then, that there were about 70,000 weavers in Ulster at that time [c.1820] and that rather more than a third of their output was produced on a large scale. The number of weavers of the three different classes (independent craftsmen, employees of small manufacturers, and employees of large firms) would not be exactly proportioned to their output; for the wage earners would give most of their time to weaving, whereas the independent craftsmen would

[9] Young, A., *Tour in Ireland*, ed. Hutton, A.W. (2 vols, London, 1892), vol. 1, 130.
[10] See pages 39 to 48.
[11] Gill, op. cit.

have to devote some time to farm work and to attending markets. Therefore, a third of the weavers, and perhaps rather more, may still have been independent.[12]

If Gill had restricted himself to pointing out the existence on a large scale of employees working for wages no-one could have disagreed with him. The county statistical surveys of the early nineteenth century refer regularly to master weavers who in towns hired journeymen to work in their workshops, or in rural areas let out small cot-takes of land to cottier-weavers who paid their rent in weaving. These two categories obscure many degrees of dependence, notably sons working for their fathers, or weavers taking yarn from jobbers either in hard times or until their own flax crop was harvested, scutched and spun.

Gill, however, was concerned rather with locating his 'manufacturing drapers', capitalists in the trade employing labour. It was not difficult for him to find damask weavers working under capitalist conditions, because large workshops or factories were required to house the considerable number of men (from six to 16) needed to set up and work a draw-loom, and to maintain regular supervision of the patterns woven into the expensive cloth. The very high standard that they could attain is now evident from a superb tablecloth woven in 1728 in Waringstown, County Down, measuring 11 feet by 9 feet and depicting a coronation procession and a map of London.[13] The number of damask manufactories, however, was very small in the eighteenth century, so their employees would have constituted a tiny percentage of the weaving population. Therefore Gill concentrated his strategy on the bleaching districts. He suggested that 'in order to gain a more exact idea of the growth of capitalism we need to distinguish between the areas of rapid change, in which production on a large scale was common, and the conservative districts, where capitalism had made little headway'. He designated the linen triangle (the south of Antrim, the centre and west of Down, and the north of Armagh) and the east of Londonderry 'as districts in which capitalism was the most fully developed'. He explained the process of evolution:

[12] Ibid., pp. 144, 162, 279. The figures for 1770 (pages 144, 162) do not tally.
[13] Lewis, E., 'An eighteenth-century linen tablecloth from Ireland', *Textile History* (1984), pp. 235–44.

The fact that so many of the employers were bleachers had an interesting effect on the grouping of population. In earlier times, when practically the whole demand for brown linen came through the open market, weavers would naturally wish to live near to a town, for convenience in selling their cloth and buying flax or yarn. But with a steadily increasing demand on *the part of bleachers for the direct supply of cloth by means of hired labour,* weavers gradually settled in larger and larger numbers in the neighbourhood of bleachgreens. The census returns [of 1821] show time after time a bleachyard, the owner's house, and a little community of bleachyard workers and weavers settled round them.[14]

To this final sentence Gill added an explanatory footnote: 'To give one example out of many, close to the bleachgreen of William Hudson, near Banbridge, nineteen households of his employees – bleachyard hands and weavers – were settled'. Yet these weavers would have been able to supply no more than a tiny percentage of the webs that Hudson finished each year in his bleachgreen. Throughout the explanation, in fact, Gill is forced to scrabble about for evidence. Contemporaries record that the linen producing districts were already densely populated by the 1760s, geared to thousands of independent weavers selling their webs of cloth in the brown linen markets held in many provincial towns.[15] To account, therefore, for concentration of settlement around bleachgreens Gill seized on McCall's mention of the migration by 1800 of weavers from towns to the countryside.[16] From which towns could they have come? Surely not from Belfast, to which weavers were migrating to earn higher wages from cotton-weaving; nor from Armagh, where weavers in 1770 composed less than two per cent of the occupations; nor from thriving towns like Lisburn, Lurgan, Newry, Banbridge or Dungannon. It is important to remember that Gill was trying to account for between a quarter and a third of all the weavers.

Gill was able to argue a more impressive case for capitalists in the

---

[14] Gill, op. cit., pp. 272, 273 (my italics). See also pages 144–5.

[15] Harris, W., *The Antient and Present State of the County of Down* (Dublin, 1744), p. 108; Kelly, J. (ed.), *The Letters of Lord Chief Baron Edward Willes* (Aberystwyth, 1990), pp. 31, 33; Crawford, W.H. and Trainor, B. (eds), *Aspects of Irish Social History 1750–1800* (Belfast, 1969), p. 92; Arthur Young confirms these trends in the late 1770s in his *Tour*, vol. 1, 120, 128, 150.

[16] Gill, op. cit., p. 272.

industry putting-out yarn to be woven for wages:

> Different yarns were often needed for warp and weft, so that a weav-
> er might have to spend many hours in an expedition in search of
> warp yarn, many more in buying weft, in addition to his day at the
> market for the sale of his web. Production could be carried on more
> cheaply if a draper or manufacturer bought the yarn, supplied it
> made up into chains or wound on pirns, and received the cloth with-
> out waste of time when it was woven.
>
> There can be no doubt then, that the supply of flax or yarn, in
> increasing quantities, in greater variety, and from a wider area, was
> one of the chief causes of change in the organisation of manufac-
> ture.[17]

Yet even here Gill overstated his case. He seems to have failed to
appreciate the significance of widespread flax-growing and yarn-spin-
ning in the rural economy not only of Ulster but of the neighbouring
counties of Leinster and Connacht. A multitude of yarn-jobbers was
able to tour the rural districts there to purchase the yarn and transport it to the brown linen markets in the Ulster towns, where it was
sold throughout the weekly market day.[18] These men were regular in
attendance and it was not difficult for a weaver to obtain the warp
and weft that he needed, knowing that the quality was guaranteed by
regular inspection as well as by the jobber's reputation. In these circumstances middlemen had few opportunities, especially as regrating
(purchasing to retail at a profit) was expressly forbidden by law.

The last people who would have been prepared to venture their capital in yarn would have been the bleachers. They needed their money
to purchase brown linens in the markets but they also had to continue to invest in improving their bleachgreens in order to remain competitive. From the early days the bleaching and finishing trades had
attracted investment, especially after the application of water power
to the wash mills and the beetling (i.e. finishing) mills.[19] In the second half of the eighteenth century the average output of bleachgreens
rapidly increased: whereas few greens in 1750 could bleach more than
1,000 pieces, there were many in the early nineteenth century that
could finish in excess of 10,000 pieces. The major factor in this

[17] Ibid., p. 155.
[18] Ibid., 38–9; 3 Geo. III, c. 34, s. 49 re sales of linen yarn and cloth.
[19] See pages 24–37, 185–8.

expansion was the introduction of chemicals that greatly reduced bleaching time and allowed bleaching round the year instead of in the summer only.[20] These improvements cut bleaching costs and caused intense competition among the bleachers so that many of the smaller firms disappeared, especially after 1800.[21] Those bleachers who remained dominated the trade.

Gill's interpretation of the structure of the brown linen trade in the early 1820s bears a marked contrast to the evidence presented to a select committee of the House of Commons inquiring into the linen trade of Ireland in 1825.[22] The whole tenor of this report is founded on the assumption, by all parties concerned, that almost all the linens woven in Ulster were sold through the brown linen markets. The select committee wanted the Irish representatives to explain why the markets were still so popular when there were obvious alternatives that would seem to have been more convenient for both buyers and sellers. Why, for instance, did the weavers not just take their finished webs to the nearest bleachgreens at their convenience instead of waiting until the next market day? Why did the buyers not just buy from local dealers who would then make it their business to keep a large stock of assorted linens? The reply from all three senior representatives of the Ulster linen industry giving evidence to the select committee was that both buyers and sellers much preferred to sell in the open markets. Because the conduct of markets had evolved over more than a century the trade had a certain rhythm. It was controlled by the bleachers who had introduced profitable techniques to bleaching in the 1730s and as a consequence had absorbed the class of drapers that had originally been the dealers and buyers in the markets. By the close of the eighteenth century the term 'draper' was applied indiscriminately to both the bleachers and the buyers whom they employed to tour the linen markets buying an assortment of linens that would enable them to fulfil their orders from Britain and abroad. As one of them explained:

[20] L'Amie, A., 'Chemicals in the eighteenth-century Irish linen industry' (MSc thesis, Queen's University, Belfast, 1984).

[21] Gribbon, H.D., *The History of Water Power in Ulster* (Newton Abbot, 1969), p. 87; PRONI Foster–Massereene Papers, D562/6225, Printed copy of John Greer's 1784 Report of the State of the Linen markets in the Province of Ulster, with manuscript notes on the comparative state of the trade in 1803: published here as Appendix 4.

[22] *Report from the Select Committee on the Linen Trade of Ireland* (British Parliamentary Papers 1825 (463) V) [hereafter *1825 Linen Trade Report*].

Buyers that attend on Monday at Banbridge market, when they have made their purchases there, and paid for them all with ready money, the next market they go to is Armagh, which is fifteen or sixteen miles distant; there they have the same business to do on Tuesday; and it produces also great expedition to the seller: there he sells his linen at once, and finds the people at once that purchase his description of goods; *as linens vary very much both in quality and fineness*. Then, after Armagh, the next market he goes to is generally on Wednesday, Tanderagee. The next day, Thursday, there is a market at Newry which he attends; and the following day, Friday, there is a market at Lurgan, which he attends. There is also one at Cootehill, he may go to, or at Belfast, there are markets on Friday at each of those three places; and then on Saturday there is a market at Downpatrick; and also in Ballymena, in the country of Antrim. Linens are sold in various parts of the country in the market towns. There is a market every day in the week ...[23]

The bleachers were satisfied that this system of markets enabled their own employees, most familiar with the marketing policies and requirements of their firms, to buy fifty or sixty webs in a three-hour period at a market, confident that their length, breadth and quality had been inspected earlier that same day by a public sealmaster licensed by the Linen Board. During the bleaching season they were able to purchase a wide variety of linens at a range of prices by touring markets and fairs, some of which were a considerable distance from their base. This was the case in 1759 when Thomas Greer of Dungannon recorded in his market-book visits not only to neighbouring towns but also to Monaghan and Cootehill. By 1825 men like John Andrews of Comber purchased linens from markets much further afield: as well as buying in Belfast, Lisburn, Downpatrick and Kircubbin, he had buyers attending the several markets in Armagh, Tyrone and Londonderry 'in order to enable us to make out a fair assortment'. He explained that his firm had to supply 'such an assortment as would enable us to hold our connections and go on with our business, for we can only hold our connections in this country [Britain] now, by supplying them with articles of all varieties'.[24] For their part the weavers preferred to attend public markets where they

[23] Ibid., 731 (my italics).
[24] Ibid., 741, 747, 790, 830.

were confident that the buyers were competing fairly for their linens, so that demand affected price.

It is quite clear from the report of the select committee that the pattern of markets had evolved to suit the structure of the industry. The committee itself was inclined to believe that the prevalence of this system of markets was due to the enforcement of a linen act of 1764 (3 Geo. III, c. 34) and even quoted a clause that linen yarn 'shall be sold publicly in some open market or fair, between the hours of eight of the clock in the forenoon and four of the clock in the afternoon', and brown or unbleached linen 'between the hours of ten of the clock in the forenoon and four of the clock in the afternoon'. However, it was informed that the law was not strictly enforced in practice, except for the clause prohibiting dealing before the bell sounded to announce the commencement of the market. When it criticised as inadequate the fixed hours and dates of the markets, it was told that weavers who had not sold all their linens in the public market usually approached a buyer afterwards to negotiate a price; between markets weavers even took their cloth direct to a bleachyard for sale. The implication was that although the 1764 act did specify that all linens had to be sold in public markets, a blind eye was turned to arrangements made privately between bleachers and weavers because they were on such a small scale.

In short, the structure of the brown-linen trade that had been endorsed by the 1764 act operated so well that it continued to be accepted in principle by all parties, even if not enforced in detail, up until industrialisation. Just as significant, in the light of Gill's conjectures, are the references by witnesses to the activities of his 'manufacturing drapers'. Although one of the most important markets for fine linens was held in Belfast, it is well known that by 1825 there were no linen weavers in the town and district because cotton weaving was more profitable. That market, however, was supplied to a large extent from the neighbouring districts of County Down by 'many extensive manufacturers in the country towns, small towns in the neighbourhood of Belfast, who bring in each week a quantity of linens to Belfast market, a distance of, from six or eight to fifteen or sixteen miles, and then they find customers'.[25] It had been reported in 1816 that 'Belfast

25 *1825 Linen Trade Report*, 741.

market is made up by rich manufacturers, who bring ten to forty pieces to it': yet 400 manufacturers attended that market to sell 1,000 pieces weekly, which would suggest that the rich manufacturers made up only about 10 to 15 per cent of the attendance.[26] A witness before the 1825 select committee, himself a substantial draper, added that the weavers preferred to deal with him in the public market-place rather than come to his warehouse, because they wanted competition between the buyers. Away from the major market towns, the same witness pointed out, it had become the practice for small manufacturers to sell to more substantial manufacturers who could afford the time to travel to markets.[27]

As well as such manufacturers buying linen in local fairs and markets to sell at a profit in major markets, there were other men mentioned in the 1825 report who might be more accurately termed entrepreneurs or capitalists. The reason for their appearance was that suggested by Gill: all of them were able to corner part of the yarn supply and put it out to weavers. This enabled them to specialise in the production of certain types of cloth for which they knew there was a ready export market. Yet, although the select committee of 1825 was anxious to learn everything about enterprises that accorded so well with their suggestions for the future of the trade, very little evidence was proffered. Smith of Seapatrick was reported to be concentrating on six quarter (i.e. 54 inch) wide sheeting, 'the best sheeting that I have ever seen made in Ireland' according to a Scottish capitalist.[28] John Cromie of Draper Hill, south of Ballynahinch in County Down, was said to be producing perhaps five to six thousand pieces annually.[29] Around Dromore other entrepreneurs were putting-out fine yarns for cambric weaving but they were selling in the market, unlike Cromie. It was said, too, that there was an extensive manufacturer about Belfast but no-one was able to inform the select committee whether he manufactured linen or linen and cotton 'unions'.[30]

---

[26] If 400 weavers were to bring only one piece each it would take a maximum of 60 of these 'rich manufacturers' to bring the remaining 600 pieces. *Minutes of the Trustees of the Linen and Hempen Manufactures of Ireland, containing the Reports of their Secretary, on a Tour of Inspection through the Province of Ulster in October, November, and December, 1816* (Dublin, 1817) [hereafter *1816 Tour Report*], Appendix, 78.

[27] *1825 Linen Trade Report*, 741, 745.

[28] Ibid., 765.

[29] Ibid., 792.

[30] Ibid., 765, 792.

The most obvious reason for capitalists to put-out yarn to weavers would have been to benefit from the production of mill-spun yarn, whether manufactured locally or in Britain. A major obstacle to the development of such a system, however, was claimed to be the imposition of considerable duties on imported flax and yarn for the protection of the Irish domestic yarn industry.[31] The other reason given is even more significant for our understanding of the trade. Mill-spun yarn was too coarse for weaving the fine linens produced in the linen triangle. As Robert Williamson, a bleacher from Lambeg near Belfast, explained to the select committee:

> Mill-spun yarn is generally adapted to the heavier fabrics ... and it is more capable of being bleached before it is woven; it is adapted to what we call ducks, which are worn in trowsers [sic], etc. to heavy diapers; to heavy damask diapers; to dowlases and different articles of that heavy kind. The hand-spun yarn is adapted to very various sorts of linen; the best indeed is fitted pretty well for those things just enumerated; but it is peculiarly adapted to the very finest linen, up as high as twenty-seven hundreds; it is peculiarly fitted for the shirting that you wear; it is adapted to lawns, and to the finest damasks; to the very lowest thin three-fourth [i.e. 27 inches] wides exported to the Brazils, Mexico, Peru, and other places in South America, and the United States; besides, the spinning of this yarn affords the chief employment to the female population of Ireland.[32]

In substantial agreement with Williamson was the evidence of John Marshall of Leeds, the pioneer and leading figure in the mill-spinning of flax. He admitted that the yarn he spun would not be suitable for anything finer than the middle quality of Irish shirtings. He admitted also that machine yarn was more expensive than Irish hand-spun yarn of similar weight by from 10 to 15 per cent; as a result his sales to Ireland were small.[33] In fact, in the year 1822 almost no mill-spun yarn was imported into Belfast.[34] Nor was mill-spun yarn produced on any scale in Ulster by 1821, although 13 dry-spinning mills had been built in Ulster in 1805–9, with financial assistance from the

[31] Ibid., 802–3.
[32] Ibid., 791.
[33] Ibid., 708, 709.
[34] National Library of Ireland, MS 376, 'Volumes of Dublin Imports and Exports' which contain the statistics for all the individual Irish ports, 1822.

Linen Board, to provide sail-cloth and canvas for the navy in the Napoleonic Wars.[35] The late Rodney Green argued that 'even before the wet-spinning system developed, large scale manufacturers of linen had appeared in County Down using millspun yarn imported from England'.[36] Although he cited several firms engaged in putting-out yarn, however, his sources are government reports of 1836 and 1840 respectively, subsequent to the introduction and rapid expansion of the wet-spinning process: by 1839 there were 35 wet-spinning mills in Ulster employing 7,768 workers.

Why was there such a critical difference between Gill's concept of the structure of the linen industry and the actual evidence presented to the select committee of 1825? The fundamental reason appears to have been Gill's presumption that the industry was evolving from a domestic to a putting-out system. This led him to view the conflict between the drapers and weavers in the linen triangle in the 1750s and early 1760s as the weavers' defence of their economic independence (in which light they certainly viewed it before 1764) and their refusal to accept the role of wage-earners.[37] This was a serious misconception. Examination of the background to the dispute, and the failure to enforce a series of regulating acts for the inspection of 'brown' linens, reveals that the real intention of the drapers and bleachers in obtaining the comprehensive legislation of 1764 had been to impose certain standard practices in the manufacture and marketing of linens that would make it possible for them to purchase linens in the public markets. They believed that the system of public markets provided them with the most practical and efficient method of obtaining the linens they required, if only they could be certain that the quality of the cloth was uniform throughout each piece and its minimum measurements guaranteed.[38]

In 1762 the Linen Board, under an act of 1733, appointed 'brown' sealmasters to execute these duties in each market, and it was their roles that were confirmed by the act of 1764 (3 Geo. III, c. 35). What

[35] Gribbon, op. cit., pp. 92–3.
[36] Green, E.R.R., *The Industrial Archaeology of County Down* (Belfast, 1963), p. 6.
[37] Gill, op. cit., pp. 138–48.
[38] Royal Irish Academy, Haliday Collection, vol. 308, no. 2, *A Review of the Evils that have prevailed in the Linen Manufacture of Ireland* (Dublin, 1762), pp. 9–23. This pamphlet refutes Gill's comments that the linen drapers had not tried to enforce the existing laws: see Gill, op. cit., pp. 106–10.

surprised everyone was the readiness of the Board to appoint weavers as brown sealmasters: indeed, within a few weeks nearly 1,300 seal-masters had been appointed.[39] The fact that the Board was prepared to permit responsible weavers to seal their own linens as well as per-forming the duties of public sealmasters was practical as well as mag-nanimous. It made them partners in the promotion of standards while permitting them to collect fees for sealing from their fellow-weavers, at no charge to the Board. The sealmasters themselves were constantly reminded of their responsibilities by their seals on which their names were engraved; dereliction of duty could mean confisca-tion of the seals and public disgrace. For its part the Board, if it felt that standards were being allowed to deteriorate, could intervene to tighten them. In 1782, for example, when it was being suggested that 'frauds in the sale of brown linens, whereby bleachers and drapers are often imposed on' were becoming too frequent, the Linen Board appointed county inspectors under the control of two inspectors-gen-eral, one for Ulster and one for the other provinces. These county inspectors or their deputies were required to visit markets, intervene in disputes, and report faults in sealing to a magistrate. They were nominated by the registered bleachers of each county but selected by the Linen Board.[40] They were encouraged in their supervisory role by local trustees of the Board and the linen drapers. In 1800 an address from the linen drapers to the Marquess of Downshire returned him 'our most unfeigned acknowledgements for the important services you have rendered to the trade, by your incessant exertions to reform and re-establish the original system of brown-sealing – a system under which the great staple of Ireland has been so eminently prosperous'. His reply contained the sentence: 'I am sensible that the brown seals were of the greatest advantage when first established, and I trust will continue to be so by their general use, if by your assistance the Linen Board shall be enabled to correct any abuse that may by negligence or fraud creep into the institution.'[41]

The relevance of this scheme even in 1825 was reflected in the number of brown sealmasters then operating throughout Ulster

[39] Gill, op. cit., p. 115.
[40] Ibid., pp. 207–8.
[41] Belfast News-Letter, 18 February 1800.

TABLE 11.1
Number of brown linen sealmasters in the service of the
Linen Board of Ireland, 1825

County	Public sealmasters	Manufacturers and others holding seals	Total
Antrim	1	99	100
Armagh	0	150	150
Down	0	137	137
Tyrone	19	0	19
Londonderry	3	0	3
Donegal	5	0	5
Monaghan	5	5	10
Cavan	5	0	5
Fermanagh	6	0	6
ULSTER	44	391	435
Louth	4	0	4
King's County	2	0	2
Longford	2	0	2
Westmeath	1	0	1
LEINSTER	9	0	9
Cork	7	0	7
Clare	2	0	2
Kerry	5	0	5
Limerick	3	0	3
Tipperary	1	0	1
MUNSTER	18	0	18
Mayo	9	0	9
Roscommon	5	0	5
Sligo	3	0	3
Galway	5	0	5
Leitrim	2	0	2
CONNACHT	24	0	24
IRELAND	95	391	486

Source: *Report from the Select Committee on the Linen Trade of Ireland* (British Parliamentary
Papers 1825 (463) V), p. 811.

(Table 11.1). Within the counties of Antrim, Down and Armagh 12
linen markets were served by 386 manufacturers and others holding
seals and only one public sealmaster; throughout the rest of Ulster
there were 43 sealmasters and only five manufacturers serving 40
markets. The term 'manufacturer' was defined by a witness to the
1822 select committee examining the laws that regulated the linen
trade in Ireland:

The word 'manufacturer', to one unacquainted with the distinctions that exist among the trade, would seem to embrace every description of person that works at the loom, whereas it means ... the very reverse of this. It is the distinguishing appellation of him 'who does not work at the loom himself, but who buys his yarn and gives it out to weavers employed by him to be woven into cloth, which he sells himself in the public market'.

In discussing the importance of these individuals with a view to assessing them as influential sealmasters, it was reckoned that the number of clients was related to 'the fineness or coarseness of the linen of the district in which they speak; thus in Belfast and Lisburn it was "five looms, or any greater number;" in Banbridge "ten looms and upwards;" and in Armagh, "twenty looms and upwards"'. These individuals might influence the bleachers but certainly not dictate to them. Their significance in society, however, was recognised. They were said to be 'men of as high character, as respectable a station in life, and of as much wordly substance, as many to whom they sell their linens; they form that link in the chain of society that in England is called its "yeomanry"'.[42] It was these manufacturers who gave the linen triangle its distinctive character within the brown linen trade. They were the men who employed other weavers, whether journeymen, cottiers, or members of their family. Yet it should be noted that each of them employed relatively few men, particularly in the Belfast, Lisburn and Banbridge areas where the finest linens were woven. The fundamental point, of course, is that these manufacturers sold their linens in the public market and the bleachers bought them there.

The pre-eminence of the brown linen markets in the structure of the trade can best be illustrated from two reports to the Linen Board, prepared in 1816 and 1821 by its secretary, James Corry.[43] For the several markets in 1816 detailed replies to a circulated list of questions were provided by the inspectors. The information includes the kinds of cloth brought for sale, with the prices they fetched, the average number of webs sold on each market day, the average number of

[42] *Report from the Select Committee on the Laws which Regulate the Linen Trade of Ireland* (British Parliamentary Papers 1822 (560), VII) [hereafter *1822 Linens Laws Report*], 493–4.
[43] Horner, J., *The Linen Trade of Europe* (Belfast, 1920), pp. 188–96.

147

weavers attending each market, and the names of the principal buyers who attended, whether from far afield or locally, with an indication of their place of origin.[44] The 1821 report is rather more limited, but as well as estimates of the number of weavers in both 'slack time' and 'busy time' it gives details of the number of pieces sealed in 1820 with an estimate of their value by the public sealmasters. It should be remembered that in the counties of Antrim, Armagh and Down the great bulk of the linens was measured by manufacturers holding brown seals and so for these counties the figures for the pieces sealed are crude estimates: this accounts for the most significant discrepancies between the two reports, the numbers of pieces reported as sold in the counties of Antrim and Armagh. The statistics for sales in the other counties are much more consistent and they emphasise the considerable scale of the markets in Tyrone, Londonderry and Monaghan by 1820 (Table 11.2).

In view of the differences between the 1816 and 1820 figures for the individual counties it is a mere coincidence that the total number of pieces sold weekly in these two years approximates to 24,000 in each case. For the year 1820 an analysis of the pieces sealed indicates that the markets handled about 43 million yards, approximately the same amount that was exported in the year ending 5 January 1821. Any estimate of total home production would have to take into account quality linens that did not go through the public markets, production in the other provinces, and linens that were retailed locally, usually by dealers, without coming to the public market. The poor quality of this latter class provoked the following comment from Belfast in the 1816 Report:

> All linens brought to the Linen Hall come in the brown state; but many other descriptions are brought grey; half-white, etc. for the use of the common people, who loudly complain of the rotten state of the linens retailed in a grey state in the streets, alleging that they give no wear from being bleached with lime.[45]

[44] *1816 Tour Report*, Appendix, pp. 29–30.
[45] Ibid., Appendix, p. 77.

Table 11.2. Average attendance and sales at brown linen markets
in 1816 and 1820

| County | 1816 | | 1820 | | 1820 |
	Weavers	Pieces	Weavers	Pieces	Length in yards sold annually
Antrim	3,400–3,700	5,960–5,970	1,540–3,270	3,225	5,161,710
Armagh	1,050	4,290	1,500–2,900	7,796	15,613,800
Down	1,309–1,319	2,058–2,060	810–2,050	2,543	3,289,750
Monaghan	1,080	2,910	930–1,740	2,291	3,109,444
Cavan	750	1,150	510–930	934	2,251,545
Fermanagh	150	200	750–1,440	183	613,800
Tyrone	3,712–3,720	4,740	2,270–4,260	3,552	8,314,366
Donegal	174	174	130–250	200	626,680
Londonderry	2,750	2,800	1,950–3,570	3,642	4,169,984
TOTAL	14,375–14,693	24,282–24,294	10,390–20,410	24,366	43,151,079

Source: *Tour of Inspection through Ulster 1816* (Dublin, 1817); J. Horner, *The Linen Trade of Europe* (Belfast, 1920).

When these reports for 1816 and 1820 are compared with those for 1784 and 1803 four distinct regions can be defined, specialising in various widths and qualities of cloth. This makes it possible for us to understand how a significant increase in production was achieved in the period between 1790 and 1825, in spite of the defection of many weavers and spinners to the cotton industry in the Belfast region. These regions were also being affected in different ways by competition that was forcing down profits to dangerously low levels.

The heart of the industry was concentrated within the triangle between Belfast, Dungannon, and Newry where the finest yard-wide linens were produced. They were bought in the markets at Belfast, Lisburn, Lurgan, Banbridge, Newry and bleached in the valleys of the Lagan and Upper Bann. The manufacture of cambrics was noted in Lurgan in 1784 and by 1803 it had spread to the neighbouring towns of Lisburn, Banbridge, Tandragee and Dromore.[46] It is said to have declined after the French wars in face of competition from that country,[47] but the 1816 report notes that the fine lawns were used for printed pocket handkerchiefs and children's wear. The fine linens

[46] See note 20 and Appendix 4.
[47] *1825 Linen Trade Report*, 802.

were popular in Britain for apparel while diapers were sold for towels and tablecloths.

This region must have suffered most by competition for weavers from the cotton industry thriving all round the shores of Belfast Lough, especially when cotton weaving was paying twice as much as linen. We do not know if the success of cotton weaving was responsible for compelling the linen drapers to concentrate on the more expensive linens. The linen triangle seems to have generated its own momentum:

> In the north of Ireland ... the object of every person who has flax, is to have it of as fine quality as he can; and the spinner's object is to spin it as fine as they can, because it pays a better price; and the manufacturer's object is to weave the finest linen that he can; for which reason, the coarse article in the north of Ireland is made only of the refuse of the flax.[48]

To the south of the linen triangle the yard-wide linens were mainly coarser and cheaper and known as 'Stout Armaghs'. This district comprised south Armagh and Monaghan as well as Cootehill in County Cavan, famous for its sheetings. The city of Armagh was the centre of the industry and was by 1820 much the busiest linen market in Ulster. Yet much of the linen it handled was at the bottom end of the market. Although it was estimated that 6,000 webs a week (or 312,000 per year) were sold in Armagh in 1820, half of them were double pieces (52 yards long compared with about 25 yards), amounting to some eight million yards and sold at 5d. or 6d. per yard. They were woven from tow yarn (made from the fibres combed away during the preparation of the flax for spinning) and exported to England, either half-bleached or in their natural state. In the term used above they were made from 'the refuse of the flax'. This indicates that south Armagh and Monaghan must have been selling much of its flax yarn, probably for export through Newry, Dundalk, or Drogheda, or perhaps to the linen triangle, if it was sufficiently fine for its weavers, leaving the tow yarn only for the local industry. This was a serious indication of the poverty of the local industry. A Scots employer who had toured Ulster and was giving evidence to the 1825

---

[48] *1822 Linen Laws Report*, 486.

commission calculated that weavers of the cheap cloth that he saw in Monaghan market could earn no more than 2s. 6d. per week, working for twelve hours each day.[49]

The part of County Antrim that lay to the north of Lough Neagh had for many decades been the home of the three-quarter (yard) wide linens, with Ballymena as its capital and Ballymoney and Portglenone as the other significant markets. These 'three-quarters' were coarse linens for general use, often made from tow yarn, and fetched low prices: they appear to have been made mainly by farmers weaving in their spare time. As a consequence the Ballymena and Portglenone markets attracted many such part-time weavers from the neighbouring counties of Tyrone and Londonderry. During the early decades of the nineteenth century this region was penetrated by drapers purchasing yard wides and 'seven-eights' yard wides in Ahoghill and Ballymena. Ballymoney, however, was said to have lost a growing market in seven-eights to Coleraine.

The most interesting developments throughout the final fifty years of the domestic spinning industry were taking place in the west of the province, stretching from Inishowen in the north to Cavan in the south. Early in the eighteenth century the Linen Board had bestowed the name 'Coleraines' on a 'seven-eights' linen.[50] Later it was applied specifically to cloth of this width woven from half-bleached yarn and suitable for good quality shirts. This marked the top end of the scale. The chief markets were Derry, Coleraine and Limavady (which collapsed before 1816), Strabane and Newtownstewart. It is probable that the making up of shirts in this region developed with this specialisation. Towards the south the quality tended to decline somewhat so that the linens were referred to first as 'Moneymores' and later as coarse and fine 'Tyrones'. The greatest market was Dungannon, with Cookstown and Stewartstown to the north and Ballygawley, Fintona, Fivemiletown and Enniskillen to the west. For all this region the cloth was purchased by bleachers on the rivers Roe, Agivey, Moyola, and Ballinderry, and on the streams around Dungannon, because there were very few bleachgreens in the whole of the Foyle basin.

Demand from these bleachers stimulated production in the west of

49 *1825 Linen Trade Report*, 763. See also appendix 5.
50 9 Anne, c. 3, s. 68.

the province, especially in the counties of Donegal and Fermanagh. Whereas the report of 1784 notes that locally-made non-commercial 'Laggans' (from the traditional name of that district of east Donegal) were still being sold in the fairs, they had disappeared from sale in 1803 to be replaced by 'seven-eights' linens. The attraction of the Derry market was so strong, however, that the growing markets of Letterkenny and Ramelton found great difficulty in establishing themselves because of jobbers who flouted the laws. The appearance by then of 'three-quarter' webs woven from tow yarns in these markets as well as those of Derry, Strabane and Newtownstewart is an indication of the phenomenon explained by John McEvoy in 1802:

> There cannot be a greater proof of the increase of the linen trade, than the great rise of flax land ... now the same quantity of land frequently brings double that sum ... Common labourers, who were not much in the habit of weaving some years ago, generally work out two or three yards of linen at night in the winter time, after the common day's labour is over.[51]

In the south of the province Cavan, with its neighbouring counties of Longford and Leitrim, seems to have represented a world of its own. Even in 1784 its fairs and markets dealt in 'seven-eights', whereas both counties Monaghan and Fermanagh, and even the market at Cootehill in Cavan, dealt in 'yards': later Fermanagh went over to 'seven-eights'. Markets at Killishandra, Ballinagh and Arva were frequented by local buyers with very few from Tyrone, Armagh and Monaghan. It may be that Cavan's linen industry resembled that of Sligo, rather than that of Monaghan which was geared into Armagh.

The totality of the responses from these four regions to changing economic conditions in the early nineteenth century suggests how industrialisation and deindustrialisation occurred simultaneously in Ulster. If the Irish linen trade had been dependent on coarse linens it would have failed in competition with England and Scotland. Only in the linen triangle did weavers produce fine linens and so they were able later to use the fine yarns produced by the wet-spinning process. Elsewhere in the province the industry appears to have reached its maximum capacity by 1820, dependent as it was on the farmer/

---

[51] McEvoy, J., *Statistical Survey of the County of Tyrone* (Dublin, 1802), p. 135.

weaver economy. Competition from cotton was forcing down the market prices. To survive, families would economise more and more strenuously, exploit themselves, their children, their servants and their cottiers. They would depend more on a diet of potatoes. They would work longer hours in their own homes at the spinning wheel and the loom. Those who had access to land would farm it more intensively, leaving weaving to cottiers and landless labourers. The number of emigrants to Britain and North America would rise, draining away the younger folk and leaving the older generation to come to terms with change.

The linen trade in Ireland was especially vulnerable to the introduction of machine-spinning because it was immeshed in the social system, especially as that system was based on agriculture. An Irish linen merchant and bleacher, Robert Williamson, explained to the 1825 commission:

> the linen trade is so constituted in Ireland and the capital so subdivided and spread abroad over the population, that the present mode is the best adapted to the circumstances of the country ... In short, it is one of those already established things which you find as it is, and you are obliged to use the best means with respect to it in your power: to alter it (were it even desirable) you must re-cast the state of society and ... re-model that of property. It is now a mixture of agriculture and manufacture, and I think it tends greatly to the health and morality of the people ...[52]

Williamson, like many other Irish people, viewed the problem in social terms. He admitted that if machinery for spinning linen were to be introduced, it would throw the manufacture into the hands of large manufacturers. This development he would have welcomed. He was aware that Ireland was already losing several branches of the manufacture to the Scots, notably strong sheeting as in diapers, coarse damask diapers and dowlas, because the Scottish mill-spun yarn, although dear, was easier to bleach and more consistent in quality. Williamson was able to convince himself that the introduction of mill-spinning into Ireland would not destroy hand-spinning

because there is room enough for both, and the population, dense as

---

[52] *1825 Linen Trade Report*, 790.

it is, requires employment in both ways. Nor is it possible to direct capital generally over Ireland for mill-spinning; I should think that the new manufacture would rather fix itself in those portions of Ireland that are richest, and extend the other back to those unfortunate districts that have not the linen manufacture, or any other.[53]

Williamson underestimated the devastating impact that the introduction of mill-spinning had on those districts that had become almost dependent on the sale of fine hand-spun yarns to the triangle. They lost not only their markets but also their entrepreneurs. Only in a few places outside the triangle would linen spinning mills be erected and yarn put out to weavers, notably at Castlewellan, Keady, Laragh near Castleblaney, and Sion Mills near Strabane.

Williamson's mention that a number of individuals had set up a subscription of £30,000 to erect a flax-spinning mill near Belfast predates Kay's invention of the wet-spinning process in the same year.[54] It suggests that Ulster capitalists were preparing to invest in machinery for dry-spinning rather than concede the industry to their English and Scottish competitors.

This study has argued that the pattern of the domestic linen trade in Ulster on the eve of the mechanisation of spinning had developed in the first half of the eighteenth century and was confirmed by an act of 1764 that specified that all brown linens had to be exhibited and sold in public markets after being measured and sealed by sealmasters licensed by the Linen Board. The movers of this act were the bleachers who believed that their interests would be best served if they or their agents were able to tour the linen markets to make a selection of those kinds and qualities of linens that they required to fulfil their contracts abroad. For this they needed an assurance that the quality and length of the linens were guaranteed. As we have seen, the bleachers were not anxious to become involved in dealing in yarn or putting-out work to weavers. Instead they made themselves an international reputation and attracted bleaching business from Britain and the Continent. Where a 'putting-out' system developed it was within the manufacturing process, but even there it was the rare individual who could command more than a score of looms.

[53] Ibid., 791.

Because the brown linen markets witnessed the transfer of all linens of commercial quality from the manufacturers to the finishers, the evidence of the four reports deserves proper consideration and analysis. The reaction of the four major regions throughout the period 1784–1820 to changing economic and social conditions provides valuable indications to the study of Ulster provincial society. Pat Hudson's agenda for research challenges us to re-examine the evidence. We now have sufficient evidence to understand how the manufacture locked in with the agrarian base through the seasons and between regions, and we know something about the institutional environment of landholding.[55] About both inheritance practices and the distribution of wealth much could be learned from analysis of the wills held in the Public Record Office of Northern Ireland, especially if they were related to the estate-archives there and to the Registry of Deeds material in Dublin.[56] Although very little research has yet been done on the nature of central and local government, there is sufficient archive material available from parish vestries, manor courts, grand juries, and even borough corporations to devise worthwhile projects.[57] The same can be said for the study of urban centres on the lines suggested by Leslie Clarkson's work on Armagh city.[58] Investigation into the history of Belfast will be boosted by the prospect of access to the computerised files of the *Belfast News-Letter* for the late eighteenth century. As for the major theme of the impact of proto-industrialisation on the family in Ireland, pioneer work has been done by

54 Ibid., 792.
55 Crawford, W.H., 'Landlord–tenant relations in Ulster 1609–1820', *Irish Economic & Social History* 2 (1975), 5–21; Roebuck, P., 'Rent movement, proprietorial incomes and agricultural development, 1730–1830', in Roebuck, P. (ed), *Plantation to Partition* (Belfast, 1981), 82–101; Wylie, J.C.W., *Irish Land Law* (London, 1975).
56 See for example the will of Thomas Christy of Moyallen, County Down, linendraper, 19 January 1780, in Crawford and Trainor, op. cit., pp. 70–71; Eustace, P.B. (ed.), *Abstracts of Wills in the Registry of Deeds Dublin*, vol. I: *1708–45*; vol. II: *1746–85* (Dublin, 2 vols, 1954–6).
57 Crawford and Trainor, op. cit., pp. 122–32; [Crawford, W.H.], *Sources for the Study of Local History in Northern Ireland* (Belfast, 1968).
58 Clarkson, L.A., 'An anatomy of an Irish town: the economy of Armagh, 1770', *Irish Economic & Social History* 5 (1978); 'Household and family structure in Armagh City, 1770', *Local Population Studies* XX (1978); 'Armagh 1770: portrait of an urban community', in Harkness, D. and O'Dowd, M. (eds), *The Town in Ireland* (Belfast, 1981).

Brenda Collins and Leslie Clarkson.[59] To co-ordinate this research we need to create a forum where students from a variety of disciplines can share their ideas and learn about potential sources from archivists and librarians.

---

[59] See especially Collins, B., 'Proto-industrialization and pre-Famine emigration', *Social History* VII, 2 (1982), 127–46.

12

A handloom weaving community in County Down[1]

PLATE 12

Perspective View of the Linen Hall in Dublin, with the Boxes and Bales of Linen ready for Exportation, the Emblems of their Industry . . .

WILLIAM HINCKS 1783

BECAUSE THE WHOLE EMPHASIS of the study of the Irish linen industry in the nineteenth century has concentrated on its industrialisation, little or no attention has been directed to the cardinal importance of the handloom weaving industry, especially in the first half of the nineteenth century. Yet it has to be recognised that after the introduction of the wet-spinning process into Ireland in the late 1820s, the great bulk of the yarns spun in Irish mills were woven into cloth by handloom weavers throughout the countryside of the province of Ulster. It has been calculated that Irish linen production increased from around fifty million yards in the early 1820s to sixty-five million yards in the early 1850s.[2] Nor did the introduction of powerlooms in the 1850s kill the handloom weaving industry at a stroke. Several decades were to elapse before powerlooms were adapted to weave the patterned damasks and then the lighter qualities of linen. The process of change was predicted in 1859 in a journal of the linen trade:

> From the enhanced value of manual labour and other causes, the supply of handloom goods is becoming less abundant and decidedly less certain, and there are many circumstances which would seem to indicate that while the days of progress in powerlooms have unquestionably set in, those of decadence in handlooms give warning of approach ...
>
> The handlooms will sustain their superiority in the fine goods, 18^{00} to 26^{00}, for years to come, though as the powerloom machinery becomes more perfect in future, I have no doubt it will gradually be creeping upwards, and encroaching on what at present is considered the special domain of handloom weaving.[3]

Although great prosperity was enjoyed by the handloom weaving industry during the boom caused by the cotton famine of the American Civil War, it could only postpone the inevitable. The spread of powerloom factories soon undermined the old rural economy that had grown up around the domestic linen industry. Yet the

---

[1] First published in *Ulster Folklife* 39 (1993), 1–14.

[2] Solar, P.M., 'The Irish linen industry', *Textile History* 21, 1 (1990), 71.

[3] Ure, A., *Philosophy of Manufactures or An Exposition of the Scientific, Moral, and Commercial Economy of the Factory System of Great Britain*, 3rd edition, 'continued in its detail to the present time, by P. L. Simmonds' (London, 1861, reprinted New York, 1969), p. 591. The superscript '00s' stand for 'hundreds': 26^{00} indicates that each ell (= 45 inches) width of cloth contains as many as 2,600 warp threads – very fine indeed.

impact was not the same in every district throughout Ulster because the products of the industry varied greatly in substance, finish, quality, and price:

> In Ireland, coarse linens for blouses, etc. and for the common kinds of export goods are chiefly made in the county of Armagh; medium and fine kinds of export cloth about Ballymena and Coleraine; damasks and diapers at Lurgan, Lisburn, and Belfast; lawns at Lurgan and Dromore; cambrics at Lurgan, Waringstown, and Dromore; heavy linens and sheetings for the home market at Banbridge; hollands in the counties of Antrim and Armagh; shirt fronts, woven in plaits, at Dromore; and the coarsest fabrics, such as bed-ticks, coarse drills, etc., at Drogheda.[4]

No study has been written yet about any of the districts affected by the rapid decline of handloom weaving. They cannot be pinpointed readily from the printed census returns although their tables on 'occupations' do identify the Poor Law Unions concerned. Often tradition is a better guide. Once located they provoke a range of questions that can be answered from readily available source material such as census returns and valuation records. How did the social structure of the townlands relate to handloom weaving? Are they associated with very high population densities? Did weaving communities, for example, flourish most in townlands where subdivision and subletting had fragmented the holdings so that they often provided little more than accommodation? Were such communities most likely to develop on marginal land? From census returns the demographic trends can be charted to determine population movements in terms of both inhabitants and inhabited houses, changes in family size, the sex ratio, the rate of population decline and its relation to the housing stock, and the experience of the several religious sects.

Such information can be of great value in the preparation of an oral history project on any of these themes, for while oral history is probably the only method of fleshing out the dry figures, they in turn inform and colour the whole approach and suggest new questions. They provide us with the information about contemporary families, their occupations and their holdings that is essential to reconstruct a

[4] Ibid., p. 599.

picture of the community's view of itself. What were the characteristics of a 'well-doing' family? What futures did such parents see for their children? What standards of behaviour did they set? What misfortune befell them? How did they farm their smallholdings? Are there any stories about the consolidation of these holdings? How did they view the Swiss-embroidery and hem-stitching enterprises? Who were the last weavers and how did they manage to carry on their craft? What traditions remain about them? The answers to these questions will help us to understand the character of the community at the present time and may provide us with some valuable information about its past.

After such an extensive vindication of this method of approaching the study of a rural community, the indulgence of the reader has to be sought for the limited aims of the actual study. It confines itself to an examination of documentary sources that are readily available for every district, in order to discover how the decline of a particular handloom weaving community was reflected in the census returns and the valuation records and how its surviving housing stock was assessed by the census enumerators.

This paper is a report of an investigation into the history of a community in the northwest of County Down that was engaged in the weaving of cambrics and damasks. Cambric weaving had expanded very quickly in the Lurgan/Dromore district in the early nineteenth century and its products sold well. 'In 1826 for every 1,000 dozen of French cambric sold in the English market 100 pieces of Irish were sold; in 1846 for every 1,000 pieces of French there were 16,000 pieces of Irish sold'.[5] Among the most notable townlands that retained the tradition of handloom weaving into the twentieth century were Ballydugan, Bleary and Clare.[6] They lie astride a main road from the mill town of Gilford that diverged at Ballydugan into a pair of roads running to Lurgan and Waringstown respectively. For administrative purposes they were defined from the seventeenth century as townlands in the parish of Tullylish in the Upper Half of the

[5] Ibid., p. 600.
[6] I knew about the handloom-weaving trade in Ballydugan and Bleary and I added Clare because, like them, it had such a large population in 1841. I overlooked the townland of Corcreeny which borders on Bleary: I had lived there for six years without being aware of its weaving tradition.

Lower Barony of Iveagh in the county of Down, and after the creation of the Poor Law Unions in 1839 they were assigned to the Electoral Division of Tullylish in Lurgan Union (although the town of Lurgan itself lay in the neighbouring county of Armagh). After 1898, as a result of the new Local Government Act, they became part of Moira Rural District Council.

This information is essential for tracing population data from 1901 and 1911 census returns (the only surviving census returns), and the printed census abstracts that provide figures for every townland from 1841 to 1926. The table illustrating population change (Table 12.1) shows not only the total number of inhabitants but also the total of inhabited houses. While decline in the population of a townland may indicate the emigration of its younger generation, the vacating of houses indicates the disappearance of whole families.

The most obvious comment contrasts the increases of both population and housing stock until the peak census year of 1861, with the rapid decline that did not end even with the outbreak of the Great War in 1914. At the outset it is surprising to realise that over the period of the Great Famine in the late 1840s, when County Down lost

TABLE 12.1
Population change based on census returns. Inhabited houses in square brackets. Acreage and valuation from the printed Valuation of Tenements for Lurgan Union in Co. Down (1864)

YEAR	BALLYDUGAN	BLEARY	CLARE	TOTAL
	948 acres	911 acres	1,334 acres	3,193 acres
	£1,305 valuation	£1,275 valuation	£1,741 valuation	£4,321 valuation
1841	1,175 [192]	1,263 [214]	1,403 [248]	3,841 [654]
1851	1,198 [219]	1,351 [224]	1,188 [206]	3,737 [649]
1861	1,190 [234]	1,408 [264]	1,062 [202]	3,660 [700]
1871	1,061 [207]	1,298 [228]	819 [167]	3,178 [602]
1881	885 [189]	976 [209]	606 [135]	2,467 [533]
1891	763 [174]	913 [202]	488 [113]	2,164 [489]
1901	579 [136]	783 [182]	409 [100]	1,771 [418]
1911	516 [127]	722 [170]	380 [99]	1,618 [396]
1926	462 [109]	589 [146]	315 [80]	1,366 [335]

more than 11% of its population, this district lost no more than 104 people out of nearly four thousand inhabitants. Indeed, the losses in terms of both houses and inhabitants can be attributed to one of the three townlands, Clare, which lost 315 inhabitants and 42 houses while Ballydugan and Bleary gained between them 111 people and 37 houses. The same trend continued in the following decade, 1851–61, when the total number of houses rose by 51 to an all-time peak of 700 while the population fell by 77. While 40 more houses appeared in Bleary, Ballydugan got 15 and Clare lost 4; Bleary's population increased by 57 but Ballydugan lost 8 and Clare 126. By 1861 the density of population in Bleary had reached almost a thousand to the square mile whereas that of Clare barely exceeded five hundred. Since Bleary and Clare belonged to the same landlord and all three were managed by the same agent, the difference cannot be attributed to his policy. It is worthwhile, however, to examine the structure of land-holding.

Characteristic of those districts in mid-Ulster that specialised in the weaving of fine linens was the high percentage of householders who held their land directly from a landlord. The phenomenon had its origins in the prosperous period enjoyed by handloom-weavers in the mid-eighteenth century. Many landlords saw their intermediate tenants profit by subletting to handloom weavers who competed for small-holdings and paid their rents with regularity. Whenever these leases came up for renewal, the landlords seized the opportunity to cut out the middlemen by letting every smallholding to its immediate occupant.[7] This process was most marked in County Armagh, where a landlord commented in 1803:

> Proprietors find it in their account to let land in small parcels, as the weaver will pay for just what suits his own convenience, in the vicinity of a good market town, much more than could be afforded for a large farm, the rent of which is to be made by the business of agriculture.[8]

The legacy of such a policy was very difficult to reverse as long as the linen industry continued to provide the cash to pay the rent. In

[7] Crawford, W.H., 'Landlord–tenant relations in Ulster 1609–1820', *Irish Economic and Social History* 2 (1975), 13–14.
[8] Coote, Sir C., *A Statistical Survey of the County of Armagh* (Dublin, 1804), p. 137.

TABLE 12.2
Size of farms in Bleary, Ballydugan and Clare as compared
to Ireland as a whole

	1–5 acres	5–15 acres	15–30 acres	over 30 acres
Three townlands	38%	40%	16%	6%
Ireland*	15%	32%	25%	28%

* Source: Crotty, R.D., *Irish Agricultural Production: Its Volume and Structure* (Cork, 1966), p. 351.

this district in County Down, for example, farms remained much smaller than the national average. In 1861 the relative figures were as shown in Table 12.2.

The average size of holdings in this district was just under ten acres but two-thirds of the tenants had farms smaller than that. On the other hand, only eighteen farms exceeded thirty acres in size: ten of them were in Clare townland whereas, by contrast, Ballydugan had only two. These discrepancies may be accounted for by the success or failure of family strategies that had left some farming families better equipped to deal with economic change.

The Valuation Records distinguish between tenants and subtenants (see Table 12.3). Tenants held their farms directly from their land-lords and the legal system encouraged them to believe that they had certain basic rights against these landlords. In their turn, however, they did not concede that their undertenants had legal rights against them. By 1864, the date of the Valuation, the subtenants actually out-numbered the tenants, although only about one third of all the ten-ants kept subtenants. In some cases subtenants were members of the same family, often sharing the same long, low cottage, but in others surnames were scattered so randomly throughout the district that the community must have had a long history of accommodating cottier-weavers who paid rents in cash from their earnings at weaving because they possessed no land. The number of subtenant cottages on each holding varied from one to sometimes as many as seven, but there were a few remarkable exceptions. Robert Urey of Clare had sixteen and Leonard Uprichard of Bleary had thirteen but William Wells of Bleary had forty subtenants on his property. We should not, howev-er, jump to a conclusion that all subtenants were packed on to marginal land or around the tenants' farmyards (although there were examples of both phenomena in this community), because in the case of William Wells's subtenants, many of them occupied good sites around a road junction complex in Bleary.

Such was the landholding structure in this district when the population statistics began their headlong plunge. In the half century that separated 1861 from 1911 County Down lost one third of its population and a fifth of its houses. This community lost more than half of its total population as it fell from 3,660 to 1,618 while the housing stock fell by two-fifths, from 700 to 396. It was dealt an immediate and severe blow in the early 1860s by the appearance of new powerloom factories during the linen boom caused by the American Civil War and its cotton famine. Whereas County Down lost 6% of its population in the 1860s and a further 11% in the 1870s, this community lost 13% in the 1860s and a further 22% in the 1870s. A quarter of its housing stock disappeared in those twenty years.

TABLE 12.3
Landholding structure

	BALLYDUGAN	BLEARY	CLARE	TOTAL
TENANT FARMERS				
Over 50 acres	0	1	4	5
30–49 acres	2	5	6	13
15–30 acres	14	13	19	46
5–15 acres	41	35	39	115
1–5 acres	51	41	19	111
less than 1 acre	10	11	19	40
TOTAL	118	106	106	330
SUBTENANTS				
House and land	3	2	2	7
House and garden	14	6	10	30
House only	95	138	84	317
TOTAL	112(46)	146(45)	96(30)	354(121)
GRAND TOTAL	230	252	202	684

Note: Figures in parentheses denote the number of tenants owning these subtenancies.

Valuation revision books indicate that they were almost all the houses of subtenants, the homes of families of landless labourers leaving the district. Yet the families that had lived in the cottier houses could have accounted for no more than three-quarters of the migrants and so the remainder would have been drawn from the children of the small farmers. A lesser factor was the amalgamation and the readjustment of holdings brought about by changes in family circumstances, usually after the death of a patriarch. During the 1880s and the 1890s the haemorrhage continued at twice the county level. In the 1891 census a note explained the decline from 614 to 444 people (137 to 115 houses) over the previous decade in the neighbouring townland of Ballinagarrick: 'The decrease is attributed to reduced employment for handloom weavers.'

The survival of the original census returns for 1901 permits a more detailed survey of the textile industry in the district.[9] Even after the great decline of weaving, linen workers still occupied three out of every four houses and averaged more than two to a house. There are, however, significant variations between the number of people engaged in the linen industry in the three townlands (Table 12.4).

The most densely populated townland, Bleary, also boasted the greatest number of weavers. Indeed, it had so many weavers that its prosperity was bound up with that of the cambric weaving trade.

TABLE 12.4
Numbers engaged in the linen industry, 1901

BALLYDUGAN
Of 579 people living in 136 houses, 211 workers from 96 of these houses
BLEARY
Of 783 people living in 182 houses, 350 workers from 152 of these houses
CLARE
Of 409 people living in 100 houses, 110 workers from 56 of these houses
TOTAL
Of 1,771 people living in 418 houses, 671 workers from 304 of these houses

9 The original census returns for both 1901 and 1911 are available for public inspection at the Reading Room of the National Archives, Bishop Street, Dublin. Microfilm copies of the 1901 census for the six counties of Northern Ireland may be examined now at the Public Record Office of Northern Ireland, 66 Balmoral Avenue, Belfast, BT9 6NY (hereafter PRONI) under the reference MIC/354.

TABLE 12.5
Textile skills of the community according to the 1901 census

	BALLYDUGAN			BLEARY			CLARE			TOTAL		
	MEN	WOMEN	TOTAL	MEN	WOMEN	TOTAL	MEN	WOMEN	TOTAL	MEN	WOMEN	TOTAL
WEAVING												
Weaver	38	44	82	2	5	7	10	5	15	50	54	104
Cambric weaver	51	53	104	132	141	273	13	15	28	196	209	405
Damask weaver	6	3	9	31	19	50	33	12	45	70	34	104
Diaper weaver	0	0	0	1	3	4	1	0	1	2	3	5
TOTAL	95	100	195	166	168	334	57	32	89	318	300	618
SEWING												
Dressmaker	0	3	3	0	6	6	0	6	6	0	15	15
Milliner	0	0	0	0	1	1	0	0	0	0	1	1
Seamstress	0	1	1	0	3	3	0	1	1	0	5	5
Veiner	0	0	0	0	3	3	0	0	0	0	3	3
Hem-stitcher	0	0	0	0	1	1	0	0	0	0	1	1
Machinist	0	0	0	1	0	1	1	1	2	2	1	3
TOTAL	0	4	4	1	14	15	1	8	9	2	26	28
Bobbin-winder	0	0	0	0	0	0	1	2	3	1	2	3
Factory-worker	7	3	10	0	0	0	0	0	0	7	3	10
Bleacher	0	0	0	0	0	0	8	1	9	8	1	9
White-collar	2	0	2	1	0	1	0	0	0	3	0	3
TOTAL	9	3	12	1	0	1	9	3	12	19	6	25
GRAND TOTAL	104	107	211	168	182	350	67	43	110	339	332	671

Clare, on the other hand, was the most extensive townland with the smallest population after 1851. Yet in 1841 its population had been the largest. It lost 340 people, however, and 46 houses over the next two decades, indicating that its farming structure was most vulnerable to the changes brought about by the Famine. In general, whereas townlands engaged in agriculture lost large numbers of both people and houses, the experience of both Bleary and Ballydugan suggests that weaving townlands were much more resilient. The corollary is that those rural townlands whose population suffered least in the Famine period were weaving townlands. Over the whole period 1841–1926 Clare suffered the heaviest losses, totalling three-quarters of its population and two-thirds of its housing stock. Some few inhabitants were employed on the bleachgreens along the River Bann. In general Ballydugan illustrated a mixture of the characteristics of the other two. The Blane family organised putting-out work to the cambric weavers but it is probable that the damask workers of both Bleary and Clare were serviced from Lurgan.

The structure of the textile skills in this community can be learned from an analysis of the 1901 census (Table 12.5).

It is a pity that the constable who supervised the census in Ballydugan was not as consistent as his fellows in Clare and Bleary in ensuring that weavers distinguished themselves as either 'cambric' or 'damask' weavers. Nevertheless, as many as 405, or two-thirds of all weavers, described themselves as cambric-weavers while one-sixth were damask-weavers. It is probable that most of those who described themselves merely as weavers were cambric-weavers: damask-weavers would have been more likely to distinguish themselves from the more common cambric-weavers. In cambric-weaving women just outnumbered men but damask-weaving engaged twice as many men as women. Before the introduction of mill-spun yarn in the mid-1820s women had concentrated on hand-spinning the yarn. Tradition had asserted that weaving was too heavy a job for them but, like cotton-weaving, cambric-weaving was not so strenuous and the introduction of the flying shuttle about 1825 relieved the exertion of throwing the shuttle by hand. In this community three hundred women were weavers in 1901 but only thirty-two engaged in other textile roles and, of these, fifteen were dressmakers and one a milliner: no-one then was engaged in embroidery except for three 'veiners' in the town-land of Bleary. Among the householders in this district who were not engaged in the linen industry, three-quarters (118 out of 158) described themselves as 'farmers' while another sixth were 'labourers'; the others comprised three shoemakers, two teachers, two grocers (one a cambric manufacturer), two carpenters, two carters, a mason, a cattle-dealer and a roadsurfaceman.

Before the next census was taken in 1911 a significant change had taken place in the composition of those engaged in the textile trades in this district. Christopher Blane of Ballydugan and his son James had established two new textile enterprises: a hem-stitching factory and a Swiss embroidery school. The Blane family were relative new-comers to the district for they had purchased a farm of some 15 acres in 1854. Family tradition claims that James Blane established a cambric manufactory in 1865. The 1901 census records that his son Christopher, then aged 74, was both a family grocer and a cambric manufacturer, putting out work from his home. In 1907 the valuation officers noted that Christopher Blane had completed developments that had increased the valuation of the buildings on his holding to £36 and by 1914 the addition of another four blocks had raised the valuation further to £83.[10] These premises were to house hemstitchers as well as a warping room for preparing the yarn beams for the weavers in their homes. They also included, however, the first school for Machine (or Swiss) Embroidery in Ireland. This school was established in 1910 with the active encouragement of the Department of Agriculture and Technical Instruction to introduce the manufacture of machine embroidery in order to employ the handloom weavers and hand embroiderers whose livelihood was being undermined by powerlooms and machinery embroidery from Switzerland.[11] The valuation officers recorded that the school had eight embroidery machines, hand-operated, and was lit by electric light 'manufactured on other premises'. The designer and teacher was a Swiss, Hans Siefert, who gave his age as 25 and condition as married to the 1911

[10] PRONI Valuation Revision Books VAL/12A/3/71 p.16 and VAL/12B/21/8E, numbers 108a & b.
[11] Fletcher, G., 'The problem of small industries with special reference to machine embroidery', *Journal of the Department of Agriculture and Technical Instruction for Ireland* 14, 4 (July, 1914), 695–9.

TABLE 12.6
Distribution of textile skills of the community according to the 1911 census

	BALLYDUGAN			BLEARY			CLARE			TOTAL		
	MEN	WOMEN	TOTAL	MEN	WOMEN	TOTAL	MEN	WOMEN	TOTAL	MEN	WOMEN	TOTAL
WEAVING												
Weaver	34	39	73	22	31	53	18	10	28	74	80	154
Cambric weaver	24	33	57	84	81	165	3	4	7	111	118	229
Damask weaver	4	4	8	36	14	50	18	12	30	58	30	88
Diaper weaver	0	0	0	6	0	6	0	0	0	6	0	6
	62	76	138	148	126	274	39	26	65	249	228	477
EMBROIDERY												
Embroidery worker	4	3	7	0	1	1	0	0	0	4	4	8
Handkerchief veiner	0	5	5	0	3	3	0	5	5	0	13	13
Hem-stitcher	0	9	9	0	2	2	0	0	0	0	11	11
Others employed in stitching factory	0	2	2	0	3	3	0	1	1	0	6	6
	4	19	23	0	9	9	0	6	6	4	34	38
SEWING												
Dressmaker	0	2	2	0	5	5	0	2	2	0	9	9
Milliner	0	0	0	0	0	0	0	1	1	0	1	1
Seamstress	0	1	1	0	1	1	0	0	0	0	2	2
	0	3	3	0	6	6	0	3	3	0	12	12
OTHER TEXTILE WORKERS												
Bobbin winder	0	1	1	0	0	0	0	1	1	0	2	2
Factory worker	5	4	9	5	1	6	3	3	6	13	8	21
Bleacher	0	0	0	0	0	0	2	0	2	2	0	2
White-collar	3	0	3	1	0	1	0	1	1	4	1	5
	8	5	13	6	1	7	5	5	10	19	11	30
TOTAL	74	103	177	154	142	296	44	40	84	272	285	557

census-taker, when he was a boarder with a local farmer in Ballydugan. In 1915 the following description was given of the school at Ballydugan and another at Maghera subsequently founded:

> These schools are well designed, light and airy buildings, offering pleasant conditions for work. No motive power is required other than that provided by the worker. The worker sits at one end of the machine, which is operated by hand and foot. The enlarged design is mounted on a board, and the operator follows it, point by point, with an indicator which operates a pantograph and moves the long frame holder containing the handkerchiefs, which are held in position by metal frames. In the six and three-quarter yards machine as many as 234 handkerchiefs are embroidered simultaneously. The needles, pointed at either end, with an eye in the middle, are held by clips in a frame which moves to and fro on wheels. The 234 needles pass through the handkerchiefs at the precise points required, and are seized by corresponding clips at the other side, which slide back, pulling taut the threads. The operator moves the pantograph indicator to the next point of the design, and, by the movement of a lever, the frames containing the needle clips repeat the operation. The needles are threaded, and the thread knotted and cut automatically by a beautiful and cunningly-devised machine.
>
> These schools have been very successful. Before they were started there were scarcely a dozen of these machines in Ulster. Now there are, I am informed, something like 140, and we are well on the way to capture the industry, and thus provide employment for our own workers.[12]

The scale of the changes induced by the enterprise of the Blane family is illustrated by a comparison of the census returns for 1901 and 1911 (Table 12.6). The total number of cambric weavers (comprising all those describing themselves simply as 'weavers') fell by 25% from 509 to 382, affecting both men and women to the same extent. At the same time, however, the number of damask weavers in 1911 would have remained almost the same as in 1901 except for a loss of fifteen men that was peculiar to the townland of Clare. It is worth noting also that of all the 477 inhabitants who described themselves as weavers, 64 or 13% had reached retirement age: this provides

---

[12] Fletcher, G., 'Ireland's industrial opportunities', *Journal of the Department of Agriculture and Technical Instruction* 15, 3 (April, 1915), pp. 482–3. The first paragraph of this quotation was taken word-for-word from the paper detailed in footnote 11.

some indication of the rate of decline that could be attributed to the ageing of the community. The impact of the new Blane enterprise can be assessed from the increased numbers in the relevant trades: there were ten more handkerchief veiners, ten more hemstitchers, eight embroidery workers, and six employed in the stitching factory.[13] While thirty-four of them were women, however, only four were men. In general, therefore, the new enterprises catered for women while men would have had to seek employment in the spinning mill at Gilford or on the bleachgreens along the River Bann that flowed through the southern townlands of the parish.

In the Ulster Folk and Transport Museum a replica of one of the handloom weaver cottages from Ballydugan has been erected to exemplify the style of housing that the weavers had developed. In order to understand the distinctive quality of this housing it is valuable to consider it in the national context.

James Donnelly in his study *The Land and the People of Nineteenth Century Cork* used census returns to argue that 'for the farming classes, these years [1851–91] formed an extraordinary era in home construction – one of the best indications of their increased material welfare.' The figures he published for County Cork are shown in Table 12.7 (percentages in brackets have been added by him),[14] along with comparable figures for County Down.

Although some dissimilarities between the two counties are striking, notably the overall scale of losses and also the percentage of fourth-class housing in 1841, we are conscious that the percentage figures for each class are converging towards 1891. They show that fourth-class housing was fast disappearing and that after 1851 third-class housing was giving way to second-class housing while the percentage of first-class housing was steadily rising. The question is, however, whether or not these changes add up to the claim for 'an extraordinary era in home construction' although there can be no doubt that they indicate that the material welfare of the population was improving.

The method used for the classification of houses had been set out first in the report of the 1841 census:

---

[13] It is probable that an equal number of Blane employees lived in the townland of Ballinagarrick which bordered on Ballydugan.
[14] Donnelly, James, *The Land and People of Nineteenth Century Cork* (Cork, 1975), p. 243.

TABLE 12.7

House construction in Counties Cork and Down, 1841–91

	FIRST-CLASS	SECOND-CLASS	THIRD-CLASS	FOURTH-CLASS	TOTAL
COUNTY CORK					
1841	3,001 (2.5)	20,309 (16.7)	37,304 (30.7)	60,896 (50.0)	121,510
1851	3,624 (4.3)	24,464 (29.0)	39,860 (47.4)	16,197 (19.0)	84,145
1861	3,945 (5.1)	26,552 (34.5)	35,196 (45.8)	11,165 (14.5)	76,858
1871	4,325 (5.8)	29,318 (39.4)	24,621 (33.0)	16,135 (21.7)	74,399
1881	4,937 (7.3)	31,507 (46.3)	27,079 (39.8)	4,561 (6.7)	68,084
1891	5,520 (8.8)	35,668 (57.2)	19,184 (30.8)	1,887 (3.0)	62,259
COUNTY DOWN					
1841	1,451 (2.2)	21,826 (33.5)	27,838 (42.8)	13,987 (21.4)	65,102
1851	2,210 (3.8)	26,352 (45.0)	27,757 (47.5)	2,114 (3.6)	58,433
1861	2,642 (4.6)	28,114 (49.0)	25,246 (44.0)	1,304 (2.3)	57,406
1871	3,234 (5.5)	32,048 (55.0)	18,791 (32.0)	4,270 (7.3)	58,343
1881	3,795 (6.8)	32,561 (58.7)	18,437 (33.0)	662 (1.2)	55,455
1891	4,344 (9.0)	29,760 (61.0)	14,305 (29.0)	332 (1.0)	48,741

The value or condition of a house, as to the accommodation it affords, may be considered to depend mainly on – 1st, its extent, as shown by the number of rooms; 2nd, its quality, as shown by the number of its windows; and 3rd, its solidity or durability, as shown by the material of its walls and roof. If numbers be adopted to express the position of every house in a scale of each of these elements, and if the numbers thus obtained for every house be added together, we shall have a new series of numbers, giving the position of the house in a scale compounded of all the elements, i.e. their actual state. We adopted four classes, and the result was, that in the lowest, or fourth class, were comprised all mud cabins having only one room; in the third, a better description of cottage, still built of mud, but varying from two to four rooms and windows; in the second, a good farm-house, or in towns, a house in a small street, having from five to nine rooms and windows; and, in the first, all houses of a better descrip-tion than the preceding classes.[15]

Although this statement clarifies the intentions of the organisers of the census, the instructions set out for the enumerating constables

[15] *Report of the Commissioners appointed to take the Census of Ireland for the year 1841*, H.C. 1843, XXIV, xiv.

were liable to provoke a variety of results. The criteria were defined for the enumerators as shown in Table 12.8.[16]

TABLE 12.8
Criteria for census enumerators, 1841

(Column 6) **WALLS:** 'If walls are of stone, brick or concrete, enter the figure 1 in this column; if they are of mud, wood, or other perishable material, enter the figure 0.

(Column 7) **ROOF:** 'If roof is of slate, iron, or tiles, enter the figure 1 in this column; if it is of thatch, wood, or other perishable material, enter the figure 0.

(Column 8) **ROOMS:** Enter in this column:

for each house with one room only	the figure 1
for houses with 2, 3 or 4 rooms	2
for houses with 5 or 6	3
for houses with 7, 8 or 9	4
for houses with 10, 11 or 12	5
for houses with 13 or more	6

(Column 9) **WINDOWS IN FRONT:** State in this column the exact number of windows in front of house.

(Column 10) Tot the figure you have entered in columns 6, 7, 8 and 9, and enter the total for each house in this column.

(Column 11) **CLASS OF HOUSE:**

When total in column 10 is:	Enter:
1 or 2	"4th"
3, 4 or 5	"3rd"
6, 7, 8, 9, 10 or 11	"2nd"
12 or over	"1st"

When this system is applied to the Ballydugan, Bleary and Clare community, the results are as shown in Table 12.9. This classification is of little value for our comprehension of the quality of the housing because it conceals the major factor of the durability of the houses as defined in terms of the material used in the construction of the house. This information, as we have seen, is available in the details collected for the classification of the houses and is readily tabulated. It throws

[16] Transcribed from Form 1B – House and Building Return, Census of Ireland, 1901. This layout was adopted for the 1881 census and was used also for 1891 and 1911. Previously, since 1841, particulars had been filled in under the same headings by the enumerators but the classification had been left to the civil servants employed at headquarters by the Commissioners.

TABLE 12.9
Application of house classification criteria to Ballydugan, Bleary and Clare for the years 1901 and 1911

	FIRST		SECOND		THIRD		FOURTH		TOTAL	
	1901	1911	1901	1911	1901	1911	1901	1911	1901	1911
BALLYDUGAN	9	12	91	87	35	27	1	1	136	127
BLEARY	4	8	105	90	72	69	1	3	182	170
CLARE	8	8	68	72	23	17	1	2	100	99
TOTAL	21	28	264	249	130	113	3	6	418	396
	(5.0)	(7.0)	(63.0)	(63.0)	(31.0)	(28.0)	(0.7)	(1.5)		

a completely new light on the whole system of classification. Although the criteria laid down in 1841 suggest that mud houses were relegated to the third and fourth class, an analysis of this community's housing reveals that more than half of the 'mud and thatch' houses were second class in 1911 while two of them were graded first class, indicating that they each contained at least seven to nine rooms and had at least eight windows in the front of the houses. Three-quarters of all the houses in the district were still thatched. By 1911, too, very few of the 'mud and thatch' houses had provided themselves with a permanent roof, which was likely to be made of corrugated iron fitted over the thatch to provide insulation against both cold and sound (see Table 12.10).

At once several discrepancies are apparent between the 1901 and 1911 figures (Table 12.11). The most significant is the considerable increase in the number of 'mud and thatch' houses and the even larger decline in the houses of brick or stone with a thatched roof. This condition is most obvious in Bleary, where the figure for 'brick or stone and thatch' fell from 67 to only 6 inside ten years. The most probable explanation consistent with the census returns is that many houses in the 1901 census were wrongly described as 'brick or stone and thatch' and that this error was rectified by the enumerators in 1911. This suggests that mud houses could look as durable as stone houses to the untrained eye.

TABLE 12.10
Classes of houses related to construction materials, 1911

	MUD AND THATCH	MUD AND PERMANENT ROOF	BRICK OR STONE AND THATCH	BRICK OR STONE AND PERMANENT ROOF	TOTAL
First	2	0	0	26	28
Second	131	9	48	61	249
Third	103	0	8	2	113
Fourth	6	0	0	0	6
TOTAL	242	9	56	89	396
(per cent)	(61.0)	(2.0)	(14.0)	(22.0)	

TABLE 12.11
Construction materials used in houses according to census returns

	MUD AND THATCH		MUD AND PERMANENT ROOF		BRICK OR STONE AND THATCH		BRICK OR STONE AND PERMANENT ROOF		TOTAL	
	1901	1911	1901	1911	1901	1911	1901	1911	1901	1911
BALLYDUGAN	74	68	1	5	41	26	20	28	136	127
BLEARY	102	123	1	3	67	6	12	38	182	170
CLARE	40	51	1	1	43	24	16	23	100	99
TOTAL	216	242	3	9	151	56	48	89	418	396
(per cent)	(52.0)	(61.0)	(0.7)	(2.0)	(36.0)	(14.0)	(14.0)	(22.0)		

Another apparent discrepancy concerns the houses built of brick or stone with a permanent roof of slate or metal. The number had increased from 48 to 89. The explanation, however, is that these new houses were built between the two censuses of 1901 and 1911 as a consequence of the Labourers (Ireland) Acts of 1883 and 1906. After the Local Government Act of 1898 the new Moira Rural District Council assumed responsibility for the housing of labourers in the Tullylish electoral district that comprised, among others, the town-lands of Ballydugan, Bleary and Clare. Early in 1900 the Council met landlords of twenty applicants for labourers' cottages and allotments and when they found that 'in the majority of cases the [immediate] landlords refused to put the house in repair and provide sanitary acco-modation', the councillors decided to formulate an improvement scheme.[17] Their ledger for the Labourers' Acts reveals that by the end of 1910 they had completed 129 houses in their rural district, of which 41 were in the three townlands: 10 in Ballydugan, 27 in Bleary and 4 in Clare.[18] Although the 1911 census records that the 26 (*sic*) houses built in Bleary and owned by Moira Rural Council were all rated in class 2, this fact shows up in any comparison of the census classifications. It is not altogether surprising, then, that the census compilers in both 1901 and 1911 collated the second class and third class figures for each county. They had outlived their usefulness and were no longer a guide for those intent on improving housing conditions in rural areas.

The new labourers' cottages, with their allotments ranging in size from a half to one acre, were available only to labourers. Yet they were built by contractors using the same kinds of materials and techniques that were being used to build new two-storey houses for the wealthier farmers. It was at this time, for example, that cement blocks began to be used in house construction while mass production was increasing the range and variety of clay and metal fittings and pipes. In contrast the occupiers of the 'mud and thatch' houses had no way of improving their houses to any significant extent without demolishing them and rebuilding in the new style. How then can we explain the regular transfer of third class houses into the second class which had been continuing since the Famine? The only factor that must have changed to any considerable extent is the number of rooms in each house – the original houses had either been extended or, more probably, internally subdivided. Alan Gailey has drawn attention to:

> the growth in internal subdivision throughout the nineteenth century. Apparently this was the outcome of a desire for greater privacy in sleeping arrangements, but it involved growing specialisation in the uses to which space was allocated within the dwelling. Separation of some of the multiple social and economic functions of the traditional kitchen was part of this same process, giving rise to the concept of the parlour or 'room' in farmhouses all over Ireland. It is another matter to try to detect the motivations underlying these changes. Certainly, changing attitudes to the quality of family life during the

[17] PRONI LA/54/2F/1, Minute Book of Moira Rural District Council: Minutes re Labourers (Ireland) Acts, 237–8, Thursday 25 January 1900.
[18] PRONI LA/54/12E/1, Labourers' Acts Ledger of Moira Rural District Council, 1900–15.

nineteenth century are involved.[19]

It is significant that Donnelly chose to support his claim that the late nineteenth century represented 'an extraordinary era in home construction' for the farming classes by pointing out 'that substantial dwellings with five to nine rooms (second-class houses in the language of the census) rose by 76 per cent between 1841 and 1891'. Gailey's explanation for 'the growth of internal subdivision', thereby increasing the number of rooms in cottages, undermines Donnelly's assertion.

Unless similar investigations are made into other handloom-weaving districts there is a danger that this study will be used to generalise about the social and economic effects of the decline of handloom weaving on Ulster communities. It should be remembered, however, that this paper concentrates on a community that was engaged in weaving cambric for handkerchiefs and damask for tablecloths: its most significant characteristics are the scale of the participation of women in weaving and the number of tenants with families engaged at the loom. In contrast it is probable that the social structure and the participation of women may have been different in the Ballymena area where handloom weaving survived into the twentieth century. It would be interesting also to apply the same exercise to districts where the shirt and underclothing trades were engaged in putting-out work, such as Donegal and Londonderry, as well as districts in Down and Donegal that were famous for embroidery: these skills were practised by women and so they were assets in a community where there were fewer opportunities for men. Comparative studies should help us to understand the significance of the factors that determined why and how some communities were involved in textile crafts while others were not.

The study of communities provides a valuable methodology for local and regional historians. It integrates and focuses many disparate studies. It enables us to compare and contrast their characters and experiences. A wide range of sources can be used to broaden and deepen the investigation. Although many local historians have used

---

[19] Gailey, R.A., 'Some developments and adaptations of traditional house types', in O Danachair, C. (ed.), *Folk and Farm* (Dublin, 1976), p. 69; see also the same author's *Rural Houses of the North of Ireland* (Edinburgh, 1984), especially Chapter 9.

provincial newspapers few have investigated the legal cases to discover the tensions within the community. How much can be learned from the records of the local board of guardians, the town commissioners and later the district councils? Valuable evidence about the community can often be uncovered from government reports or 'blue books' as well as the journals and annual reports issued by government departments such as the Local Government Board.

And it is at this level too that we have to examine local politics and the relationships between the religious sects.[20] It is not difficult to understand why in the Ballydugan district in the decade 1910–19 two halls were built by the Ancient Order of Hibernians as well as a third Orange Hall. Local people will know the background to their construction and the names of the individuals who organised local politics. An intimate knowledge of such grassroots politics would deepen our understanding of the contemporary crisis in Ulster.

---

[20] See, for example, Fitzpatrick, D., *Politics and Irish Life 1913–21: Provincial Experience of War and Revolution* (Dublin, 1977).

APPENDIX 1

Thomas Turner
New methods of improving flax
and flax-seed and bleaching cloth[1]

(P. 3) DIRECTIONS FOR THE IMPROVEMENT OF
FLAX AND FLAX-SEED

It is found by experience, that when flax-seed is sown on a thin and poor soil (which is frequently done) the roots meeting with a gravel or cold clay, the growth of the flax is starved, it grows short and weak, and the seed degenerates.

We may also frequently observe yellow, red and brown rows, and much sprit in cloth, all which faults arise from the poorness and thinness of the soil in which the seed was sewn, that is not able to nourish the root, so that the flax has generally but a weak stem; which by the heat of the sun and weather (p. 4) turns of a brownish or reddish colour long before it be ripe.

For remedy whereof, make choice of fresh land and good soil, which for some years past has been grazed upon. In the months of September or October, lay it over with dung, digging or ploughing it down soon after. In December following or thereabouts, as the weather proves open and fair, harrow it well and cross plough it after. If the land be of a clayey substance it will require four ploughings; but if otherwise, three will serve. After the last ploughing and harrowing, lest the land should want depth to give the seed its full growth, divide the land into ridges of fifteen or sixteen feet broad or less, but that according to the wetness or dryness of the land, marking it out as is most convenient for carrying off the water. Between each ridge mark out eight foot, the mould of which is to be thrown on the ridges on each side, so as to make the (p. 5) mould on the ridges one third

179

thicker, which will cause a furrow between each ridge, resembling a potato-garden. To prepare the flax-seed for sowing, you must steep it in new milk about two days, which will nourish and swell it, then sow it, taking one fourth less than is commonly used in this kingdom, viz. instead of four bushels to an acre take but three, and so in proportion to the quantity of ground to be sowed. By this method the flax will be long and strong, the seed good, and yield a good increase. This kind of flax will make the best sort of cloth, and take a better colour, and sooner than that which is produced by a thin soil, and the charges sufficiently recompensed.

SOME CAUTIONS TO BE OBSERVED IN WATERING FLAX

The blackish and bluish rows in cloth always arise from watering the flax in black turf-bogs that yield red ashes. These bogs contract a black (p. 6) slimy dirt at the bottom of the water which dyes or stains the flax, so that it will never bleach to a true white, which is only to be prevented by making choice of good water. The best in my opinion, is in your turf-bogs, commonly called flow-bogs, that produce great quantities of white fog growing in the water: flax watered in this comes soon to a good colour. Loughs are very proper, or ponds drawn from rivers so contrived, that they may easily be drained to bring fresh water to your flax. Rather under water than over water your flax, and when you spread it on the grass do it very thin, and turn it according to your discretion to prevent its mildewing, which is another very frequent cause of rows in cloth.

NEW DIRECTIONS FOR THE BETTER BLEACHING
LINEN-CLOTH AND YARN

Buck [wash] your hollands or other linen-cloth either with green buck, or with leys [lye or detergent] made of fern-ashes, kelp or (p. 7) pot-ashes, or both fern-ashes and kelp mist [mixed?], or pot-ashes alone, according to the common methods; but be sure at the end of every bucking before you lay them on the bleach-yard to bat and rench [English dialect for rinse] the leys very clear out of the cloth, which must be done on the batting-plank and planking-floor hereafter both described. For the common practise of spreading it with leys in it, is no manner of benefit to it; but on the contrary the leys drying in the cloth, stain it and give it a yellowness, the taking out of which will oblige you to let it lie longer in the sower [sour from buttermilk], than otherwise would be necessary, and consequently weakens it.

When you have given your cloth the first buck, carry it to the batting-plank, which must be thus prepared. Take a plank of oak, ash, or fir, if the other two cannot easily be had, they being most proper and lasting; let it be ten or twelve inches broad and five feet long, rather longer than shorter, which plank may be called a cleansing or batting- (p. 8) plank. Cut in it a round or square hole of three inches diameter within a foot of the end, and equidistant from the two sides. Prepare also a kieve or vessel near three foot high and about as much diameter. Prepare also a small hand batt, being a flat piece of wood about twenty inches long, four broad, and one and a half-thick, part of it being cut into a handle. Place the plank cross the top of the kieve or vessel to be ready for the work, first putting cold water into it. The cloth being bucked the first time ready to be taken out of the bucking-kieve, take one or more pieces and put them into the vessel that is under the plank, soaking them in the cold water; then take one piece and put the two ends of it up the hole laying it on the plank, holding it with one hand, and turning it as it is gently beaten with the bat. This loosens the ley bucking, and cleanses the cloth from it. Continue drawing it through the plank and batting it in this manner until the whole piece be cleansed, (p. 9) letting the cloth as it is batted pass down into the vessel out of which it was drawn.

Having thus far cleansed one or more pieces on the plank, they must be carried to the planking-floor, which must be thus prepared. Take ten or twelve deal boards, plane and nail them upon a frame of several strong joists, as is done in flooring. Place this frame on the brink of a good watering place, bring your cloths to this floor, lash fair water on all parts of it, beating it with your planking-poles, such as are used by dyers, till it appear well renched from the ley-buck. Then lay it on the bleach-yard, water and expose it there in the usual manner four days or a week. Take it up when near dry, and let it undergo a second course of bucking as before, repeating it to four or five times for fine and thin cloths. Others will require six or seven of those ley-bucks, all which must be governed by observation.

NEXT FOLLOWS SOAP-BUCKING

(p. 10) Take the cloth to the kieve that lies under your batting-plank, and being wet with fair water, draw it by the two ends up the hole over the plank, that you may rub soap on it all over, letting it fall into the same kieve of water. Then draw it by the two ends up the hole in the plank, beating it gently with the batt as it is turned with the other hand, letting it fall into the vessel again; by which means the soap will pierce through all parts of the cloth. Four pounds of soap will serve for twenty pieces of holland, of twenty three yards each. When this is done, lay it in the bucking kieve, bucking it with warm water, in the same manner as the ley-bucking. Continue this soap bucking but five hours, then batt it on the plank, rench it on the floor, and lay it on the green, watering and letting it lie four days. When it is dry, it is ready for sour liquor, which is thus prepared.

TO MAKE A GOOD SOUR

(p. 11) Put fair [clean] warm water into a kieve or vessel of size sufficient to contain the pieces of cloth in hand. To the quantity of each half barrel of water, put eight quarts of wheat or oat-meal, or of both mixed, or of any other grain if you have not of the former, mixing the meal or warm water well. Cover up the vessel very close for twenty-four hours, or thereabouts, till the liquor becomes sour, adding four quarts of buttermilk to each half barrel of water, or more if to be had. And to increase the sharpness, add the juice of three or four handfuls of sorrel: when that is not to be had, you may instead put three ounces of burnt alum, or any other innocent [innocuous or harmless] sharps. The sour being thus prepared, well stirred up, and mixed with the meal which lay at the bottom, put the cloth therein, and in an open manner the better to receive the liquor, and either with staves or men's feet, it may be so worked as to (p. 12) become full of the liquor. Let it remain thus forty-eight hours. Place your plank over this kieve if not too large, else over its usual vessel or kieve. Then bring a piece of the cloth out of the sour, drawing it double up the hole in the plank, and batting it as before. Then put it into the same sour, let it lie forty-eight hours more; take it thence and batt it a second time. Then take it to the planking-floor to water out all the sour liquor. This course must be repeated a second, third or fourth time according as the cloth requires. Between the souring and soaping, you may give hollands a bucking of leys made of pot-ashes, always taking care to batt and rench the leys well out before you spread them on the bleachyard. When your cloth is come to a perfect good colour, take some buttermilk, and three times as much water, handle your cloth well in it, then rench it clear in water only, and so take it up. The use of this buttermilk is not only for the (p. 13) colour, but to make it handle well and like Dutch hollands. Make use of stone and powder-blue mixed, and the finest starch you can get, and observe, that light blueing is best for very white cloth.

DIRECTIONS FOR HIGH WHITENING YARN IN A SHORTER TIME THAN HAS YET BEEN PRACTISED, FIT FOR DOWLASS, TAPES, TICKS, ETC.

After yarn is soaked in cold water, batt, rench and wring it according to the usual method, then lay it in the bucking-kieve. Spread several courses one above another to the thickness of eight or nine inches. Spread thereon ashes of the country make, the quantity of a bushel to one layer, if the kieve be five foot broad and so in proportion. Then lay a like course of yarn and a like course of ashes, till the kieve be full. A strong ley of ashes being prepared, the kieve of yarn must be bucked therewith. (p. 14) Following the buck [leave it] twenty-four [hour]s day and night. Take it thence and lay it in cold water to soak a while, then batt it gently turning it on the plank, thence to the planking-floor, which will cleanse it from all the first bucking, then wring it and spread it thin on the bleaching green, letting it lie there two weeks, turning it each week. Then proceed to a second bucking, putting no ashes between the courses of yarn in the kieve; but instead place a sheet over the head of the kieve, and therein put about a bushel of fern-ashes only, the quantity more or less according to the size of the kieve. Follow this second bucking (but with a weaker ley than the first) for one day, then gently batt and rench out the ley, spread it on the grass, and let it lie as before. Repeat this course a third time. When that is finished, prepare a good suds of soap, dissolved and beat up in warm water, in which lay your yarn, then batt it gently on the plank, turning it as before. Then give it a bucking with water and soap without any ley, then rench the soap, buck out in fair water and lay it on the green. If this do not make it white enough, you must repeat another soap buck, renching it and laying it on the green as before. When you take it up you must rench it in fair water, wring it and hang it up to dry.

[1] Printed by Andrew Crooke, Printer to the King's Most Excellent Majesty, in Copper Alley, Dublin, 1715 [Hanson 2116]. Punctuation and spelling modernised.

APPENDIX 2

The case of the linen manufacture of Ireland, relative to the bleaching and the whitening the same [1]

Humbly offered and submitted, to the wisdom and consideration of the Right Honourable, and Honourable, the Trustees thereof.

That our linen manufacture is in an increasing, and not declining, state, may appear by an abstract, taken from the Custom House books, from the year 1723 when the quantity exported was 3,864,987 yards, to the year 1749, when it was 9,504,339 yards. That although in the intermediate years, this increase has not been always proportionable, some years being less than those preceding, yet this is easily accounted for, by considering the price of grain in each year: it being certain that when grain was scarce and dear, the quantity was greater; and when cheap, the less – cheap grain making always idle hands. And it is remarkable in said Custom-House returns, that the great decline between the years 1745 and 1746, was occasioned by the rebellion being in Scotland, and French privateers being on our coasts; and in 1747, when those obstructions were removed, the surplus of the year 1746, being exported in 1747, made the exports of that year greater than in any other year. Some check was also given to the growth of this manufacture, by the great number of weavers, not less than 2,000, enlisting as soldiers, during the late war, who, had they stuck to their looms, would have wove, at least, 50 pounds worth of cloth each in the year, amounting to 100,000 pounds yearly, loss to this kingdom. And many of their wives and children, who were spinners, followed them out of this kingdom; and few of them have again returned. But what seems most worthy of observation under this head is, that for a course of several years past, the exporters have never met with any material discouragement, in regard to exportation, from their goods continuing unsold at the close of the year,

185

there still appearing to them a full demand for whatever quantity of goods their country can find hands to manufacture and send to market.

That the well-bleaching of linen is the greatest improvement of the trade; and whilst the manufacture was in its infancy in this kingdom, was found the most difficult to be brought to perfection, and was not only tedious but also expensive and hazardous in the performance.

That many years ago a person of ingenuity, by trying many experiments for the improvement of the colours of our linen, found out a method of improving the colour by rubbing the same with soap on boards, that on this improvement of colour, and not before, our linen began to gain reputation abroad. And as this method of rubbing improved, our linens were likewise improved in colour and made better; and it was found by experience that they might be bleached thereby with much more expedition than by any other means. That by a constant practice of this method, and by observing the benefit on the one hand, and the inconveniencies on the other hand attending it, some person, more sagacious than the rest; considering that the cloth was sometimes damaged by the rubbing, thought of a method of preventing that damage by altering the manner of working with said boards; and, instead of rubbing the cloth, as first practised, contrived to make the cloth to roll between the boards with a sufficient quantity of soap rubbed thereon. And when, by experience, it was found that the finest linen and cambrics would undergo the operation of these boards much longer than was necessary to bring them to a complete colour, without hurting the fabric or injuring them in any material degree. And as a further improvement, the said rubbing, or rather rolling-boards, were wrought by the equal uniform power of water-mills, whereby much labour is saved. And this method has been found, by experience, so advantageous that great numbers of persons have, at a very great expence, erected mills of this kind and have brought the bleaching to be a very considerable branch of trade, many persons of substance having embarked their fortunes in that way; and by means of those mills, the manufacturers of this kingdom are enabled to go to market with their linens much sooner than they otherwise could, and can, with proper care and diligence, make THREE RETURNS in the year; but without them, not more than ONE. And the disproportion, in point of labour, is still greater, as by the help of those mills more pieces of linen can be bleached with ten hands than fifty hands would do by our former, or even in the Dutch methods.

That some years ago it was objected that the Dutch made as good or better colours in Holland without the assistance of rubbing boards, than we in Ireland do with them. Whereupon several pieces of Irish linen were privately sent to Holland and put to bleach there, without permitting the Dutch to know from whence they came. And though they kept them a much longer time in bleaching than we do, yet when they came back, they were not near so good colours as those bleached here, though our bleaching be performed much sooner than the Dutch do, or can do by their methods.

That it is well known to all persons skilled in bleaching, that the longer linens lie on the grass, and the stronger and more corroding the lees are made, and the sharper the sours, etc. used to them are, they are by so much the more damnified, made more tender, and rotted thereby; and that without long lying on the grass, and frequent boiling in strong lee, linens cannot be brought to a high colour and sufficient white, without the help of those mills.

That those mills are of a very plain and simple construction, little liable to go out of order, and easily kept in repair, and the quantity of soap necessary to keep the linen perfectly safe, is insignificant when compared with the labour, insomuch that nothing but the most extreme carelessness and ignorance in the person using or attending them, occasions any damage to the linen in the use of them. That it is found by happy experience, that the colours of Irish linens now equal, if not exceed the Dutch, and that the Irish linens are come into such reputation for strength and colour, that no linens sell preferable to them in foreign markets, so that the increase of our linen trade is chiefly owing to our improvement in bleaching.

That these mills are come into a very high and great reputation in Scotland, insomuch that several persons have come from thence to view our mills, and procure models of them, and have taken millwrights from this kingdom to erect mills of the like kind in Scotland, and have accordingly erected several rubbing mills there.

That were those mills to be laid aside, it would be, in a great measure, the entire loss of the bleaching trade of this kingdom, as without the help of rolling mills, fine linen cannot be made a high white; and as the carriage of our linen to Scotland, and bleaching it there by mills, would be cheaper and more expeditious than the bleaching could be performed here by any other method yet known to us.

That many experiments have been tried in relation to the bleaching of linen and cambrics with and without these mills, all of which have convinced the persons concerned, that bleaching with the help of mills is the most expeditious, the cheapest, and best way of bleaching linen: the most expeditious, because performed in half the time; cheapest, because it doth save three parts in four of the labour; best, because it doth give the highest white to the linen, equal, nay superi-or to the Dutch, and with less injury to the fabric, than by any other manner of bleaching yet discovered.

All the considerable dealers concerned in the manufacturing and bleaching of linen, are now fully satisfied, by frequent experience, that provided a due quantity of soap be made use of, and the rolling mills be rightly formed, and well attended, no damage whatever can arise from the mills, nor can any lint or cotton fall from the cloth, whilst it is kept moist and well soaped; and they are persuaded that no man of common sense or honesty would hazard the spoiling of his cloth by saving a little soap of small value, which may be bought cheaper and better for the purpose in Ireland than in any other country in Europe, considering that tallow and fern-ashes, of which it is made, may be had in great abundance among us.

It is not pretended that our mills and engines are as yet brought to the highest degree of perfection, as they are capable of great improve-ments; and it is not to be doubted but that in a few years, by the art and contrivance of ingenious men, they will be brought to a much greater degree of perfection, which will make ample amends for the unfitness of our climate, and put us more than on a level with other countries, who have greater natural advantages for bleaching linen.

---

[1] c.1750 [Hanson 6429] Endorsed: A state of the case in relation to the rolling boards made use of in the linen manufacture of Ireland.

APPENDIX 3

*Serious considerations on the
present alarming state of agriculture
and the linen trade, by a farmer*

INTRODUCTION

Students of eighteenth-century Ireland know Arthur Young's famous diatribe against the linen industry in Ulster written after his celebrated tour in the late 1770s. It opens:

> Change the scene, and view the North of Ireland; you there behold a whole province peopled by weavers; it is they who cultivate, or rather beggar the soil, as well as work the looms; agriculture is there in ruins; it is cut up by the root; extirpated; annihilated; the whole region is the disgrace of the kingdom; all the crops you see are contemptible; nothing but filth and weeds. No other part of Ireland can exhibit the soil in such a state of poverty and desolation.

The tone of this comment does not accord well with Young's observations as he made his way through Ulster, and nowhere does he spell out the evidence for his criticisms. It may be that his recollections were coloured by comments that had been made to him by agricultural improvers during his visit. He might even have read this pamphlet dedicated to Richard Robinson, Lord Rokeby and Primate of All Ireland (Church of Ireland), one of his most influential informants, and published only a few years before his visit.

The writer of this pamphlet claims that his reasons for considering the subject sprang from a discussion about the causes of 'the great emigration of the lower kind of people to America'. He traced them back to the fundamental economic and social problems brought about by the rapid spread of the domestic linen industry throughout the countryside. In contrast to Young, however, he has explained how and why farmer-weavers managed to 'beggar the soil'. Their major problem was lack of capital to stock the smallholdings – for farms averaging ten acres belie any other appellation – buy their seed, and allow their crops to reach maturity before harvest. The writer describes the difficulties of new families in establishing their farms as well as maintaining production of cloth.

The author deals only with the earliest stage of the family cycle, however, pointing out how the nursing of children deprived a man of the help of his wife in the field and at the loom. To recover from these expensive years there was a strong temptation for a couple to use the labour of their children as soon as it became available. A girl could spin by the age of four while a boy could assist his father at the loom until he was strong enough to weave about the age of fourteen. Especially in their teens children proved a real asset to the fortunes of a family. Problems returned when they wished to marry. If the parents wished to retain their support they had to set up the couple on a patch of land cut out of their own holding. Subdivision among members of the families was the consequence so that farms continued to be fragmented. An alternative to exploiting one's own family was to let land out to cottiers. In return for working for the farmer-weaver they might be allowed the use of a 'dry cot-take' for planting potatoes, or a 'wet cot-take' that would include sufficient grass for a cow.

In the long term such continuous, intense subdivision produced great population densities, especially in north Armagh where the finest linens were produced. The 1841 census records the population of the barony of Oneilland East in the north-east corner of the county, including the town of Lurgan (4,205 persons) as 23,391 people living on 20,890 acres, a density of 716 to the square mile. A thousand people to the square mile was considerably exceeded in several rural townlands.

THE PAMPHLET

(p. v) To His Grace Dr. Richard Robinson, Primate of All Ireland, &c.

My Lord,

A very principal gentleman of this county, in whose company I had the honour of spending a few hours (p. vi) some time since, asked me, what

I thought might be the cause of the great emigration of the lower kind of people to America?

The question, I found upon reflection, involved matters of the utmost consequence to this Kingdom – agriculture and the linen trade; for which reason, I have bestowed some time and pains in considering it; and, if I have been able to discuss it with accuracy and precision, I trust it will be found not altogether unworthy of your Grace's attention and patronage.

The many great and lasting improvements, planned and executed by your Grace, for the public good, (p. vii) while they fill us with wonder and gratitude, are a certain pledge of your receiving favourably any attempt to follow, though at the most humble distance, your Grace's patriotic example.

I am, with the most profound respect, My Lord, Your Grace's most devoted, most obedient, and most humble servant, A FARMER. Armagh September 1, 1773.

(p. 9) In this age of improvement of the arts and sciences, it will not I hope be thought presuming, or impertinent, in one who affects no higher character than that of a rational practical farmer, to point out (p. 10) to the public, a scheme of profitable agriculture, which, while it enriches the farmer, will diffuse plenty of all sorts of provisions, through this manufacturing country, at a much cheaper rate, than they can now be sold for, from the wretched pitiful crops that we see yearly produced, by the present barbarous method of tilling the ground.

My ideas, which I shall endeavour to prove to be founded on facts, will probably expose me to much censure; but relying wholly on the integrity of my heart, and conceiving it to be the duty of every honest man to contribute, as much as in his power, to the Public Good; I shall not scruple to lay down the following axioms:

First, That the present mode of letting small farms to weavers, is extremely injudicious and prejudicial to this kingdom; and next, that such farms are never cultivated, in that spirited masterly manner, as is necessary for procuring that plenty of the fruits of the earth, which the providence of God, in His great bounty and goodness to man, hath given it a capability of.

To illustrate what I have to say on that subject, I must beg leave to suppose a tract of one thousand (p. 11) square acres of land, inhabited by one hundred weaving families each supported, in some measure, by the produce of its little farm of ten acres. This supposition will, I believe, be allowed to be no unfair representation of the whole of this manfacturing country, with some very few exceptions; and if I can demonstrate, that these little farmers, from their inability, by reason of their poverty or ignorance, do not raise above one-fourth part of the provisions, which their land would produce under a spirited rational culture; one of the points which I endeavour to establish, will be allowed me, and the other must of necessity fall in with it.

Let us then observe the weaver seated in his little farm, what will be his management of it? He begins generally with a capital not exceeding four pounds, including his loom, and with his wife's fortune, (seldom so much, but scarce ever more) he may possibly add a small cow, and some wretched furniture for his cabin. Unable to keep a team, or even a single galloway, he must with patience wait till his more (p. 12) wealthy neighbour hath finished his spring labour, and then, when his corn should be four or five inches above ground, he hires the farmer's jaded team to scratch up the surface of four acres of his little farm for oats from a lay of three years when it has been perfectly exhausted by his predecessor. On this he sows twenty bushels of seed which by giving him three months credit for, the farmer hath supplied him with, at twenty-five shillings per boll of ten bushels, when the price for money is only twenty shillings. And if he hath been fortunate and diligent enough to scrape up from about his door a little dung, (well stored with dock and nettle seed) he must hire a horse to carry it out, and with two days of his own labour, to spread it in the lazy-bed way, and the help of another as poor as himself, and his wife to lay the sets, he plants four bushels of potatoes, which he is to pay for, in about a month, at the rate of eighteen-pence per bushel, the current price being then only thirteen-pence, or fourteen-pence. (But I have known them buy potatoes upon credit for two shillings per bushell, when I was selling some of a much superior kind at (p. 13) sixteen pence.) The drawing out his dung, as well as the help he hath had in setting his potatoes, together with the ploughing and harrowing of his little spot under culture, must all be paid by his own labour; for the farmer, to avoid disbursing any money, makes it a condition to be paid for the use of his horses, by the weaver's help, in setting and weeding his potatoes, and digging them out, and assisting in making his hay, turf, &c. to the unspeakable loss of the linen trade.

He hath found too in his farm, a rood of potato ground; this he gets laboured on the same terms as for his oats, and sows it with two pecks of flax seed, which some conscionable retailer of that commodity hath generously granted him a few months credit for, at the moderate advance of one or two shillings per week, above the ready money price; and if the credit given is for a longer time, the price rises beyond all (p. 14) degrees of proportion, so as to amount frequently to the double of what it sold for in the sowing season. His little spring labour being thus slovened over, his wife can then and not before, sit down to her wheel, and he to his loom, for five or six weeks, after which it will require the full exertion of their joint labours, to keep his little farm tolerably clean from weeds, and repay the engagements which he is under for tilling it. Five acres remain under grass, if such it may be called, which hath been perfectly exhausted by his predecessor; however such as it is, he contrives, with it and the assistance of the high road, to keep his little beast from starving the first year: he hath besides about half an acre of flat, wet, spritty ground, which he calls meadow. About the middle or latter end of July, impelled by hunger and want of credit, he begins to dig up his potatoes though not half arrived at maturity, so that by the end of November, they are above two-thirds consumed. If the linen trade hath been favourable to him, (that is if a number of (p. 15) commissioners, who lay out other folk's money, or ignorant foolish young men, who are vain of shewing what large quantities they buy, have been busy in the markets) our little motley man, half weaver, and half farmer, hath contrived not to run in debt above two or three pounds.

His oats of four acres with the wretched culture they have had, do not produce more than one hundred bushels, which, if he hath not been forced to sell on the spot to pay his debts and rent, must now be disposed of, at the best price he can (at that cheap season) get for it, seldom exceeding thirteen-pence per bushel: he then sits down to his loom and his wife, as much as her state of pregnancy or nursing, will permit, to her wheel, and if the linen trade hath still continued favourable to him, that is, if he hath got for his web more than every true friend of this country should wish it to be sold for, who opens his eyes to future events and sees that the many powerful rivals we have in that branch, should induce, us, by every honest means, to undersell them; if this, I say, hath been the case, he may, perhaps, notwithstanding (p. 16) his loss in farming, have wrought himself clear of debt, by the time his spring labour comes round again.

This loss upon his farm, together with his expenses in housekeeping, for at least one-half of the year, must all be paid for out of the profits of his weaving; a melancholy reflection to the true friends of this unhappy infatuated country; especially when we consider, that the major part of the linen made here is coarse, and that the weaving farmer cannot by reason of his many avocations, work above fifteen double pieces in the year, consequently, there is an unnecessary load of near three shillings and six-pence laid on each piece, which is about one penny per yard, a trifle under.

(p. 17) (1) Dr. the Weaver's Farm of 10 acres, at 14s. per acre rent & taxes

	£	s.	d.	Cr.	£	s.	d.
To rent and taxes	7	0	0	By ten bolls of oats, @10s. 10d.	5	8	4
Ploughing for oats, four acres@ 5s. per ditto	1	0	0	6 stone of scutched flax @ 5 1/2 d. per pound (great produce)	1	18	6
20 Bushels oats, seed, @ 2s. 6d.	2	10	0	1/2 acre of hay (high price)	1	0	0
Sowing, harrowing @ 2s. 6d.	0	10	0	Grazing for hire, a small heifer	0	10	6
Drawing out dung for potatoes, and spreading	0	3	10	35 bushels of potatoes, at 8d	1	3	4
2 men setting, a boy to lay	0	2	1	Straw	1	17	0
4 bushels potato seed, @ 1s. 6d.	0	6	0		11	17	8
Ploughing and sowing one rood for flax	0	2	0				
2 Pecks, flax seed, @ 2s. 6d.	0	5	0				
Weeding corn, flax and potatoes	0	10	0				
Reaping oats	0	15	0	Lost this year by the farm, (besides victualling women who attended the flax)*	2	11	11
Tythe of oats, @ 2s. meadow, and small dues 2/6	0	10	6		14	9	7
Pulling flax, 2 women 1 day	0	1	1				
Drowning, Lifting, spreading	0	1	1				
Drying with turf, beetling	0	3	3				
6 Women scutching	0	3	3				
Digging potatoes	0	2	8 1/2				
Cutting meadow, 6 1/2 d., winnowing hay 1s. 1d., bringing home, and stacking, 2s. 2d.	0	3	9 1/2				
	14	9	7				

(p. 18) His second year's management is a transcript of the former, except that he takes from his pasture a rood of ground for potatoes, and sows with oats that which was nearly exhausted last year by his flax: this, while it diminishes his pasture, makes but a poor amends by tillage, as the oats after his flax do not yield above five bushels, and then he turns it out to rest for at least three years: His crop of four acres of oats, being the second from lay, is rather more favourable than the former, and he reaps one hundred and (p. 19) twenty bushels at the harvest. But as his family increases, the labour of his wife is consequently less, and though the linen trade hath still been brisk yet it requires his whole diligence and activity to wipe himself clear of debt by the following spring; for notwithstanding his crop of oats hath exceeded that of the former year twenty-five bushels yet the loss of the greater part of his wife's labour, hath deprived him of all the advantage of it.

(p. 20) Dr. the Weaver's Farm the second year

	£ s. d.	Cr.	£ s. d.
To rent and charges as before	14 9 7	By produce as before	11 17 8
Ploughing and sowing with oats one rood of last year's flax ground	0 1 10 1/2	Additional produce more than last year on 4 acres of oats	1 1 8
5 Pecks of seed oats for it	0 3 11	5 Bushels on a rood of flax	0 5 5
Additional tythes	6	Additional straw more than last year, 37 stooks @ 3d	0 9 3
	14 15 1	Lost this year by the farm	1 1 1
			14 15 1

But the third year is the most distressful, for then, as his family increaseth in number, his crop decreaseth in quantity, as well as quality.

(p. 21) Dr. the Weaver's Farm the third year

	£ s. d.	Cr.	£ s. d.
To rent and charges as before	14 15 1	By 8 bolls of oats @ 9s. 9d.	3 18 0
		Flax, hay & potatoes as before	3 17 5 1/2
		By straw, 160 stooks @ 2d	1 6 8
		*Lost this year by the farm	5 12 11 1/2
			14 15 1

*Which upon 15 pieces of linen is a tax of 7s. 6d. each, above 2d. per yard.

(p. 22) His four acres, which are still in oats, produce no more than eighty bushels of a poor starved grain; and his wife's inability, by her increase of family, to assist as before, obliges him to hire a boy, to attend his loom, and help to weed his crop, which from an injudicious course of slovenly tillage, requires it more than ever. More provisions must be had, and unable as he is to buy them, but from hand to mouth, he must in the spring, provide as he wants them, at an extravagant rate. Happy if the high price of linen enable him to stand his ground, indebted only four or five pounds. Every year afterwards, his circumstances grow worse and worse; so that to escape a jail, he makes a moon-light flitting, as it is called, and flies to England or America, or perhaps attaches himself to the service of some more wealthy neighbour, with whom he ever after-wards lives in a state of wretched dependence, of absolute beggary and vassalage. And here I appeal to most country gentlemen, whether they do not find many such about them; for my own part, I employ three of them in my little farm, and occasionally several of their children, (p. 23) who must otherwise have starved or gone a begging, and a great part of those whom I call in at hay and corn harvest, &c. consists of such. What then, will it be asked, shall we do with this very useful body of men to whose skill and labour we are indebted for our (only free) trade? I answer, if you wish the linen trade to flourish among us let them stick to their looms and, if they must have land, let them hold no more than is neces-sary for one or two cows' grass. Throw your estates into farms from one to three hundred acres to be let to men who are able to cultivate them to the best advantage. Let these be discouraged under the most severe penalties, viz. double rents, from letting any part of them beyond a cot-ter's take of three or four acres to one family, and oblige them also to pay an advanced rent for all their meadow and pasture beyond a certain pro-portion of their farm so as always to have at least two-thirds of it in labour. Let a judicious course of tillage be laid down for them and con-strain them under heavy penalties to observe it. No more scratching the ground for three successive crops of oats and then (p. 24) leaving it, as they term it, to rest, as naked as the high road, five acres of which would scarcely keep a cow in flesh. Instead of that, substitute the following course or something similar, so as never to have two crops of white corn succeeding each other.

1 Potatoes with plough or dibble, to be cleaned with horse or hand-hoe
2 Bere or barley
3 Clover one year for meadow

4 Wheat
5 Peas or beans, well-hoed
6 Oats
7 Turnips, well-hoed, and a slight dressing for
8 Wheat or barley
9 Flax, and then potatoes as before.

With such a course the farmer would take treble crops from the ground and would consequently be enabled to sell provisions at a much cheaper rate than he can now raise them for. The weaver having no avocation from his loom, could give up his whole time and attention to it and make at least eight or ten (p. 25) pieces more in the year, and of better cloth, than he can do now; and by the low price of provisions he could afford to sell his linens at such a rate as to command a constant foreign demand for them. Whereas (I shudder at the thought) if things are suffered to go on in the same course in which they have moved for some time past, we shall be undersold in all foreign markets; and when once the Dutch, French, German, and Russian linens have obtained some time, we shall find it next to impossible to get sale for ours. Let us not flatter ourselves. Our good friends the English and Americans will never think themselves obliged to take our goods if they are dearer or of an inferior quality to what they can import from other manufacturing countries. All that they owe us and indeed all that we have a right to expect from them, is to give us the preference of their money, the price and quality of our goods considered. I have now in my possession some remnants of hempen and flaxen Russian linens which I bought in London, at the third hand from the importer, where no doubt every man had his profit, (and which, moreover, had paid a heavy duty) which (p. 26) are cheaper and better than any I can procure in this manufacturing country. And yet it is a favourite maxim with many of our country gentlemen, that our brown linens can never be too high, not once reflecting upon the number of our competitors ready to undersell us nor that a trade where the profits between buyer and seller are not reciprocal must be of short duration. About thirty months since, when upon some expected demand for the American markets (in which however we were sadly disappointed) our brown linens rose to an extravagant price, I have known many gentlemen overjoyed at it, not considering that so unnatural a rise in the staple trade of a manufacturing country must in the nature of things soon subside and that lands then taken at the extreme high rents which the unthinking weaver then foolishly imagined the profit of his web would enable him to pay, must consequently sink as much below their real value whenever such a reverse as we now feel, happened; inasmuch as by far the greater part of their estates are let to such who are now so absolutely dispirited that they have not yet determined how low they would reduce their rents.

(p. 27) But I think I hear the landed gentry say, 'Can you seriously advise us to lower our rents at least one third of their present value?' No gentlemen, I am not so unreasonable. I would, on the contrary, wish to secure to you an advantageous and certain value of your lands independent of the accidental fluctuations of trade, without being exposed to the failure of the tenantry on the one hand or laying yourselves, as is now likely to be the case, at the mercy of a set of poor desponding, dispirited weavers who are for the present utterly unable to secure to you above one-half of your late rents. The farmer, such as I have mentioned, can very well afford to give you thirteen or fourteen shillings per English acre, and where he is not above one or two miles removed from good, natural manures, he will grow rich by it (if at a greater distance, some abatement should be made him) and I dare say that most gentlemen would be well satisfied with such rents. I know indeed some poor wretches who engage to pay twenty shillings and a guinea per (p. 28) acre; but they hold in general the third or fourth removed from the lord of the soil under a set of unfeeling task masters who keep them naked and half starved in a perpetual state of bondage. Would gentlemen take the trouble of informing themselves of the wretched condition of such people, they would not fail to prevent, by every public means, that kind of subdivision of their farms. But some mistaken advocates of the weavers will say, 'What, sir, would you degrade this very useful body of men into the abject state of cotters?' Mistake me not, good sirs, I look upon them as a very useful and necessary body and would go as far in their service as anyone, but yet I would not wish to see them landholders, not because I despise but because I love and esteem them and therefore would wish to see them employ their time more beneficially for themselves and their families than they can possibly do by attending to their little farms. I would have them live as weavers do in England, with plenty and comfort. I have travelled through a great part of the manufacturing counties there, not altogether an unattentive observer, (p. 29) and particularly in Yorkshire about Leeds, Wakefield and Halifax, and in Lancashire about Preston, Warrington and Manchester, I observed the country for some considerable distance round these towns to be thickly inhabited by weavers and I can with truth affirm that not one of those of whom I occasionally asked the question, possessed a single foot of land beyond a garden. The farmer supplied them daily with milk, butter, cheese, flour, potatoes etc. and the butcher with flesh meat; for there the weavers, except the dissolute and debauched, not only possess the necessaries but enjoy also many of the comforts and some few of the luxuries of life which are here the lot of only our wealthier folks and are utterly unknown to our weavers and small farmers. But many will ask, 'How is this total change of things to be brought about?' Not all at once I confess. Such an improvement must come by degrees. The landed gentlemen, were they even unanimous in desiring it, could not effect it of a sudden. Leases would interfere and render such a scheme for the present impracticable in its full extent. But something might be (p. 30) done, even now, to open men's eyes to their own interests. Many gentlemen have it at this instant in their power to let perhaps more than one such farm as I mention. Let them look out for an occupier and publish the conditions in England. Men of property and judgment might be found there who would consent to come among us for a good farm, especially if gentlemen could be prevailed upon to relinquish those slavish clauses which are now too generally introduced into leases such as duty work, with duty corn, and fowls, besides grinding our grain at certain mills at an extravagant price; terms and conditions utterly unknown among the sensible spirited gentlemen and farmers of England, which, while they strongly stigmatize the slavish souls of the wretches who submit to them, throw a shade on (otherwise) the fairest characters.

I am sensible of the delicacy of this subject and that it is scarcely possible to speak of it as the thing deserves without giving offence, where of all things I could wish to avoid it, and I know too how very (p. 31) difficult it is to get over the prejudice of old customs, especially where they seem to favour our interest. But my desire is by no means to abridge the landed gentry of any part of their revenues, On the contrary, I would wish to allow them the full value of their estates that they may be enabled to live with all that dignity, ease, and hospitality, which are so much the distinguishing characteristics of the gentlemen of this kingdom. The rents which they now receive under the slavish name of duties, I know do not exceed four-pence per acre and the forced rent of their mills cannot exceed two-pence more. Abolish these and we are ready and willing to advance your rents six pence per acre. The tenant who will not, let him continue still in fetters; he does not deserve to be free. Your mills, however, would still let at near two-thirds of their present value though not a single tenant were bound to them, and these would be more fairly and honestly dealt by if the millers knew they might go to what mill they pleased. But should it, upon trial, be found impracticable to induce an English farmer to settle among us from the horror he (p. 32) must conceive of the slavish condition of that state in this kingdom, I would advise to accept of the offer so often made by Mr Young of Northmines, and receive from him an intelligent husbandman to whom I would wish to see consigned the management of a farm of one, two, or three hundred acres; and by keeping an exact diary of the profits and expenses of a farm under such management, I doubt not it would be found more advantageous than any rent it would possibly let for either to weaver or farmer. A few such examples would soon be universally followed, and instead of that distress and misery which in our present low state of the linen trade we are daily witnesses to, we should soon see the whole face of the country changed, the rents liberal and well paid, the farmer enriched by plentiful crops, and the weaver with a full command of money to procure to his family all the necessaries and many of the conveniences of life. But I have occasionally heard it objected to this scheme that the experiment hath been already tried and found to be ineffectual. Some gentlemen, it is said, have been at the expense of (p. 33) building neat convenient factories for weavers to be supported merely by their loom and the experiment hath constantly failed. These objectors, however, must allow me to say that the gentlemen who have attempted such establishments have failed, not through any defect in the plan, but from an error in the execution of it. They have built factories, it is confessed, but have neglected to establish near them one or more sensible spirited farmers from whom their little manufacturing colony should have derived its support; whereas, were farms first settled, the weavers would have no avocation to take them from their looms, no temptation to call them from their natural employment, and would consequently greatly increase and improve our linen manufacture. The command of money which this increase of trade would give them, would be an alluring inducement to the farmers to vie with each other for their custom and thus these two very useful bodies of men would be linked together by the firmest bands of society, their mutual wants and interests.

(p. 34) It will not here, I hope, be required of me to prove that where men are wholly employed in the practice of any one trade they will make a greater proficiency and improvement in it than they could possibly do were their attention frequently called off to other pursuits. But should anyone be so unreasonable as to put me to the proof of it, I would beg leave to instance to him in the articles of pins or watches that the former, though seemingly of the most simple construction, is notwithstanding the work of several distinct trades not one of which infringes on the business of the other; the person who cuts the wire into proper lengths hath nothing to do with the polish or silvering of it; another gives it the point; a fourth forms the heads; and I believe a fifth puts them on. The watchmaker, too, buys his wheels from one, his chains from another; a third furnishes springs; a fourth provides screws; a fifth rivets and pins; and, if I am not mis-informed, that elegant, useful little machine is a composition of the joint labours of ten or a dozen different tradesmen. If any one doubts that both one and the other are better & cheaper than if they were (p. 35) the work each of one man, the watch- or pin-maker will soon undeceive him. But still there will be found many objectors to this plan merely on account of the novelty of it, or perhaps that they imagine that there can be no better method of cultivating the ground than the good old one which they see daily practised by men grown grey in the business of farming; They will not upon such occasions fail to instance a few men who have seemingly amassed wealth in the practice of it, not considering that among the very few who hold large farms of good land at a low rent and are worth, perhaps, two or three hundred pounds (here deemed a fortune), they cannot instance one who hath not had the advantage of some lucky hit in the linen-flax-seed, meal malting, or other trade, or perhaps hath dabbled not a little in lending out small sums at an exorbitant interest; or, in fine, saved a little money by living like a brute and denying himself all the comforts and many of the necessaries of life. Strip him of these helps and by the mere business of farming, as it is here practised, I will undertake to prove him to be no gainer. For instance in the single (p. 36) article of potatoes, that most useful, most beneficial of all roots, whether we consider it as food for man or beast or as the best preparation in nature for a subsequent crop of bere or barley, he cultivates them in the old lazy bed way, often without one single previous ploughing, but scarce ever more than one. Allured by the cheapness and ease of that slovenly kind of culture, and never keeping a register of the profits and expenses of his farm, he is well assured, by a gross guess, that by keeping them up to the spring season he can then sell them among the weavers and small farmers (for all others have enough for their own seed) at such a price as to give him some profit. But this method, besides that it doth not half labour or mellow his land, is so extremely slovenly and imperfect that it is next to impossible to keep it tolerably clean from weeds. For my own part, I never yet saw a subsequent crop of barley or wheat where I could not have traced the shape of the old potato ridge merely by the luxuriant growth of couch grass and other weeds, which had been pared indeed, but not eradicated from the brows or borders of (p. 37) the old ridges. Besides that, it is utterly impossible with that imperfect slovenly culture (if indeed it deserves the name of culture) to raise such a crop of potatoes as may enable the grower to sell them at a reasonable price to the consumer and to make at the same time such a profit by it as to pay the wear and tear of his horses and farming implements and to lay up anything towards defraying the charges of accidental contingencies.

	£ s. d.	Cr.	£ s. d.
To rent and taxes	14 0	By 140 bushels, being the middle crop between 120 and 160, which should not be higher to the consumer than 10d. per bushel, but as things are now managed are sold at 1s. 1d. in the spring, and sometimes as high as 2s. However, as 1s 1d. is a good price to the grower, I shall calculate upon it.	7 11 8
Ploughing & harrowing	7 6		
6 horses and 4 men dunging	12 4		
16 bushels of seed at 18d which is the middle price in spring	1 4 0		
10 men, with 2 boys setting	9 2		
6 men shoveling	5 0		
First weeding (very imperfect) 8 men	6 8		
Second ditto 6 men	5 0		
12 men digging up & 12 gatherers	15 0		
Drawing home & housing(2 cars & 2 men)	4 8		
	5 3 4		
Profits on this acre	*2 8 4		
	7 11 8		

(4) Dr one acre of land cultivated in the most approved lazy-bed way
*When we reflect on the expenses attending this little crop, and that in every farm there must of necessity be some land from which the tenant cannot derive any the smallest profit, such as the land under drains and hedges, with that under his yard, buildings and high road; and that how-

ever diligent he may be, there will be still some part of his farm that is not worth the rent; that besides it will be almost impossible for (p. 39) him to provide manures for above one-tenth part of his land for the culture of potatoes. When all this is attended to, the profit of £2 8s.4d must be allowed to be very pitiful and trifling.

The author's plan indeed is much more expensive, (about seven pounds to the acre) but his crops are answerable. He can prove beyond a doubt, that he raised 1351 bushels from two acres and one half of ground; his crop this year has every appearance of being much more considerable.

Upon the whole, though I have bestowed some pains in the investigation of this subject, as considering it (p. 40) of the utmost importance to this distressed country (nothing less indeed, than whether we shall become a wealthy, happy people, or dwindle from bad to worse into a state of absolute beggary and bankruptcy, to which we seem now to be hasting with great strides) yet will I not venture to conclude it to be wholly exempt from errors. Some it is possible there may be (though I am not conscious of any) because among those who here affect to call themselves farmers, there is not perhaps one (I am sure I know not one) who keeps a regular account of the profits and expenses of his farm.

But supposing, as I really do, that my premises are right, the conclusions which I have drawn from them will, I hope, appear to be natural and unforced; and as I have no manner of interest in hazarding this little publication which may possibly provoke much censure from the better kind of people and abuse from the lower, the candid public will, I hope, excuse such inaccuracies as may be found in it.

FINIS

---

[1] Printed for W. Watson in Capel Street, Dublin, 1783.

APPENDIX 4

The report of John Greer,
Inspector General for Ulster, of the state of
the linen markets in said province
[1784]

TO THE RIGHT HONORABLE AND HONORABLE

The Trustees of the Linen and Hempen Manufactures in Ireland,

THIS REPORT OF THE STATE OF THE LINEN MARKETS

OF THE PROVINCE OF ULSTER[1],

is respectfully offered, by John Greer

COUNTY ANTRIM

ANTRIM. Market on Thursday; formerly a very considerable weekly linen market, but being much decreased, an attempt was made to establish a linen market, on the last Thursday of every month, which has not succeeded; as the monthly average is only about £200 of yard wide linens, from ten to eighteen hundred, and some few seven-eighths wide.
1803. No linen market now here.

BALLYMENA. Market on Saturday; very few yard wide linens, but the greatest market of three-quarter wide linens in the province, from 5d. to 1s. 8d. per yard; the weekly average upwards of £1,000.
1803. Little increase, presently average being £1,200.

RANDALSTOWN. Monthly market on the first Wednesday of every month; yard wide linens from twelve to sixteen hundreds, but mostly three-quarter wide linens, from 7d. to 1s. 1d. per yard; the monthly average £1,200.
1803. Increased especially in yard-wide linens, monthly average £2,000.

PORTGLENONE. Monthly market on the first Tuesday of every month; seven-eighths linens of a light, neat fabric from ten to fourteen hundreds; the monthly average about £600.
1803. No linen market, being removed to Ahoghill, and held on the first Friday; monthly average £900.

BALLYMONEY. Monthly market on the first Thursday of every month; three-quarter wide linens of a very coarse poor fabric, but improving, from 4¹/2d. to 9d. per yard; and quantities of seven-eighth linens, of a good fabric, from eleven to seventeen hundreds, chiefly thirteen, fourteen, and fifteen hundreds; the monthly average £2,500.
1803. Decreased, the finer seven-eighth wide linens mostly sold at Coleraine, the monthly average £1,000.

BELFAST. Market on Friday; yard wide linens from fifteen to twenty hundreds, principally fine, and well manufactured; the market pretty regular and the weekly average about £1,000.
1803. This market very much increased, the weekly average full £3,000.

LISBURN. Market on Tuesday; yard wide linens, some very coarse, being seven and eight hundreds and of an indifferent manufacture, but principally are from fifteen to twenty hundreds of an excellent fabric; the weekly average £2,000.
1803. Increased by the addition of lawns and cambrics, the weekly average of the whole £2,800.

BALLYCLARE.
1803. A small monthly market on the third Wednesday of every month; average £100.

OBSERVATIONS

The three-quarter wide linens of this county are chiefly bleached and finished in the neighbourhood of Ballymena and Antrim; some few of the finest sorts are finished in the neighbourhood of Belfast; many of the seven-eighth wide linens are bleached in the interior parts of the county; but the greatest part of that width, and those of the best quality, are bleached in the neighbourhood of Belfast and Lisburn, and finished in the highest order, together with the principal part of the yard wides, which compose a very large share of the fine trade of the province.
1803. Sixty-six bleachgreens in the county capable of finishing 327,000 pieces yearly.

COUNTY ARMAGH

LURGAN. Market on Friday; yard wide linens of a coarse fabric, say seven and eight hundreds, and quantities of a good fabric from twelve to twenty hundreds, principally fifteen, sixteen, and seventeen hundreds; also seven-eighth and yard wide lawns or cambrics, from 1s. to 6s. per yard; and likewise diapers, of various widths and fineness: the weekly average of this market is full £2,500 exclusive of sundry drapers resident in the town, who manufacture and bleach lawns, diapers and tickens, to the amount of £400 and upwards, weekly average.

1803. Decreased, no coarse linen, and the finer giving way to lawns and cambrics, which are now manufactured up to 10s. per yard; narrow diaper only sold and the whole weekly average £2,500.

TANDERAGEE. Market on Wednesday; yard wide linens, from seven to eighteen hundreds, but principally twelve to fifteen hundreds; the weekly average £500.

1803. Increased and with the addition of lawns and cambrics, now averages weekly £1,700.

RICH-HILL. Market on Saturday; yard wide, and a few odd pieces seven-eighth linens, scarce worthy of notice; the yard wide linens from seven to sixteen hundreds; the coarse kinds of an indifferent fabric, and of the finer principally twelve, thirteen, and fourteen hundreds; the weekly average £600.

1803. Decreased, the best yard wide linens being sold at Tanderagee; and the weekly average only £100.

ARMAGH. Market on Tuesday; yard wide linen, from seven to twelve hundreds; few of the coarse or fine sorts, but the first market in the province for nine, ten, and eleven hundreds of the best fabric; the weekly average full £1,800.

1803. Increased and increasing in finer kinds; the weekly average £4,000.

KEADY. Market on Friday; yard wide linens, eight and ten hundreds, of a strong fabric, and the market, though small, is likely to increase, from the number of bleach-greens in the neighbourhood; the weekly average at present, full £150.

1803. This market totally dropt.

OBSERVATIONS

The bleach-greens of this county are principally situated in the neighbourhood of Armagh and Keady; where they bleach and finish those strong yard wide linens known by the name of *stout Armaghs*; and are in high repute but mostly come too dear to market. There are many other bleach-greens scattered through the county, but the bulk of the finer linens from twelve hundred upwards, manufactured and sold in this county, are bleached on the Rivers Lagan and Bann in the counties of Antrim and Down.

1803. Forty bleach-greens in the county capable of finishing 168,500 pieces yearly.

COUNTY CAVAN

COOTHILL. Market on Friday; linens and sheetings, being the only market for the latter in the province; the linens yard-wide, ten to twelve hundreds, principally twelve hundreds, of good stuff and neat fabric; the sheetings five quarters wide, and some few six quarters wide, nine to fourteen hundreds; the coarser sorts of indifferent stuff, the fine neatly made; but both these and the linens are defective in stoutness, being too light a texture; the weekly average of the whole full £1,000.

1803. This market much increased and improved, the weekly average being of sheetings £1,200, and of yard wide linen £1,000.

BALLIHAYS. No linen market, but some seven-eight wide, of eight and nine hundreds, sold at the quarterly fairs, chiefly to jobbers; say £30 to £40 value at each fair.

CAVAN. No linen market, but seven-eight wide linens sold at the fairs; about the same average as Ballihays.

1803. These fairs dropt and a weekly market for seven-eight wide linens held at Ballinagh on Saturday. Weekly average £600.

KILLISHANDRA. Market on Wednesday; seven-eight and yard wide linens, seven to ten hundred, principally nine and ten hundreds and seven-eight wide, of a rough fabric and too light; the weekly average about £300.

1803. This market increased and the weekly average now £600.

BALLYCONNELL. No weekly linen market, but some linens seven-eight wide and yard wide, sold at the fairs, say about £150 yearly value.

1803. The manufacture increasing and a monthly fair established, and average £250.

BELTURBET. Some linens sold at the fairs, the yearly value full £500.

1803. No linens now sold here.

1803. ARVAGH. Market on Friday, coarse seven-eight wide linens. Weekly average £150.

OBSERVATIONS

The bleach greens in this county are few and much scattered, the manufacture does not seem to improve, and regular markets are much wanted.

1803. Fourteen bleachgreens in the county capable of finishing 62,000 pieces yearly.

COUNTY DONEGAL

LETTERKENNY: Market on Friday; seven-eight wide linens, nine to twelve hundreds, and some yard wide fourteen to seventeen hundreds, all made of good stuff, but sleayed rather too light, and the linens exposed to sale in double pieces; the markets very uncertain, some being large similar to fairs, and the weekly average of the whole about £120.
1803. Increased so as to average weekly £350 in seven-eight wide linens, and £50 in 3/4 wide; no yard wide.

RATHMILTON: Market on Tuesday; seven-eight wide, and yard wide linens, much like Letterkenny market in regard to quality, although there are some of a coarser fabric; the weekly average full £150 and the market held regularly: but a great misfortune attending these two (the only linen) markets in the county is, they are chiefly occupied by jobbers, who buy up the linens for Londonderry market, and it is extremely difficult to enforce the laws.
1803. Much increased, the weekly average in 3/4 wide linens £50, and of 7/8 wide £450.

OBSERVATIONS

CONVOY, STRANORLAN, BALLYBOFAY, CASTLEFIN: No regular linen markets; but that species of linens known by the name of Lagans, is principally manufactured in the neighbourhood of these towns; they are twenty-six inches wide, of good stuff, wove in long pieces, and the weaver or manufacturer cutting the pieces in lengths of ten yards each, whiten them without the use of mills, and thus expose them for sale; but through knavery this manufacture is declining, and the present yearly value about £2,000.
1803. A market now held at Stranorlan on Saturday, seven-eight wide linens; weekly average £50. No Lagans now manufactured; seven bleachgreens now in the county, capable of finishing 27,500 pieces yearly.

COUNTY DOWN

BANBRIDGE: Market on Monday; yard wide linens principally twelve to fourteen hundreds, and some of a coarser fabric; the weekly average about £500.
1803. Increased in value, lawns being now sold as well as linens, weekly average £1,000.

NEWRY: Market on Thursday; yard wide linens from seven to fifteen hundreds, but chiefly twelve hundreds, of a good stout fabric; weekly average about £1,000.

1803. Much increased, weekly average £1,500.

KILKEEL: Market on Wednesday; yard wide linens, nine to twelve hundreds, principally ten hundreds, of a stout fabric; the weekly average about £200.
1803. The present weekly average £250.

CASTLEWILLAN: Market on Monday; yard wide linens eight to twelve hundreds, chiefly nine and ten hundreds, but are not improving; the weekly average scarce £80.
1803. The present weekly average £150.

DOWNPATRICK: Market on Saturday; yard wide linens from eight to sixteen hundreds, of a poor fabric; weekly average about £300.
1803. Much increased, and also the fabric improved, weekly average £1,500.

PORTAFERRY: Market for linens on the first Thursday in every month; yard wide linens from eight to sixteen hundreds, but chiefly twelve, thirteen and fourteen hundreds, of a tolerable fabric; and the monthly average scarce £200.
1803. This market dropt.

KIRCUBBIN: A market has been attempted here on the second Wednesday of every month, for the sale of yard wide linens, but it is not yet thoroughly established, and if it succeeds must hurt the market at Portaferry.
1803. This market continued and averages monthly £300.

BALLYNAHINCH: Market on Thursday; yard wide linens from eight to eighteen hundreds, very few of the finer sorts, as the principal part is eight, nine, and ten hundred linen, and the fabric improving; the weekly average full £300.
1803. The market decreasing, the present weekly average £150.

HILLSBOROUGH: Market on Wednesday; remarkable for yard wide linens of a neat light fabric, seven, eight, and nine hundreds for exportation unbleached, the yarn being well purged. There are also yard wide linens twelve to eighteen hundreds sold here, but of these a small quantity; the weekly average of the whole about £350.
1803. Weekly average 'as formerly' £350.

RATHFRILAND: Market on Wednesday; yard wide linens from twelve to sixteen hundreds, of a strong fabric, and some few coarse linens but not good; the weekly average full £100.
1803. Increased owing to six great fairs in the year on Wednesdays, and the weekly average is now £200.

1803. DROMORE: market Saturday for lawns, weekly average £25.

OBSERVATIONS

In this county there are great numbers of bleach greens, particularly on the River Bann, where, in the course of seven miles, passing by Banbridge, Gilford, and Moyallen, are twenty bleach greens, which on the whole finish full ninety thousand pieces annually.

1803. Sixty six bleach greens in the county capable of finishing 238,500 pieces yearly.

COUNTY FERMANAGH

ENNISKILLEN. MAGUIRE'S BRIDGE: There are some good nine and ten hundred linens yard wide, made in the neighbourhood and sold at the fairs of these towns, but no regular markets.

1803. ENNISKILLEN: From an increase of the manufacture, a market now held every fortnight on Thursdays, the monthly average £800.

1803. MAGUIRE'S BRIDGE: Two fairs, viz 16th Jany and 5th July, average £600 each fair.

BROOKEBOROUGH: Market on the second and last Monday of the month, yard wide linens from eight to twelve hundreds, principally nine and ten hundreds, of a good fabric; the average value sold is about £300 per month.

1803. The market much decreased, the average per month only £100.

OBSERVATIONS

There are only four bleach yards in this county, and one linen market, but the county abounds with spinners and good flax-yarn.

1803. No bleach green at work for three years past.

COUNTY LONDONDERRY

DUNGIVEN: Market on Saturday; seven-eight linens, of a strong fabric, from nine to twelve hundreds; the weekly average about £60.

1803. Weekly average rather increased being £100.

LONDONDERRY: Market on Wednesday; seven-eight wide linens, from ten to fifteen hundreds, some finer, but chiefly twelve and thirteen hundreds; mostly from the County Donegal; the weekly average about £1,000.

1803. Much increased by the addition of coarse three-quarter wide linens, the weekly average of the whole £2,000.

NEWTOWNLIMAVADY: Market on Monday; seven-eight wide linens, inferior in quality to those in Derry; and the weekly average about £300.
1803. Weekly average £500.

COLERAINE: Market on Saturday; seven-eight wide linens, chiefly fine, but greatly decreased in quantity; the present weekly average scarcely £75.
1803. Much increased in fine seven-eight wides and also three-quarter wide linens; the weekly average £600.

MAGHERA: Monthly market, second Tuesday of each month; seven-eight wide linens, from ten to thirteen hundreds, of a light fabric; the monthly average about £500.
1803. Also greatly increased and fabric improved; the market now on the first Tuesday, and the monthly average £1,000.

MAGHERAFELT: Monthly market, second Tuesday of each month; seven-eight linens, from nine to twelve hundreds, but mostly ten and eleven hundreds; the monthly average £600 to £700.
1803. Increased, the monthly average being £1,200.

MONEYMORE: Monthly market, 21st of the month; seven-eight linens, from seven to twelve hundreds; the finer of a light fabric, the coarser chiefly from the County Tyrone; the monthly average about £1,000.
1803. Increased, the monthly average fully £1,500.

1803. KILREA: a market now held on the second and fourth Wednesdays in the month for three-quarter wide linens, monthly average £600.

OBSERVATIONS

The bleach-greens in this county are principally situated in the neighbourhood of Newtownlimavady, Coleraine, Moneymore, and Cumberbridge; the linens sold in Dungiven, Derry, Newtownlimavady, and Coleraine, are of that species called Coleraines, when bleached; and the markets principally attended by drapers of the counties of Londonderry and Donegal.
1803. Forty-nine bleach-greens in the county capable of finishing 290,000 pieces yearly.

COUNTY MONAGHAN

MONAGHAN: Market on Tuesdays; yard wide linens, ten to twelve hundreds, principally (though there are some few coarser) of a strong, rough fabric, the yarn not being sufficiently purged; the weekly average, about £700.
1803. Market now held on Monday and thereby much increased, the fabric also improved and the weekly average £1,100.

CASTLEBLAYNEY: Market on Wednesday; yard wide linens, nine to ten hundreds, with some few finer, but of a rough fabric; the weekly average about £200.
1803. Increased and improved, the weekly average £500.

CLONES: Market on Thursday; yard wide linens ten to twelve hundreds, rather of a light fabric, and of course cheap for the thread; weekly average about £600.
1803. Decreased, the weekly average only £400.

BALLIBAY: Market on Saturday; yard wide linens, nine to thirteen hundreds; principally ten to twelve hundreds, of a good fabric, being stronger than the linens of Clones; the weekly average about £500.
1803. Much increased, the weekly average being £900.

OBSERVATIONS

There are few bleach-yards in this county; although I apprehend from the appearance of lakes and rivers, that several good situations might be had; those already erected are chiefly at the Crieve and the neighbourhood of Ballibay; the linens bleached and finished in the county are of the species of Armaghs; but the greatest part of their brown linens are purchased by buyers from the counties of Armagh, Antrim, and Down; and it is supposed one full eighth of the manufacture of the county is bought by jobbers and re-sold in other counties.
1803. Twelve bleach greens in the county capable of finishing 73,700 pieces yearly.

COUNTY TYRONE

CALLIDON: Formerly a weekly linen market on Monday; but this is dropt, and linens sold at the fairs, of which there are eight in the year; and average full £400 each fair; yard wide linens, nine to twelve hundreds, principally ten and eleven hundreds, of a good fabric.
1803. Entirely ceased.

AUGHNACLOY: Market on Wednesday; seven-eight and yard wide linens, mostly yard wide, and ten hundreds; the weekly average about £500.
1803. Increased and chiefly seven-eight wide linens now sold, the weekly average £800.

NEWTOWNSTEWART: Market on Monday; seven-eight wide linens, from nine to twelve hundreds, mostly ten and eleven hundreds; the weekly average about £600.

1803. Increased with an addition of three-quarter wide linens, total average £1,000.

STRABANE: Market on Tuesday; seven-eight wide linens from ten to fourteen hundreds, few of the latter, being mostly twelve hundreds, the weekly average about £700.
1803. Also increased and an addition of three-quarter wide linen total average £1,500.

COOKSTOWN: Market on Saturday; seven-eight wide linens, eight to ten hundreds, and increasing in quantity; present weekly average about £120.
1803. Much increased of late; the weekly average £500.

STEWARTSTOWN: Market on Wednesday; seven-eight linens, from eight to eleven hundreds, mostly ten hundreds, of a good fabric; the weekly average full £800.
1803. A small increase, the weekly average £1,000.

DUNGANNON: Market on Thursday; seven-eight and yard wide linens; great quantities of the former, and from seven to ten hundreds, yard wides; chiefly ten hundreds, and increasing in quantity; the weekly average of the whole, from £1,200 to £1,500.
1803. Much increased (very few yard wide linens now sold) the weekly average £3,500.

MOY: A monthly fair on the first Friday of every month; seven-eight wide and yard wide linens; the former a coarse indifferent kind, the yard wides eight to twelve hundreds, pretty good and improving; the monthly average full £700.
1803. Decreased, few, if any, yard wide linens now sold and the monthly average about £300.

1803. FINTONA: A monthly fair on the second Friday of every month for seven-eight linens, the monthly average £1,000.

1803. FIVEMILETOWN: A small monthly fair for coarse seven-eight wide linens; held on the second Friday of every month and averages £150 monthly.

OBSERVATIONS

The bleach greens of this county are principally situated in the neighbourhood of Dungannon, Cookstown, and Stewartstown, and from Castlecaulfield to Strabane, in the north-west part of the county, there are only two or three bleach greens; the principal part of the linens finished in the county are seven-eight wides, of the denomination formerly of Moneymores, but may now be called coarse and fine Tyrones, and of an

inferior quality to those seven-eight wides called Coleraines.
1803. Forty-one bleach greens in the county capable of finishing 192,000 pieces yearly.

[1] Printed by Mat Williamson, printer and stationer to the . . . Trustees of the Linen Board, Dublin, 1784.
An interleaved copy annotated for 1803 is located in the Public Record Office of Northern Ireland, D562/6225. Its manuscript comments for 1803 appear in italics at the relevant places in the text.

APPENDIX 5

Report made to the Linen Board
by Mr Kirk of Keady, 1822[1]

ARMAGH HAS LONG BEEN CONSIDERED the largest inland market in this kingdom. About 328,000 pieces of linen cloth are annually sold there, making an average of about 6,300 pieces each market day; of these, about 400 pieces are of the sets of four-hundreds; 1,800 pieces are five-hundreds; 1,100 pieces are six-hundreds; 400 are seven-hundreds; 500 pieces are eight-hundreds; and about 1,200 pieces from nine-hundreds to twelve-hundreds linens. These, with about 900 pieces of four-quarter-wide lawns, make about the quantity I have mentioned. They are generally bought by 170 buyers, and sold by about 2,000 sellers. A very considerable quantity of these goods are brought to market by what are called manufacturers, persons who buy the yarn, employ a number of weavers to have it made into cloth, and then bring the cloth to market in considerable quantity to sell. These manufacturers are, in general, sealmasters; but when they are not, it is their usual practice to stamp, on each piece of their cloth, the length and breadth thereof at home, then bring it to market, and previous to its commencement, get a sealmaster (of whom there are numbers) to affix his seal on whatever quantity they have, without the sealmaster either measuring or examining them; the manufacturer, at the same time, guarantees the sealmaster that, in case of fine, he will pay it, which, when fines are struck, they almost invariably do. Another very considerable quantity is brought to market by what are called jobbers – persons who make a trade of attending the markets of Clones, Cootehill, Ballybay, Monaghan, etc., every week, and have whatever goods they buy in those markets spouted over with sugar and water, etc., turn-lapped, and then brought to Armagh for sale every market day, contrary to law. These persons, also, like the manufacturers, get their linens made up at home, and the lengths and breadths put on by themselves or their assistants; and, like them, they get a sealmaster in Armagh to affix his seal on each piece, without his either measuring or examining it; they give him a like guarantee. The remaining quantity is brought to market in single pieces, like other markets.

I stated that the linen sold in Armagh was generally bought by 170 buyers – I mean about 170 buyers usually attend the market to buy – of these, about 120 are principals and 50 commissioners. The former may be again divided into twenty registered bleachers, forty buyers who get their goods bleached, and about sixty 'keelmen'. From my first statement, it will be seen that Armagh is principally a coarse market; it is also understood to be a four-quarter wide market. But in the low-priced goods the most shameful irregularities as to the lengths and breadths prevail. In many instances, goods purporting to be four-quarter-wides are sealed 33.5 inches when brown, and will not seal more than 32.5 when white or half-white; and you are obliged to purchase and pay all lengths from 24 to 32 yards. This is owing to a variety of causes, an alleged defect in the Act of Parliament not regulating the length or breadth of any piece of four-quarter-wide linen under the set of eight-hundred, the irregular system of sealing so many years carried on with impunity, the extent of the market itself, and the number of strangers resorting there to buy, who often come forty miles to the market, and either have not time or patience to correct the many errors they cannot but perceive.

The 'keelmen' were so called from the first persons who got into the trade being very illiterate, and unable to write in ordinary characters, they marked on each piece of linen the price at which it was bought with 'keel', that is 'iron ore', which makes a red mark that will not rub out. Those buyers were originally a peculiar race of travelling pedlars, who went over to England to retail linens, which, seventy years ago, they generally bought from the bleachers, but now they buy them in the brown market, half bleach them with lime in a corner of one of their fields, get them a few hours beetling in a neighbouring bleach-field, and, when ready, go with them to England, retail them there, and return to buy again. From their mode of living, and the exchange of English bills [because the English guinea was worth £1. 2s. 9d. in Ireland], they have generally made money; and, so great is this trade just now, that I am certain they buy in Armagh market alone from 1,500 to 1,700 pieces weekly. They can now pretty generally read and write, though, to this day, it is not uncommon to see some of them putting on his hieroglyphics with 'keel', as formerly.

[1] Published in H. McCall, *Ireland and her staple manufactures* (Belfast, 1870), 3rd edition, pp. 245–6.

Index

Milton Keynes UK
Ingram Content Group UK Ltd.
UKHW012001110224
437614UK00002B/24